TIME

ANNUAL

By the Editors of TIME

2002

TIME
ANNUAL

STEVE LISS FOR TIME

2002

By the Editors of TIME

CONTENTS

TIME ANNUAL 2002

Cover photography credits
Front cover, top, left to right: Ettore Malanca—Sipa Press; Peter Mountain—Warner Brothers; Stuart Westmorland—Stone; Mark Seliger—Corbis Outline. Front cover, center: Lori Grinker—Contact Press Images. Back cover: Daniel Hulshizer—AP/Wide World

FROM LEFT: SHANNON STAPLETON—REUTERS—TIMEPIX; ETTORE MALANCA—SIPA PRESS; SION TOUHIG—GETTY IMAGES; PAUL KOLNIK; GREGORY HEISLER; CLIVE BRUNSKILL—ALLSPORT; JURGEN VOLLMER—STAR FILE

TIME ANNUAL 2001

MANAGING EDITOR	Kelly Knauer
DESIGNER	Ellen Fanning
PICTURE EDITOR	Patricia Cadley
RESEARCH DIRECTOR/WRITER	Matthew Fenton
PRODUCTION EDITOR	Michael Skinner
COPY EDITOR	Bruce Christopher Carr

TIME INC. HOME ENTERTAINMENT

PRESIDENT	Rob Gursha
VICE PRESIDENT, BRANDED BUSINESSES	David Arfine
EXECUTIVE DIRECTOR, MARKETING SERVICES	Carol Pittard
DIRECTOR, RETAIL & SPECIAL SALES	Tom Mifsud
DIRECTOR OF FINANCE	Tricia Griffin
MARKETING DIRECTOR	Kenneth Maehlum
ASSISTANT DIRECTOR	Ann Marie Ross
EDITORIAL OPERATIONS MANAGER	John Calvano
ASSOCIATE PRODUCT MANAGERS	Jennifer Dowell, Meredith Shelley
ASSOCIATE PRODUCT MANAGER	Michelle Kuhr

SPECIAL THANKS TO:

Victoria Alfonso, Suzanne DeBenedetto, Robert Dente, Gina Di Meglio, Peter Harper, Natalie McCrea, Jessica McGrath
Jonathan Polsky, Emily Rabin, Mary Jane Rigoroso, Steven Sandonato, Bozena Szwagulinski
Marina Weinstein, Niki Whelan

THE WRITING OF THE FOLLOWING *TIME* STAFF MEMBERS AND CONTRIBUTORS IS FEATURED IN THIS VOLUME:
Bernard Baumohl, Mark Bechtel, Lisa Beyer, Hannah Bloch, Massimo Calabresi, Margaret Carlson, James Carney,
Howard Chua-Eoan, John Cloud, Adam Cohen, Matthew Cooper, Richard Corliss, Andrea Dorfman,
John F. Dickerson, Michael Duffy, Daniel Eisenberg, Philip Elmer-DeWitt, Michael Elliott, Steven Erlanger,
Christopher John Farley, Andrew Ferguson, Thomas Fields-Meyer, Nancy Gibbs, Frank Gibney Jr., Elizabeth Gleick,
Frederic Golden, Andrew Goldstein, Dan Goodgame, Christine Gorman, Paul Gray, Karl Taro Greenfeld, John Greenwald,
Lev Grossman, Anita Hamilton, John Heilemann, James O. Jackson, Leon Jaroff, Daniel Kadlec, Jeffrey Kluger,
Richard Lacayo, Tim Larimer, Michael D. Lemonick, Eugene Linden, Belinda Luscombe, Scott MacLeod, Ellin Martens,
J.F.O. McAllister, Jeannie McCabe, Terry McCarthy, Johanna McGeary, Tim McGirk, Jodie Morse, J. Madeleine Nash,
Daniel Okrent, Michele Orecklin, Tim Padgett, Priscilla Painton, Alice Park, Alex Perry, James Poniewozik, Eric Pooley,
Paul Quinn-Judge, Josh Quittner, Joshua Cooper Ramo, Romesh Ratnesar, Matt Rees, Amanda Ripley, Simon Robinson,
Timothy Roche, Thomas Sancton, Richard Schickel, Elaine Shannon, Janice C. Simpson, Joel Stein,
Ron Stodghill II, Robert Sullivan, Chris Taylor, Mark Thompson, Karen Tumulty, Josh Tyrangiel, David Van Biema,
Douglas C. Waller, Michael Weisskopf, Richard Zoglin

SPECIAL THANKS TO:
Ken Baierlein, Sue Blair, Howard Chua-Eoan, Barbara Dudley Davis, John Dragonetti, Dick Duncan,
Ed Gabel, Arthur Hochstein, Ed Jamieson, Kevin Kelly, Joe Lertola, Nancy Mynio, Richard K. Prue, Aleksey Razhba,
Jennifer Roth, Michele Stephenson, Lamarr Tsufura, Lon Tweeten, Cornelis Verwaal, Miriam Winocour

2001
Images

September 11

Outlined against the shards of the World Trade Center, a trio of New York City fire fighters hoists the flag only hours after the collapse of the Twin Towers. The moment was captured by Thomas E. Franklin, a photographer for the Bergen (N.J.) *Record*, who later said, "As soon as I shot it, I realized the similarity to the famous image of Marines raising the flag at Iwo Jima. The shot immediately felt important to me. It said something to me about the strength of the American people and about what these firemen had gone through battling the unimaginable."

Photograph by Chris Usher for TIME

September 13

Some years we store in our memories as sound tracks: 1956 is Elvis; 1964 is the Beatles; 1977 is the Bee Gees. But we may remember 2001 not as a snippet of melody but as a palette of three colors: red, white and blue. In the wake of the deadly terrorist attacks on the World Trade Center and the Pentagon, Americans found common cause in rallying around the flag. Within days of the strikes, the grand old banner was everywhere—including the front yard of a house outside Dover, Del., left. The only place you probably *couldn't* find the Stars and Stripes: at your sold-out local flag shop.

September 12

Ground Zero: Silhouetted against a shard of the once-majestic north tower of the World Trade Center in Manhattan, New York City firemen struggle to bring some order to the chaos that surrounds them, still a vision of hell 36 hours after the twin towers of the complex were destroyed by hijacked airplanes. Somewhere in this colossal pile of debris are the remains of 343 of their fellow fire fighters, who supervised the orderly evacuation of the burning towers that saved tens of thousands of lives, then remained in the buildings to fight the fires. Swearing in a class of 307 new recruits to the fire department five weeks later, New York City Mayor Rudolph Giuliani said, "The reality is that we're mournful, we're sorrowful, we're crying and we always will, but we are stronger than we were before."

Photograph by Christopher Morris—VII for TIME

September 13

Flyers plastered with portraits of people missing after the Sept. 11 attacks on the World Trade Center compose a mosaic of loss, memory and hope at the entrance to New York City's Bellevue Hospital. Part bulletin board, part shrine, the area became known as the "wall of prayers." Asked soon after the attack how many had died, New York City Mayor Rudolph Giuliani replied, "More than we can bear." When TIME ran this picture in September, the number of those believed killed in the attacks was more than 6,000. But the passage of time brought better news: far fewer had died than officials originally feared. By December, the estimated death toll in the New York City attacks was around 3,000. Some survivors found their names still present on official lists of the dead weeks, even months, after Sept. 11.

November 19

In Kunduz in the north of Afghanistan, a woman does the once unthinkable: lifts her veil in public to show her face to her child. As the Taliban fled city after city, women began to shed the burka—the head-to-toe garment, to Western eyes a kind of body bag for the living—made mandatory by the defeated religious zealots. From the moment in 1996 when the Taliban took power, it sought to make women not just obedient but also nonexistent. On Nov. 20, only days after the Taliban left Kabul, 200 women gathered outside the apartment of Soraya Parlika, Afghanistan's best-known woman activist, and—in a simultaneous motion—lifted their burkas.

April 11

From the front lawn of his house inside Pearl Harbor Naval Base, Commander Scott Waddle watches the U.S.S. *Greeneville* nuclear attack submarine head out to sea for the first time since it collided with the Japanese fishing boat *Ehime Maru* on Feb. 9, claiming nine lives. Waddle was relieved of his command of the sub but allowed to retire with an honorable discharge. Just before this picture was taken, the crew of the *Greeneville* sounded the whistle in tribute to their ex-skipper. On the bridge, replacement captain Tony Cortese waved to his predecessor, who raised his right arm in a stiff salute. "That was the hardest thing I have done in my life," Waddle told TIME. "It was like the last nail in the coffin."

October 30

Jordan's back! And he wants the ball as his Washington Wizards take on the New York Knicks in Michael's first game on the hardwood since he left us with a storybook finish, scoring the game-winning basket as his Chicago Bulls stunned the Utah Jazz to win the NBA title in 1998. Now 38, Jordan teased fans all summer with hints that he might return, shedding 25 lbs. as well as his part ownership of the Wizards (the NBA doesn't allow playing owners). But the comeback trail proved rough: though MJ still had his shot, the young Wizards endured an eight-game losing streak early in the season.

"It was cool, man. But I'm a little depressed that they didn't have a buffet ready"
TONY SIRAGUSA, left, Baltimore Ravens' 340-lb. tackle, on his visit to the White House

"It's either one of the best things I've ever done or one of the dumbest."
JANET RENO, on her candidacy for the governorship of Florida

"You win some, you lose some, and then there's that little-known third category."
AL GORE, campaigning for Minneapolis Mayor Sharon Belton

"I should have sent him somewhere as an ambassador. The world's a big place."
MIKHAIL GORBACHEV, expressing regret at not having kept Boris Yeltsin's ambitions under control

"Miss Cleo should have seen this coming."
JAY NIXON, Missouri attorney general, on a suit against a TV psychic

"I'm from Boston."
MICHAEL BLOOMBERG, N.Y.C. mayoral candidate dodging questions on whom he roots for: Mets or Yankees

"In the end, he wanted to hug me . . . and I said, Mr. Condit, I cannot permit you to do that"
SUSAN LEVY, Chandra's mother, on her meeting with Representative Gary Condit

"We all need to take a deep breath and think about being a Bush daughter and having that cross to bear. I'd go out and have a couple of drinks too."
JULIA ROBERTS, on the "Margaritagate" troubles of First Daughters Jenna and Barbara

"They got the willies, they got the buckwheats, their knees wobbled, and we gave it up." DAN RATHER, on CBS producers' insistence that he end his two-month refusal to do a story on the Chandra Levy case, which he maintained was just a missing-person story

"Women are my biggest defenders. It's that bad-boy syndrome. Now girls chase me."
O.J. SIMPSON, on life since his 1995 acquittal for murdering his wife and her friend

"Well, I can wear heels now."
NICOLE KIDMAN, 5 ft. 10 in., on life after Tom Cruise (officially 5 ft. 9 in.)

BEATING AROUND THE BUSH

"Someone very strange, with very little promise, has taken charge of the leadership of the great empire that we have as a neighbor." FIDEL CASTRO, in a nationally broadcast speech, on President Bush

"'Bush the father' and 'Bush the son' leaves you wondering who the Holy Ghost is." ROBIN LAKOFF, a U.C. Berkeley linguist, bemoaning the challenge of referring to both men in the same sentence

"To those of you who received honors, awards and distinctions, I say well done. And to the C students, I say you too can be President of the United States."
GEORGE W. BUSH, addressing cheering grads at Yale's commencement

"We all drink Evian, but what about the people who can't afford Evian?" MIKE MEDAVOY, Hollywood producer, lamenting President Bush's decision to delay reduction of acceptable levels of arsenic in drinking water

"Picasso had his blue
period. And I am in my
blond period."
HUGH HEFNER,
currently squiring eight
twenty-something girlfriends

"Nobody demonstrates
against me anymore.
This is fun!"
BILL CLINTON, to protesters
in Northern Ireland

"When you get over 95,
every day is your day."
BOB HOPE, newly 98,
on L.A.'s declaring his
birthday "Bob Hope Day"

"If you set aside Three
Mile Island and
Chernobyl, the safety
record of nuclear is
really very good."
PAUL O'NEILL,
Treasury Secretary, supporting
the Bush energy plan and its
advocacy of nuclear power

"Do not mistake bribe
taking for corruption."
VLADIMIR RUSHAILO, former
Russian Minister of Internal
Affairs, defending officials in his
department who sold influence.
He was later replaced

"I'm starting to
mistrust my judgment."
LEONA HELMSLEY,
on learning that boyfriend
Patrick Ward is gay

AFTER SEPTEMBER 11

"They're telling us you should fly again.
I'm not flying unless they build a
highway wide enough so they can roll
the plane from here to L.A."
CHRIS ROCK, at a World Trade
Center comedy benefit

"We're not running out of targets. Afghanistan is."
DONALD RUMSFELD, Secretary of Defense, on the U.S. bombing campaign

"It is not our proudest product placement.
But it shows that the Taliban is looking
for the same qualities as any truck buyer:
durability and reliability."
WADE HOYT, Toyota spokesman,
defending the pickup choice of Afghans

"I could probably drop a package of Sweet'N Low and evacuate this building."
KEN PINEAU, Collier County, Fla., emergency director

"I don't want any woman to go to my grave at all . . . I don't want a
pregnant woman or a person who is not clean to say goodbye."
MOHAMED ATTA, terrorist, in the will found in his suitcase

"It's incredibly positive for the Internet."
RAYMOND J. OGLETHORPE, president, America Online, on the
fear surrounding anthrax in the mail, adding that the
deaths were "unfortunate"

"It's a sorry man that would sit still during a hijacking now."
DONALD AVERY, airline passenger

"It's beyond my ability
to express it in socially
acceptable terms."
TOM BROKAW,
on his assistant's
contracting anthrax,
probably from a letter

"Four thousand donkeys are on the way from Tajikistan."
ANDREW NATSIOS, head of the U.S. Agency for International
Development, on the relief effort for Afghanistan

"It's nice to be in a disclosed location for a change."
VICE PRESIDENT DICK CHENEY, at the Alfred
E. Smith dinner at the Waldorf Astoria in New York City

"No, we are not with you, and we are not terrorists."
AYATULLAH ALI KHAMENEI, Iran's supreme religious leader,
on his country's refusal to support the attacks on the U.S.

"I don't have anthrax."
GEORGE W. BUSH, U.S. President

DREW FRIEDMAN FOR TIME

TONY BLAIR

When mad cow departed, as per his wish,
Hoof-and-mouth started. Care for the fish?

MARK FREDRICKSON FOR TIME

CALIFORNIA'S GRAY DAVIS

His lot in life just didn't seem right
Asking for aid, when his burden was light

ANITA KUNZ FOR TIME

GEORGE BUSH

The reluctant warrior shouldered a gun
O fateful symmetry: Like father, like son!

C.F. PAYNE FOR TIME

MARC RICH

Ex-pat to President: "Fill me with joy!
I've got billions—so pardon me, boy!"

ISTVAN BANYAI FOR TIME

FBI SPY ROBERT HANSSEN

No laughs here: we'll catch you later—
There's nothing funny about a traitor

JOSEPH SALINA FOR TIME

TOMMY THOMPSON

The Secretary of Health faces age-old ills
Like: Who's gonna pay for Grandpa's pills?

JOSEPH SALINA FOR TIME

DICK CHENEY

An unspoiled forest, a pristine shore?
The V.P. don't care—Let's drill for more!

DANIEL ADEL FOR TIME

SENATOR JIM JEFFORDS

His dance with Daschle rebalanced power
And left Trent Lott a Senate wallflower

TIM O'BRIEN FOR TIME

KOFI ANNAN

Hail, Kofi! May your tribe increase:
The Nobel folks say you're Prince of Peace

MICHELLE CHANG FOR TIME

COLIN POWELL

As Middle East woes trouble his brain,
He's feeling nostalgic for Saddam Hussein

TIM BOWER FOR TIME

CARLY FIORINA

Hewlett-Packard needed no surgery
Until Compaq did urge her to merger-y

VANCE YPSILANTI FOR TIME

SHAWN FANNING

Napster's rebel was, like, totally bugged—
The labels cried foul; now he's unplugged

ROBERTO PARADA FOR TIME

DONALD RUMSFELD

He tickled reporters with briefings so slick
Why speak softly, if you carry a big stick?

ANDREA VENTURA FOR TIME

SLOBODAN MILOSEVIC

Ethnic cleansing? He invented the term
Now he's on trial—so turns the worm

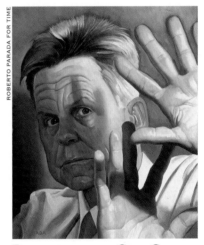

ROBERTO PARADA FOR TIME

REPRESENTATIVE GARY CONDIT

O dandy doyen of romantic duplicity,
For one so clean, you sure fear publicity

EDEL RODRIGUEZ FOR TIME

MULLAH OMAR

Sorry, Omar, we won't tell you twice
You harbor terror, you pay the price

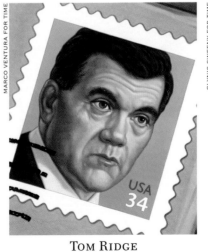

MARCO VENTURA FOR TIME

TOM RIDGE

Save us, Director of Homeland Security:
Only you can stamp out postal impurity

GLYNIS SWEENY FOR TIME

JOHN ASHCROFT

Hey, Sherlock, you missed the solution!
The case: "Who Stole the Constitution?"

September 11, 2001: A Day

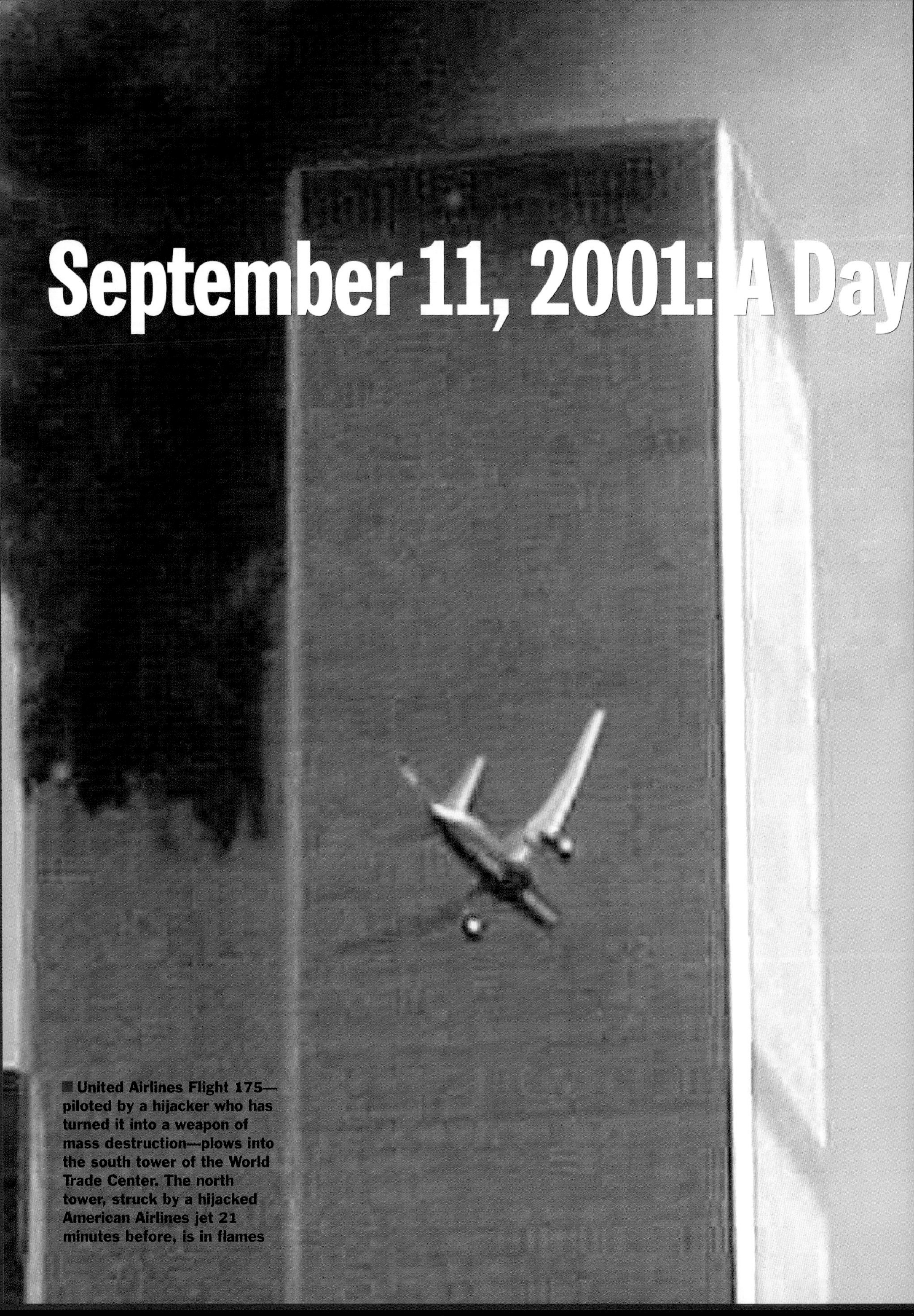

■ United Airlines Flight 175—
piloted by a hijacker who has
turned it into a weapon of
mass destruction—plows into
the south tower of the World
Trade Center. The north
tower, struck by a hijacked
American Airlines jet 21
minutes before, is in flames

That Will Live in Infamy

TARGET: AMERICA

It was the bloodiest day on American soil since our Civil War, a modern Antietam played out in real time. We couldn't move—that must have been the whole idea—so we had no choice but to watch, to watch in horror as our tall towers fell. But the terrorists who thought that by toppling buildings they could topple a nation were wrong: in the ashes of the towers Americans found new unity and fresh resolve. New York City Mayor Rudolph Giuliani was describing his constituents—but he was really speaking for all Americans—when he said, "We have never been braver. We have never been stronger."

■ Shrouded in dust, New Yorkers trudge to safety after the collapse of the World Trade Center towers. "A huge plume of smoke was chasing people, rushing through those winding streets of lower Manhattan," said Charlie Stuard, 37, an Internet consultant who worked in the area. "It was chaos, a whiteout"

In a desperate search for survivors, New York City police and fire fighters swarm over the vast heap of rubble that was the World Trade Center on the night of Sept. 11. Though local hospitals braced for thousands of wounded, the awful truth slowly sank in: there were very few survivors among those present when the towers collapsed

A NATION UNDER SIEGE

Thousands die, the towers
of the World Trade Center
collapse, and U.S. citizens
are shaken as terrorists
hijack four airliners
and crash them
into the centers
of American power

Sept. 11, 2001, was a perfect autumn day along America's East Coast: 70° as four airplanes slowly climbed into beautiful clear skies, all four on transcontinental routes, each plump with fuel, ripe to explode—and each bearing a squad of terrorists, plump with hate, ready to die in order to topple the symbols of America's financial and military prowess and hoping to spread terror across the land by taking as many innocent Americans as they could to their deaths with them.

It was a Boeing 767 from Boston, American Airlines Flight 11 bound for Los Angeles with 81 passengers, that first got the attention of air-traffic controllers. The plane took off at 7:59 a.m. and headed west, out over the Adirondacks, before taking a sudden turn south and diving toward the heart of New York City. Meanwhile American Flight 77 had left Dulles at 8:10; United Flight 175 left Boston at 7:58; and United Flight 93 left Newark at 8:01, bound for San Francisco.

The first plane, Flight 11, hit the World Trade Center's north tower at 8:45, ripping through the building's skin and setting its upper floors ablaze. People thought it was a sonic boom or a construction mishap; at worst, a horrible airplane accident. But as the gruesome rains came—bits of plane, a tire, office furniture, glass, a hand, a leg, whole bodies—people in the streets all stopped and looked and fell silent. As the smoke rose, the ash rained gently down, along with lost flocks of paper shuffling from the sky to the street below.

Almost instantly, a distant wail of sirens came from all directions, even as people poured from the building, even as a second plane bore down on lower Manhattan. Louis Garcia was among the first medics on the scene. "There were people running over to us burnt from head to toe. Their hair was burned off. There were compound fractures, arms and legs sticking out of the skin. One guy had no hair left on his head." Of the six patients in his first ambulance run, two died on the way to St. Vincent's Hospital.

Workers tore off their shirts to make bandages and tourniquets for the wounded; others used bits of clothing

ALERT Card delivers the bad news

as masks to help them breathe. Whole stretches of street were slick with blood, and up and down the blocks you could hear the screams of people plunging from the burning tower. People watched in horror as a man tried to shimmy down the outside of the tower. He made it about three floors before flipping backward to the ground.

Gilbert Richard Ramirez worked for BlueCross Blue-Shield on the 20th floor of the north tower. After the impact, he ran to the windows and saw the debris falling, and sheets of white building material, and then something else. "There was a body. It looked like a man's body, a full-size man." The features were indistinct as it fell: the body was black, apparently charred. Someone pulled an emergency alarm switch, but nothing happened. Someone else broke into the emergency phone, but it was dead. People began to say their prayers. An orderly evacuation began.

"Relax, we're going to get out of here," Ramirez said. He prodded everyone out the door, herding stragglers. It was an eerie walk down the smoky stairs, a path to safety that ran through the suffering. They saw people who had been badly burned. Their skin, he says, "was like a grayish color, and it was like dripping or peeling, like the skin was peeling off their body." But there was heroism amid the horror: as the workers descended, they were passed by fire fighters and rescue workers, panting, pushing their way up the stairs in their heavy boots and gear. "At least 50 of them must have passed us," said Ramirez. "I told them, 'Do a good job.'" When he got outside to the street, there were bodies scattered on the ground, and then another body came plummeting down, and another.

Even as people streamed down the stairs, cracks appeared in the walls as the building shuddered and cringed. Steam pipes burst, and at one point an elevator door burst open and a man fell out, half burned alive, his skin hanging off. People dragged him out of the elevator and helped get him to safety.

After leaving Boston, United Flight 175 headed to Los Angeles. Past the Massachusetts-Connecticut border, it made a 30° turn and then an even sharper turn and swooped down toward Manhattan, where it impaled the south tower at 9:06. This plane hit lower, and it seemed to hit harder; maybe that was because by now every camera in the city was trained on the towers, and the crowds in the street, refugees from the first explosion, were there to see it. Desks and chairs and people were sucked out the windows and rained down on the streets below. Men and women, cops and fire fighters, watched and wept.

The first crash had changed everything; the second changed it again. Across America, television sets were tuned to the tragedy—and anyone who thought the first impact had been an accident now knew better. This was not some awful, isolated episode, not Oklahoma City, not even the first World Trade Center bombing in 1993. This felt like a war, and the system responded accordingly; the emer-

gency plans came out of the drawers and clicked one by one into place. The city hunkered down: traffic stopped, bridges and tunnels were shut down at 9:35 as warnings tumbled one after another; the Empire State Building was evacuated, as was the United Nations. First the New York airports were closed, then Washington's, and then the whole country was grounded for the first time in history.

AT THE MOMENT THE SECOND AIRPLANE WAS SLAM-ming into the south tower, President Bush, on a routine junket to promote his education program, was being introduced to the second-graders of Emma E. Booker Elementary School in Sarasota, Fla.; he had already learned of the first strike from National Security Adviser Condoleezza Rice. As he was getting ready to pose for pictures with the teachers and kids, chief of staff Andy Card entered the room, walked over to the President and whispered in his right ear. The President's face became visibly tense and serious. He nodded. Card left the room, and for several minutes the President seemed distracted and somber, but then he resumed his interaction with the class.

When the President emerged from the room, he made a brief comment to waiting cameras. "This is a difficult time for America," he began. He ordered a massive investigation to "hunt down the folks who committed this act."

Then he and his party rushed to Air Force One and hurriedly took off—with no clear destination in mind.

Even as the President spoke, a second front opened. Having hit the country's financial and cultural heart, the killers went for its political and military nerve centers in the capital. David Marra, 23, an information-technology specialist, had turned his BMW off an I-395 exit from the highway just west of the Pentagon when he saw an American Airlines jet swooping in, its wings wobbly, looking as if it was going to slam right into the Pentagon: "It was 50 ft. off the deck when he came in. It sounded like the pilot had the throttle completely floored. The plane rolled left, then right. Then he caught an edge of his wing on the ground." There is a helicopter pad right in front of that side of the Pentagon. The wing touched there, then the plane cartwheeled into the building. By great good fortune, it struck a portion of the huge structure that had just been remodeled and reinforced; many offices were vacant. Though 189 people would die—125 in the building itself and 64 crew and passengers (including the five hijackers) on the plane—the terrorists might have claimed many more lives had the hijacked jet struck another part of the building.

But that was not all; there was a third front as well. At 9:58 the Westmoreland County emergency-operations center, 35 miles southeast of Pittsburgh, received a frantic cell-phone call from a man who said he was locked in the rest room aboard United Flight 93. Glenn Cramer, the dispatch supervisor, said the man was distraught and kept repeating, "We are being hijacked! We are being hijacked!" He also said his claim was not a hoax, and that the plane "was going down." Said Cramer: "He heard some sort of explosion and saw white smoke coming from the plane. Then we lost contact with him."

The flight had taken off at 8:01 from Newark, N.J., bound for San Francisco. But as it passed south of Cleveland, Ohio, it took a sudden, violent left turn and headed inexplicably back into Pennsylvania. As the 757 and its 38 passengers and seven crew members blew past Pittsburgh, air-traffic controllers tried frantically to raise the crew via radio. There was no response. The rogue plane soared over woodland, cattle pastures and cornfields. Finally, at 10:06, it smashed into a reclaimed section of an old coal strip mine. The largest pieces of the plane found intact were barely bigger than a telephone book. Gradually, investigators would piece together some of the story of the plane's final moments, concluding that a heroic effort by its passengers foiled the hijackers' plans before it could reach Washington (*see box*). Its intended target, officials suspected, was either the White House or the U.S. Capitol.

BACK IN LOWER MANHATTAN, THE CHAOS WAS ONLY beginning. Convoys of police vehicles raced downtown toward the cloud of smoke at the end of the avenues. The streets and parks filled with people, heads turned like sunflowers, all gazing south, at the clouds that were on the ground instead of in the sky, at the fighter jets streaking down the Hudson River. The aircraft carriers U.S.S. *John F. Kennedy* and U.S.S. *George Washington*, along with seven other warships, swung into ready positions off the East Coast.

Then the Twin Towers fell. Each tower's structural strength came largely from the 244 steel columns that formed the perimeter of each floor and bore most of the weight of all the floors above it. The floors higher than the level of the plane's impact—each floor weighing millions of pounds—were resting on steel that was softening from the heat of the burning jet fuel, until the metal could no longer bear the load above. "All that steel turns into spaghetti," explained retired Bureau of Alcohol, Tobacco and Firearms

AP/WIDE WORLD

■ HEROES IN THE SKY

From onboard United Airlines Flight 93, Tom Burnett leveled with his wife Deena: "I know we're all going to die. There's three of us who are going to do something about it." Burnett was one of 38 passengers and seven crew members aboard the hijacked flight, and he was not the only person to speak with a loved one. Mark Bingham, a p.r. exec, spoke with his mother: "Three guys have taken over the plane, and they say they have a bomb," he told her. Jeremy Glick phoned wife Lyzbeth to say, "Three Arab-looking men with red headbands" had taken over the cockpit.

CAN DO Burnett

Flight 93 was the last of the hijacked planes to meet its fate. All three passengers had been told of the attacks in New York City. Did they band together to fight their captors and ditch the Boeing 757 before it could harm untold thousands—or wipe out the White House or U.S. Capitol? Those closest to Burnett, Bingham and Glick believe they did. All three were large, athletic, decisive types. Bingham, 6 ft. 5 in., played rugby when at the University of California, Berkeley, and still played for the San Francisco Fog, a gay amateur team. Glick, 6 ft. 4 in., was a national collegiate judo champion. Burnett, 6 ft. 1 in., was a former high school football player. "We're going to rush the hijackers," Glick told his wife. Then he hung up.

agent Ronald Baughn. "And then all of a sudden that structure is untenable, and the weight starts bearing down on floors that were not designed to hold that weight, and you start having collapse … It didn't topple. It came straight down. All the floors are pancaking down, and there are people on those floors." The south tower collapsed at 10, fulfilling the intent of 1993, when the terrorists had tried to bring it down. The north tower came down 29 minutes later, crushing itself like a piston. The lower New York skyline was swathed in a chalky cloud. The towers themselves were reduced to jagged stumps; the atrium lobby arches stood tattered, like shards of a bombed-out cathedral.

The streets filled with masked men and women, cloth and clothing torn to tie across their noses and mouths against the dense debris rain. Some streets were eerily quiet. All trading had stopped on Wall Street, so those canyons were empty, the ash several inches thick and gray, the way snow looks in New York after it's been on the ground awhile. Sounds were both muffled and magnified, echoing off buildings, softened by the smoke. Fire fighters pushed people further back, north and east to the rivers. Mayor Rudolph Giuliani was

THE SEARCHERS
Investigators look for clues in the wreckage of Flight 93

GARY TRAMONTINA—AP/WIDE WORLD

THE PATHS OF DESTRUCTION

Four passenger jets, taking off within 15 minutes of one another from three East Coast airports, were transformed by hijackers into fuel-laden missiles. Two pierced the World Trade Center towers, minute apart, causing their collapse. Another pierced the Pentagon; a fourth crashed near Pittsburgh

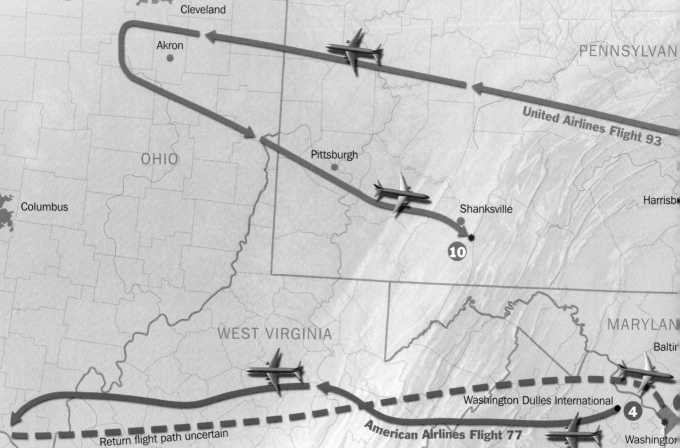

Detroit

Cleveland

Akron

PENNSYLVAN

United Airlines Flight 93

OHIO

Pittsburgh

Columbus

Shanksville

Harrisb

10

WEST VIRGINIA

MARYLAN

Baltir

Washington Dulles International

American Airlines Flight 77

4

Washington

Return flight path uncertain

1 **7:58 a.m.**
United Airlines Flight 175, a Boeing 767, departs Boston's Logan Airport for Los Angeles with 56 passengers and 9 crew

2 **7:59 a.m.**
American Airlines Flight 11, a Boeing 767, also departs Boston bound for Los Angeles, with 81 passengers and 11 crew

3 **8:01 a.m.**
United Airlines Flight 93, a Boeing 757, leaves Newark for San Francisco with 38 passengers and 7 crew

4 **8:10 a.m.**
American Airlines Flight 77, a Boeing 757, departs Washington Dulles Airport for Los Angeles with 58 passengers and 6 crew

5 **8:45 a.m.**
American Airlines Flight 11 crashes into the north tower (1 WTC) of the World Trade Center

6 **10:00 a.m.**
United Airlines Flight 175 slams into the south tower (2 WTC) of the World Trade Center

7 **9:40 a.m.**
American Airlines Flight 77 hits the Pentagon

8 **10:00 a.m.**
The south tower (2 WTC) collapses

9 **10:29 a.m.**
The north tower (1 WTC) collapses

10 **10:37 a.m.**
United Airlines Flight 93 crashes in Shanksville, Pa., 80 miles southeast of Pittsburgh

11 **5:25 p.m.**
A third building in the World Trade Center complex collapses

American Airlines Flight 77 **7**

Mall entra

Helicopter landing pa

VIRGINIA

North Carolina

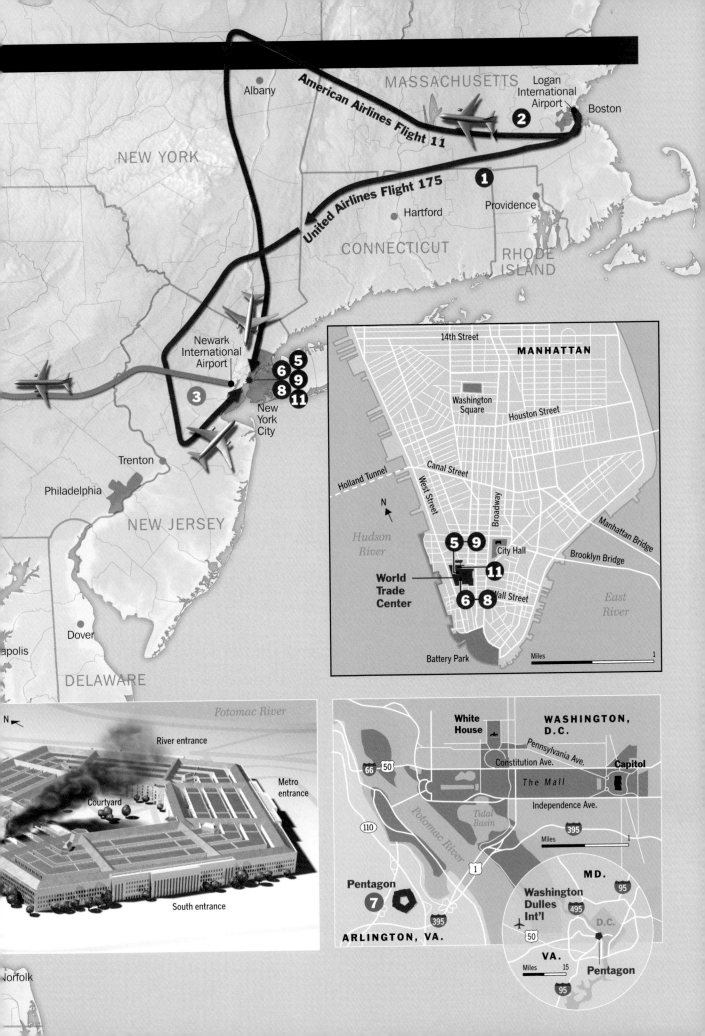

American Airlines Flight 11

2

Logan International Airport

Boston

MASSACHUSETTS

Albany

1

NEW YORK

United Airlines Flight 175

Hartford

Providence

CONNECTICUT

RHODE ISLAND

Newark International Airport

5
6 9
8 11

New York City

3

Trenton

Philadelphia

NEW JERSEY

Dover

DELAWARE

apolis

Norfolk

MANHATTAN

14th Street

Washington Square

Houston Street

Canal Street

Holland Tunnel

West Street

Broadway

Manhattan Bridge

N

City Hall

Brooklyn Bridge

Hudson River

5 9

11

World Trade Center

6 8

Wall Street

East River

Battery Park

Miles 1

N

Potomac River

River entrance

Metro entrance

Courtyard

South entrance

White House

WASHINGTON, D.C.

66 50

Pennsylvania Ave.

Constitution Ave.

Capitol

The Mall

Tidal Basin

Independence Ave.

110

Potomac River

395

Miles 1

1

MD.

95

Washington Dulles Int'l

495

D.C.

Pentagon

7

395

ARLINGTON, VA.

50

VA.

Pentagon

Miles 15

95

THE ATTACK

STANDING TALL Bush visits ground zero on Sept. 14

and security agencies believed the White House and Air Force One were both targets. Bush, the Vice President insisted, should immediately head to a safe military base. The plane's TV monitors were tuned to local news broadcasts; Bush was watching as the second tower collapsed.

About 45 minutes after takeoff, a decision was made to fly to Offut Air Force Base in Nebraska, site of the nation's nuclear command and one of the most secure military installations in the country. But Bush and his aides didn't want to wait that long before the President could make a public statement. Secret Service officials and military advisers in Washington consulted a map and chose a spot for Bush to make a brief touchdown.

Air Force One landed at Barksdale Air Force Base, outside Shreveport, La., at 11:45 a.m., with fighter jets keeping watch beside each wing throughout the descent. The perimeter was surrounded by Air Force personnel in full combat gear: green fatigues, flak jackets, helmets, M-16s at the ready. A sign on the glass windows of several doors, in large black type, read THREATCON DELTA. That is the highest possible state of military alert. Bush made his second remarks at 12:36 p.m. from a windowless conference room in Building 245, in front of two American flags hastily arranged by Air Force privates. "Freedom itself was attacked this morning by a faceless coward," he began, then spoke for two minutes before leaving the room.

ACROSS THE COUNTRY, HOUSES OF WORSHIP FILLED with grieving citizens singing *America the Beautiful,* wiping away streams of tears. Within hours of the attacks, Americans felt united as many said they had never felt before: older citizens compared the aroused national mood with the days following the Japanese attack on Pearl Harbor in 1941. Revulsion at the hideous crimes directed at innocent civilians brought Americans together across every division of politics, race, age and creed. Within a few short days, flags would sprout everywhere—on cars, in shop windows, on front porches—and "United We Stand" would become the rallying cry against terrorism.

At 7:30 p.m. Tuesday, with the Pentagon still in flames, members of Congress gathered on the Capitol steps. Republicans hugged Democrats as they broke out into a chorus of *God Bless America.* But some of them were angry: Why, they wanted to know, had the President spent the day seemingly spooked and on the run, invisible except for two brief appearances, and not in Washington? Only 24 hours later, after taking a wave of criticism for the delayed return, did aides claim there had been "credible evidence" that the White House and Air Force One were targets.

Bush did return that evening. He strode across the South Lawn of the White House and delivered a reasonably effective national address from the Oval Office. But it wasn't until the following day that he stepped up the intensity of his rhetoric and branded the attacks "acts of war." And he declared his determination to find those who were behind them and bring them to justice.

Who were the hijackers? Even before the smoke had cleared, it was obvious that the culprits knew their way

forced to evacuate his $13 million emergency command center in one of the Trade Center's auxiliary buildings. Now he took to the streets, one more fugitive from the wreckage, walking through the raining dust and forcefully ordering people to evacuate the entire lower end of the island. Medical teams performed triage on the street corners of Tribeca, doling out medical supplies and tending the walking wounded.

The refugee march began at the base of the island and wound up the highways, tens of thousands of people with clothes dusted, faces grimy, marching northward, away from the battlefield. There was not a single smile on a single face. But there was remarkably little panic as well— more steel and ingenuity as people wondered: Where am I going to sleep tonight? How will I get home?

Meanwhile, aboard Air Force One, the mood could not have been more tense. White House staff members, Air Force stewards and Secret Service agents all were subdued and shaken. One agent sadly reported that the Secret Service field office in New York City, with its 200 agents, was located in the World Trade Center.

Bush was in his office in the front of the plane, on the phone with Rice, FBI Director Robert Mueller and Vice President Dick Cheney and the First Lady, who had both been hurriedly evacuated to a bunker in the White House complex. Cheney told the President that law-enforcement around a Boeing cockpit—and all the security weaknesses in the U.S. civil aviation system. The enemy had chosen the quietest travel day of the week for the operation, when there would be fewer passengers to subdue; they had boarded westbound transcontinental flights—planes fully loaded with fuel. They were armed with knives and box cutters, had gained access to the cockpits and herded everyone to the back of the plane. Once at the controls, they had turned off at least one of the aircraft's self-identifying beacons, known as transponders, a move that renders the planes somewhat less visible to air-traffic controllers. (*For details of the hijackers' lives in America, see p. 37.*)

By Tuesday afternoon, the spooks were already making progress. Eavesdroppers at the supersecret National Security Agency had picked up at least two electronic intercepts indicating the hijackers had ties to veteran terrorist Osama bin Laden, the Saudi-born militant and "guest" of the radical Taliban regime in Afghanistan, who was believed responsible for the bombing of two U.S. embassies in Africa in 1998 and the attack in Yemen on the U.S.S. *Cole* in 2000. Less than 12 hours after the attacks, U.S. officials told TIME that their sense bin Laden was involved was as high as 90%.

On Sept. 20, President Bush spoke to both houses of Congress, vowing, "Whether we bring our enemies to justice or bring justice to our enemies, justice will be done." Fingering bin Laden as mastermind of the attacks, Bush called for the Taliban regime to hand over bin Laden and close his network of terrorist camps in Afghanistan. Bush also thanked British Prime Minister Tony Blair, who was in attendance. Blair would prove an important ally in the days ahead, as U.S. diplomats began to cobble together a multinational alliance—much like the one the President's father had built before the Gulf War in 1991—to wage war against the terrorists. Bush also created a new Cabinet-level position, the Office of Homeland Security, to guarantee the nation's safety, and he named Pennsylvania Governor Tom Ridge as its first director.

LORI GRINKER—CONTACT PRESS IMAGES

Missing from 2 World Trade Center 104th fl.

HOPING A New Yorker seeks her fiancé

Bush's powerful speech helped cement a changed national mood. As he put it, "Our grief has turned to anger and anger to resolution." A weighty burden—to bring the terrorists to justice—had been placed on the nation. But with the burden came potent new sources of strength that the masters of terror might not have anticipated. For the vast, smoking heap of rubble they had created in lower Manhattan had been the scene not only of horrific suffering but also of deeds of extreme courage and sacrifice, deeds that inspired Americans with a renewed sense of the power and purposes of freedom, deeds that consecrated this plot of ground as forever hallowed. ◼

Moments after the first hijacked jet struck the north tower of the World Trade Center, New York City's extensive medical and emergency-response teams mobilized. At Bellevue, the city's largest trauma center, an extra burn unit was set up. The night shift was called in early. The psychiatric-department staff, the biggest in the world, was mobilized to meet the survivors and families. "We actually have too many doctors now," chief medical officer Eric Manheimer reported in midafternoon. "We thought we would have more patients." By 5:40, only 159 patients had been admitted—which suggested not how few people had been injured in the towers' collapse, but how few of them could be saved.

In the hours to come, rescue workers began the grisly business of sorting through what used to be two 110-story buildings—more than 2 billion lbs. of steel and glass and concrete—compressed into a mound nine stories high. Five-fingered grapples fixed to the end of 40-ft. metal arms peeled back each layer, gently removing crisscrossed pillars piled like giant pickup sticks. Welders clambered around with acetylene torches to cut through the metal until they found a void, or pocket of air. When a fire fighter's body was found, "there is dead silence," said fireman Jeff Silver, 34. "All the machinery is cut off, and everybody takes their helmets off while a body bag is brought over and brothers from his station come, and carry him away." In all, 343 New York City fire fighters and 60 police officers died in the attack.

While the rescuers dug, Manhattan streets filled with friends and relatives of the missing, many of them bearing handmade posters with a picture of a loved one. Soon the posters blanketed the city's windows and lightposts, memos of sorrow and loss. Union Square Park, at 14th Street, for more than a century a gathering place for New Yorkers, became a candle-lit center of mourning. At firehouses and in other city parks, impromptu memorials sprang up, featuring poems and prayers, tokens and tributes, flowers and children's drawings.

As the weeks went on, the grim task of assessing the death toll in a case where so many bodies might never be found continued. But here, at last, came welcome news. The body count at the World Trade Center, which began with estimates as high as 7,000, steadily fell. Soon the count of missing and presumed dead was 5,000. By mid-December the count was close to 3,000, proving that the orderly evacuation of the towers had been hugely successful. A full count is impossible, but as many as 27,000 people who had been in the buildings on that fateful day may have escaped with their lives.

TRAIL OF A ZEALOT

How a child of wealth and privilege became a mass murderer

AS A BOY, HE WAS—BELIEVE IT OR NOT—CALLED "Sammy." Osama bin Laden was born to a Westernized mother (some say she was Syrian; others believe she was Palestinian) who favored Chanel suits and a father smart enough to amass a fortune of more than $1 billion but so unschooled that he couldn't write his own name. Easily overlooked among Mohamed bin Laden's 52 children, the young boy is remembered as serious, smart and unfailingly polite. Early pictures show him decked out in expensive jewelry, loud colors and bell-bottom pants. In his native Saudi Arabia, bin Laden attended élite schools where he studied English; he often vacationed with this family in Europe. So how did this unremarkable child of wealth

grow up to become a cold-blooded murderer, a zealot who massacred civilians in the name of his god, and the most wanted criminal in the world?

If the 1960s was a time of political ferment and radicalized youth in the West, the same was true for the Middle East in the 1970s. Within a few short years, a culture that had undergone little change for centuries was jolted by tectonic shifts, driven by a gusher of oil money, successive wars with Israel and increasing contact with the West.

Pious from childhood, bin Laden, like most Saudis, is a member of the puritanical Wahhabi sect of the Sunni branch of Islam. By the time he entered King Abdel Aziz University in Jidda in 1974, he had become convinced that Arab culture was being destroyed by external influences.

BIN LADEN'S WAR ON AMERICA

CARNAGE In the late 1990s, al-Qaeda's attacks on U.S. installations and personnel grew bolder. In 1998 U.S. embassies in Kenya, left, and Tanzania were bombed, killing 244 people. In 2000 suicide bombers attacked the U.S.S. *Cole* at a port in Yemen. Seventeen U.S. sailors died

The increasingly radical student came under the influence of Abdullah Azzam, a Palestinian academic who preached that only through violent confrontation could the decadence and evil of Western influence be purged from the holy lands of Islam. Azzam would later start the Maktab al Khidmat organization to aid the *mujahedin* of Afghanistan; it eventually morphed into al-Qaeda.

By 1979 bin Laden's world view had crystallized: he was entranced as Islamic radicals overthrew the pro-Western government of Iran in February, and he cheered in November when heavily armed Muslim fundamentalists laid siege to the grand mosque in Mecca. Before the year was out, Soviet tanks had rolled into Afghanistan, and the young millionaire had found the cause he had long sought.

Within months, bin Laden left Saudi Arabia for Pakistan, where the anti-Soviet resistance was based. He soon became a key figure, albeit more for his financial resources and organizational ability than for his distinction in combat. For the next decade, bin Laden worked with his mentor, Azzam, training the legions of Muslim militants who had come to Afghanistan to fight for their faith.

When the Soviets retreated from Afghanistan in 1989, bin Laden went home to Saudi Arabia. Though he found he had gained a mythic reputation among Islamic radicals there, he was now a holy warrior without a war. But within a year, bin Laden found a new jihad. Iraq had invaded Kuwait, and its army stood poised at the Saudi border, seemingly ready to overrun that country too. The hero of Afghanistan approached the pro-West Saudi royal family with an offer to raise an army of tens of thousands of the faithful to defeat Saddam Hussein, and was bitterly disappointed when the offer was declined. But his chagrin metastasized into cold, bloodthirsty rage when the royals invited troops of the U.S.—the embodiment of all that bin Laden saw as evil—to defend the kingdom.

When bin Laden began agitating for revolution in Saudi Arabia, King Fahd forced him into exile in Sudan. It was there that the radical began building the network that would soon bring him infamy. In 1993, 18 U.S. soldiers were murdered in Somalia, and the horrified U.S. quickly withdrew, convincing bin Laden that America was a paper tiger. U.S. officials now suspect he may have played a financial role in the bombing of the World Trade Center by a group of Egyptian radicals that year. In 1995, after a truck bombing in Saudi Arabia (apparently directed by al-Qaeda) killed three Americans, the Saudis and the U.S. urged Sudan to expel the radical. He fled to Afghanistan, where the radical fervor of the new Islamic rulers, the Taliban, meshed perfectly with bin Laden's own apocalyptic fantasies.

The next year, bin Laden issued a "Declaration of Jihad," setting for himself the goal of overthrowing the Saudi government and driving U.S. forces out of the holy land. In 1998 he called on the Muslim faithful to kill Americans, civilians included, wherever they could find them. Later that year his operatives exploded car bombs at the U.S. embassies in Kenya and Tanzania, killing 224 people, mostly Africans. The attack provoked a U.S. cruise-missile attack on an al-Qaeda base in Afghanistan that missed bin Laden and only burnished his image as an authentic hero to many Muslims.

Bin Laden denied any connection to the embassy bombings; two years later he denied involvement in the attack on the U.S.S. *Cole*. He also initially denied involvement in the Sept. 11 attacks on America. Few listeners found his denials convincing, but even the most cynical observers were appalled when, in early December, a videotape surfaced on which bin Laden brags about his role in the attacks and even seems to laugh at some of the hijackers who may not have known theirs was a suicide mission.

A Palestinian journalist who interviewed bin Laden in late November reported that he was no longer laughing. His beard had gone gray, the journalist said, and the serene cadence of his voice had turned shrill. He had even recanted his edict to kill U.S. civilians; his fight was with their leaders, he said. But such fine distinctions must have mattered little to Osama bin Laden and his followers as his long-anticipated rendezvous with martyrdom drew closer. ∎

A TERRORIST'S ODYSSEY

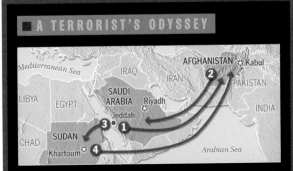

1 SAUDI ARABIA The son of a rich contractor, bin Laden inherits $80 million and is set for a life of ease. But in 1979, jihad calls.

2 AFGHANISTAN From 1980 to 1989, bin Laden battles Soviet invaders, largely by raising money and Islamic recruits.

3 SAUDI ARABIA Bin Laden returns home, agitates against U.S. troops and ends up in trouble with a nervous Saudi government.

4 SUDAN In exile, bin Laden begins to organize his old Afghan war comrades into the al-Qaeda terror network. In 1996 he is expelled.

5 AFGHANISTAN As a guest of the Taliban, bin Laden expands his syndicate and declares a holy war against Americans.

TENTACLES OF HORROR

Ruthless and patient, deceptive and defiant, the terrorists of the radical Islamic network al-Qaeda have spun a complex web of hatred that spans the globe

THE NAME IS ARABIC FOR "THE BASE" (AS IN MILITARY headquarters). New members are inducted with a secret ceremony strikingly similar to that performed by Cosa Nostra recruits. The candidate meets with a senior member and recites, "In the name of God the Merciful, the Compassionate. I promise to ally myself to Osama bin Laden for the sake of God." Within days of the Sept. 11 attacks, U.S. officials declared that the 19 hijackers who carried out the plan had sworn this very oath—to the terrorist network al-Qaeda.

Founded in the mid-1980s to wage Islamic holy war against the Soviet presence in Afghanistan, al-Qaeda was in decline by 1989. The war that was its raison d'être was winding down and its founder, Palestinian academic Ab-

dallah Azzam, was dead from a bomb blast that has never been fully explained. Waiting in the wings was Azzam's protégé, the Saudi-born millionaire Osama bin Laden, who went from providing mere financing to furnishing an entirely new vision: al-Qaeda would combat the enemies of Islam not just in Afghanistan but around the world. At first, this meant attacks primarily against the pro-West regimes in Egypt and Saudi Arabia. But when the radical Taliban regime, led by zealous cleric Mullah Omar, came to power in Afghanistan, bin Laden expanded his training camps—and his dreams. In 1998, he joined forces with Ayman al-Zawahir, an Egyptian doctor who led Al Jihad (or Egyptian Islamic Jihad), an organization that had the real-world experience to put bin Laden's deadly schemes into practice on a much larger scale. The synergies of the merger soon become apparent. Later that year, the group's operatives exploded truck bombs at the American embassies in Kenya and Tanzania, killing 12 Americans and hundreds of locals. In 2000 the group masterminded the bombing of the U.S.S. *Cole* in Yemen that killed 17 U.S. sailors.

Why has al-Qaeda been so successful? By being different from most radical Islamist groups, in both mind-set and method. Many of bin Laden's operatives subscribe to a school of Islamic thought called Takfir wal Hijra ("Anathema and Exile"). Takfir has two unusual features: first, adherents are taught to despise fellow Muslims with differing interpretations of the faith as much as they hate nonbelievers. Second, operatives are taught to assimilate completely into the country they intend to attack, even defying Muslim prohibitions against alcohol and gambling.

Operationally, al-Qaeda is different because its initiatives often percolate from the bottom up rather than being handed from the top down. Al-Qaeda picks and chooses among the best and the brightest (read: the most ruthless and committed) Islamic terrorists around the world. It furnishes them with skills and funding that make them independent contractors of fear—and far more effective and deadly than they ever could have been on their own.

Funds for terrorist operations come from sources as diverse as the Middle Eastern honey trade, wealthy sympathizers in Islamic nations and unknowing contributors in the U.S., who often believe they are supporting humanitarian missions. Funds are moved through a traditional Middle Eastern system of money exchange called *hawala* (the Hindi word for "trust"), in which a secret code is used to identify the recipient and the amount of a cash transfer. This paperless, wireless network leaves no records and is nearly invisible to law enforcement.

This also makes al-Qaeda almost impossible to track down. U.S. officials believe there are dozens, perhaps hundreds, of cells hidden in as many as 60 nations around the world—from Europe to Indonesia—and none of them knows very much about the others. So even when investigators put one team out of business before it strikes (as they have more than once), it doesn't necessarily follow that progress has been made against any of the others. Even if the group's leaders are rooted out of Afghanistan, the battle to eradicate its branches may prove a long one. ∎

MULLAH OMAR A rare photo of the cleric, third from left

THE HIJACKERS

LEAD HIJACKER Atta

They came from Saudi Arabia, most of them, but also from Egypt, Lebanon and the United Arab Emirates —we think. Their number included two sets of brothers and a pair of cousins—we think. But the truth is that beyond a handful of positive identifications, we may never know much more about the foot soldiers who perpetrated the horrific Sept. 11 attacks on the U.S. Their traces are shrouded in a welter of stolen passports, forged credentials, multiple aliases and names like Alshehri that—even if genuine—are as common in the Middle East as Smith and Jones in the U.S.

Here is what we do know about the 19 people behind the bland, expressionless faces that stare out of the photos culled from passport files and driver's license records. They came to the U.S. as long ago as 13 years and as recently as four months. They seem to have entered and left the U.S. without difficulty, even though two (Khalid Al-Midhar and Nawaq Alhamzi, Flight 77) were on an FBI watch list as suspected terrorists. At least seven of them had some training as pilots. Fully half of them left no written record whatsoever of their lives in America: there isn't a paper trail to indicate that they ever crossed a U.S. border, used a credit card, rented a home or applied for a driver's license.

They trained relentlessly at flight schools and in local gyms. Some of them showed an unusual interest in crop-dusting airplanes. But not all of them may have been prepared to die for their cause: U.S. investigators suspect that the nonpilots among the hijackers, whose job on each plane was to overpower the crew and keep the passengers under control, may have believed that these would be "ordinary" hijackings (in which the plane returns to the airport and the terrorists make demands) and thus didn't realize they were going to die that morning. One of them (Abdulaziz Alomari, Flight 11) had a wife and four small children in Vero Beach, Fla.

They ate pizza, used automatic teller machines, blended in with their communities, lived modestly. The Florida team drove a Toyota Camry that was nearly a decade old, but were sometimes picked up by limousines in the middle of night. Defying the strict tenets of the religion in whose name they killed, some of them drank alcohol, gambled and caroused with strippers in Las Vegas. Yet they never seem to have lost sight of the goal they were secretly working toward—to kill Americans and to dwell in paradise as martyrs. As Mohamed Atta (Flight 11), their suspected leader, wrote in a note to himself not long before Sept. 11, "Before you enter [the plane], start praying and realize that this is a battle for the sake of God, and when you sit in your seat, say these prayers ... When the plane starts moving, then you are traveling toward God and what a blessing that travel is."

GERM WARFARE

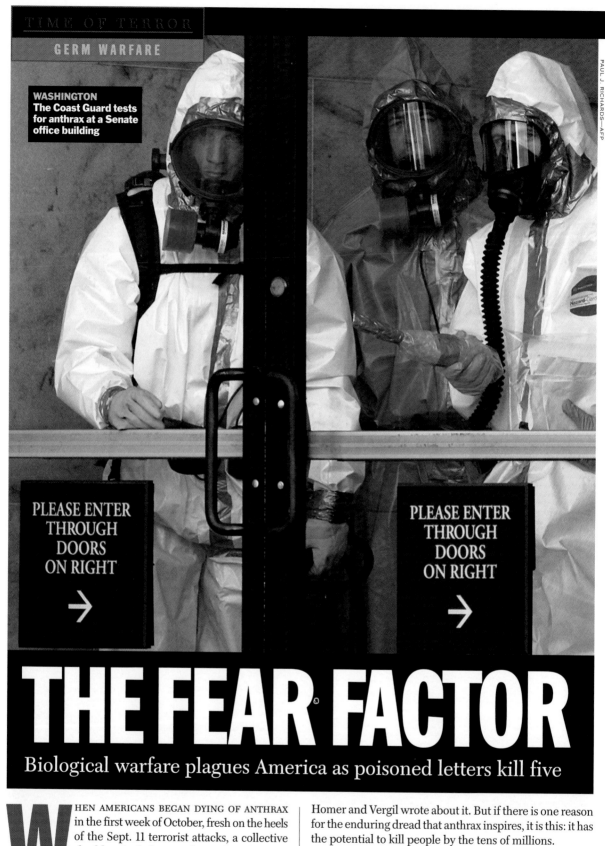

WASHINGTON
The Coast Guard tests for anthrax at a Senate office building

PLEASE ENTER
THROUGH
DOORS
ON RIGHT
→

PLEASE ENTER
THROUGH
DOORS
ON RIGHT
→

THE FEAR FACTOR

Biological warfare plagues America as poisoned letters kill five

WHEN AMERICANS BEGAN DYING OF ANTHRAX in the first week of October, fresh on the heels of the Sept. 11 terrorist attacks, a collective shudder rippled across the nation. For a microbe that few laymen know anything about, *Bacillus anthracis* has long gripped the human imagination: it was the fifth of the 10 Old Testament plagues that God visited upon the Egyptians, and both

Homer and Vergil wrote about it. But if there is one reason for the enduring dread that anthrax inspires, it is this: it has the potential to kill people by the tens of millions.

Robert Stevens, a photo editor at tabloid publisher American Media in Boca Raton, Fla., died of inhalation anthrax on Oct. 5—the first U.S. case of the disease since 1976. More than 40 of his colleagues later tested positive for anthrax exposure, and within weeks, anthrax-laced letters were found at other media companies (NBC, the New York *Post*) and government offices (those of Senators Tom Daschle and Patrick Leahy). But in the capital, anthrax killed not politicians but two postal workers, Joseph Curseen and Thomas Morris, who worked in the sorting facility that handled the letters. A delay in recognizing the potency of the anthrax cost Curseen and Morris their lives. Within days of their deaths, as many as 20,000 people were taking antibiotics at government urging, and unknown thousands more were taking medication on their own.

By early December, a total of five people had died and six others had contracted the inhaled form of the disease, its deadliest variety, which kills victims in as little as 48 hours by overloading the immune system. At least seven others were being treated for cutaneous anthrax, a milder form contracted through contact with the skin.

VICTIM Thomas Morris, above, was one of the two capital postal workers killed by tainted letters

Investigators had no idea who was behind the mailings or how the deadly substance had been obtained. And no thread linked the disparate victims: Kathy Nguyen (a New York City hospital worker) and Ottilie Lundgren (an elderly Connecticut woman) had no connection to power. Investigators suspected these two were infected because their mail had been sorted in the same facilities as letters sent to more prominent targets. Trace amounts of anthrax were also detected in other postal facilities in the Northeast.

What investigators could say for certain was that all the anthrax seemed to come from the same source, the so-called Ames strain (an especially lethal variety that was first isolated in Ames, Iowa, in the late 1970s). Different government spokesmen gave contradictory accounts about whether the disease had been "weaponized" (refined so that in powder form, it would disperse freely, rather than clumping together, and thus threaten a far greater number of people). And the letters that accompanied the deadly powder contained threats that linked the attacks to Sept. 11: "This is next/ take penacilin [sic] now."

But FBI profilers discounted foreign terrorists as suspects. Agents believed the perpetrator was probably a lone domestic operator who had not been involved in the Sept. 11 attacks but may have been set off by them. He was likely an angry male, they said, who shunned human interaction and had some scientific background. It is also probable that English was not his first language.

If the American public was not reassured by the extent to which this profile would narrow the list of suspects, they were even more unnerved by the conclusion of at least one expert from the Centers for Disease Control and Prevention: four letters were unlikely to have created the widespread contamination detected by mid-December, so it was quite possible more tainted letters might be found. ■

■ BATTENING THE HATCHES

When anthrax-tainted letters began arriving in U.S. mailboxes, some Americans invested in gas masks, while the Federal Government began planning to vaccinate every American against smallpox and to stockpile anthrax vaccine. Helping lead attempts to heighten security and stifle terrorist networks, Attorney General John Ashcroft called for extraordinary measures, some of which were seen as curtailing civil liberties in the name of national defense, raising serious constitutional issues.

● **DETENTIONS** Federal agents detained more than 800 foreign nationals, mostly for outstanding immigration violations, and held them for months without filing any serious charges—tactics they could not employ against U.S. citizens. FBI agents also began canvassing college students from Middle Eastern countries, while federal prosecutors sent letters to some 5,000 men of Middle Eastern descent, asking them to report for interviews.

● **SURVEILLANCE** The Bush Administration announced that, in certain cases, federal agents would eavesdrop on conferences between criminal defendants and their attorneys. Meanwhile, gun-rights activists objected to proposals to cross-check the watch list of suspected terrorists with the names of gun buyers.

● **MILITARY TRIBUNALS** The White House reserved the right to try captured foreign terrorists before military tribunals, rather than civilian courts, in part to protect the secrecy of evidence. Civil libertarians branded such proceedings as unconstitutional "kangaroo courts."

● **AIRLINE SECURITY** After a rancorous political debate over the shabby state of security on airport check-in lines, the White House and Congress agreed before Thanksgiving to a compromise plan that would hire and train 28,000 new federal employees to handle baggage  **ASHCROFT On the spot** screening at most airports for a period of three years. An expanded corps of sky marshals would be hired and trained for undercover posting aboard some flights.

AMERICA STRIKES BACK

An aroused, grieving nation declares war on the Taliban, the radical rulers of Afghanistan—and the guardians of the suspected mastermind of the Sept. 11 attacks, Osama bin Laden

For a new kind of war, it had an old sort of start. In the places where soldiers and sailors live—in Norfolk, Va.; Fort Bragg, N.C.; in a hundred other towns of the Republic and far beyond its shores—the rhetoric of impending battle was rendered in the humdrum details of military life. Bills were paid; kit bags packed; wives, husbands and children hugged. Patriotism hung in the air, as palpable as the first chills of fall; flags sprouted on a million lapels and fluttered from a thousand taxicabs in a wounded but defiant New York City as George W. Bush went to the U.S. Capitol and, in a speech to Congress, braced Americans to prepare for a war against terrorism, "a lengthy campaign unlike any other we have ever seen … the hour is coming when America will act."

In his remarks on Sept. 20, Bush spoke directly to the Taliban, the radical Islamic regime in Afghanistan that harbored Osama bin Laden, leader of the al-Qaeda network and prime suspect behind the Sept. 11 atrocities. The President demanded that the Taliban hand over all the terrorist leaders to U.S. authorities. The Afghans refused, demanding, in turn, firm proof of bin Laden's guilt. Evidence came soon enough, provided by British Prime Minister Tony Blair. On Oct. 4 his government released a white paper that built a case connecting bin Laden and al-Qaeda to the Sept. 11 attacks.

ANTHONY SUAU FOR TIME

WARRIORS: Northern Alliance troops fire at the Taliban front lines

The devastating assault on America sparked a dramatic shift in the Bush team's strategy. An Administration that just a month or two before had emphatically believed in going it alone—walking away from the Kyoto Protocol, pushing its missile-defense scheme no matter who said what—would be driven by terrorism into creating a multinational coalition to fight a war abroad against an elusive enemy.

Support from America's NATO allies was immediately forthcoming. Other allies were more surprising: early on, Bush spoke twice with Russian President Vladimir Putin, who pledged his aid; even Libyan dictator Muammar

INCOMING U.S. soldiers take cover during the revolt by surrendered Taliban at Qala-i-Jangi, near Mazar-i-Sharif

Gaddafi denounced the attacks. America's allies in the Arab Middle East, Saudi Arabia and Egypt, came on board, but quietly: each nation faced strong Islamist elements within. Indeed, as many as a dozen of the 19 hijackers who died in the attacks had lived in Saudi Arabia.

Ironically, the ally the U.S. needed most was the nation that had helped the Taliban take power in the first place: Pakistan. On Sept. 11, Bush called President Pervez Musharraf. The U.S. President's language was friendly but firm as he asked if Pakistan could help hunt down bin Laden. Musharraf faced a stark choice: if he agreed, he might face a major reaction at home from irate militant Islamists. If he refused, the U.S. response could be harsh. Musharraf, 58, a low-key soldier with tolerant views, was aghast at the suicide attacks. He did not hesitate. "I'll face tremendous difficulties, but I'll support you," he told Bush.

With his coalition intact, Bush made good on his threat. On Oct. 7, U.S. planes, backed by British cruise missiles, swooped down from the skies and dropped their payloads on poor, doomed Afghanistan, where war of some kind or another has been a fact of life since the Soviet invasion of 1979. As the bombs dropped, Bush had one eye on the response from Muslims around the world, a concern that had led him to feather his engines longer than he had planned.

The situation within Afghanistan was complex. The ruling Taliban, a Pashtu term for Islamic students, had emerged in 1994 from the rural southern hinterlands of Afghanistan under the guidance of the reclusive yet charismatic onetime village preacher Mullah Mohammed Omar. Winning military and political support from Pakistan, the largely Pashtun Taliban rose to power by promising peace and order for a country ravaged by corruption and civil war and by aiming to restore traditional majority-Pashtun dominance.

THE ALLIANCE The Taliban's present foes, the loose coalition of rebels known as the Northern Alliance, were in many cases the bloody warlords who took power after the Soviets withdrew, only to be overthrown later by the Taliban. The Alliance forces were mainly composed of ethnic Tajiks and Uzbeks; they were supported by the leaders of their homelands to Afghanistan's north, the former Soviet republics Tajikistan and Uzbekistan. Both nations declared they would aid the U.S. cause.

As the war began, Alliance forces held some 10% of the land in the nation, all along Afghanistan's northern rim. For purposes of fighting the Taliban, the U.S. would make common cause with them, but they were allies of convenience: the Bush Administration understood that simply

ENDGAME **Captured Taliban fighters are moved between Kunduz and Mazar-i-Sharif**

A LAND AT WAR

Operation Enduring Freedom began on Oc with major airstrikes b U.S. planes and cruise missiles. Within two months, the Taliban ha been routed from pow across Afghanistan

- Approximate area of Taliban control, Nov. 24
- Relief convoys
- Refugee concentrations

ISLAM QALA
Returning refugees reportedly being arme the Northern Alliance

HERAT
The Northern Alliance captured Herat after the Taliban pulled out on Nov. 12. Its former governor, Ismail Khan, took over. More than 200,000 refugees surrounded the city

FARAH
More than 50,000 refugees wer encamped around the town as of Dec. 1

100 mi.
100 km

Sources: United Nations; U.S. Defense Department; Reuters; Associated Press; Agence France-Presse; news reports; East View Cartographic: www.cartographic.com
TIME Map by Jackson Dykman and Joe Lertola

replacing one set of tyrants with another was no answer to Afghanistan's grave long-term problems.

The first week's bombing runs were carried out by B-2 Stealth bombers flying halfway around the world from Missouri; B-1 and B-52 planes based on Diego Garcia, a tiny island in the Indian Ocean; and Navy F-18s flying off the U.S.S. *Carl Vinson* and U.S.S. *Enterprise.* Cruise missiles were fired from surface vessels and submarines. The attacks hit more than 60 targets: air-defense systems, weapons dumps and training camps run by both the Taliban and al-Qaeda.

After six days, the bombing slowed, in part for observance of Friday prayers at mosques. By the third week of the air war, the number of U.S. sorties over Afghanistan doubled to about 100 a day, but it had been clear from the beginning that air strikes alone probably wouldn't budge the Taliban, who seemed able to withstand hits against strongholds and replenish its forces. And for all the talk of teamwork between the U.S. military and the Northern Alliance, the two would-be partners were marching out of sync. While Alliance leaders refused to work together to coordinate their attacks and called for more U.S. air support, U.S. brass branded the Alliance's loose-knit guerrilla bands as inexperienced, plagued by ethnic infighting and hooked on hashish.

SECOND WIND They weren't the only ones bickering. Scant weeks into the conflict, the U.S. war effort came under fire from a global chorus of critics who said the campaign was hurtling toward either humiliating defeat or inescapable quagmire. Many in the Muslim world focused on the deaths of innocent civilians caused by American bombs—deaths they conveniently failed to link to the horrific strikes on civilians that sent U.S. bombers over Afghan air space in the first place.

Meanwhile, critics in the U.S. blasted the Pentagon's campaign as sluggish and unfocused. "War is a miserable business," said Arizona Senator John McCain. "Let's get on with it." Some Europeans were also wavering in their support for the U.S. effort. Then the Pentagon stepped on the gas. The war's critical turn came on Oct. 21, when U.S. B-52s began hammering Taliban front lines dug in near Mazar-i-Sharif, a key northern stronghold; Kabul, the capital city; and further north, along the Tajik border. It was a new phase in the war: Pentagon strategists were now coordinating attacks with the Alliance rebels, and U.S. planes began air-dropping them guns, money and horse feed.

The number of American special-ops spotters deployed to the front more than doubled, to almost 100. Target guides on the ground enabled the U.S. to pulverize Taliban troops with B-52 carpet bombings and BLU-82 "daisy cutters"—15,000-lb., minivan-size killing machines carried one at a time in the belly of MC-130 cargo planes. When detonated 3 ft. above the ground, the bomb's slurry of ammonium nitrate and aluminum dust wipes out everything within a half-mile radius.

MAZAR-I-SHARIF
The Taliban's key northern stronghold fell on Nov. 9. Hundreds of trapped soldiers were killed, many shot while trying to surrender. A revolt of surrendered prisoners at the fortress of Qala-i-Jangi was quelled after 3 days of fighting

TERMEZ
Western aid was bottled up at this Uzbek bridge crossing until Uzbek authorities agreed to open it on Dec. 9

KUNDUZ
After Alliance forces marched into a Taliban trap and suffered losses on Nov. 13, the U.S. heavily bombed Taliban positions. Kunduz fell into Alliance hands on Nov. 25

TAKHAR PROVINCE
Thousands of refugees fleeing Kunduz and Taloqan reached camps along the Tajikistan border in late November

PAKISTAN
More than 2 million Afghan refugees are in Pakistan, and an estimated 155,000 more crossed the border between Sept. 11 and Dec.

CENTRAL HIGHLANDS
As winter set in, Western officials feared thousands might be stranded in remote areas without access to relief supplies

JOURNALISTS KILLED
Four Western journalists were killed on the road. Others have been robbed at gunpoint

KABUL and JALALABAD
Once Mazar and Kunduz fell to Alliance troops and after weeks of steadily more precise U.S. bombing, Taliban soldiers surrendered the capitol on Nov. 13 without putting up much of a fight

DAR-I-SUF
A bitter guerilla war between Alliance and Taliban troops raged here until Nov. 8

TORA BORA
A host of al-Qaeda fighters, and perhaps Osama bin Laden, were believed to have taken shelter in this remote, formidable region

BAMIYAN
Here the country's worst humanitarian crisis unfolded. Refugees fleeing both the Taliban and a withering three-year drought were starving and freezing on the sides of surrounding hills

Termez
Mazar-i-Sharif
Sheberghan
Faizabad
Taloqan
Kunduz
Chaghcharan
Bamiyan
Kabul ★
Jalalabad
Ghazni
Khost

PAKISTAN

AFGHANISTAN

Area of detail map

NDAHAR
e last major Taliban onghold held firm for eeks longer than the rthern cities. Then shtun opposition troops unted an offensive, and S. Marines set up a base amp Rhino) 70 miles thwest of the city. Forces al to designated interim me Minister Hamid Karzai k control of the y on Dec. 8

HUNTING OSAMA
The U.S. concentrated the search for bin Laden in eastern Afghanistan, in the Tora Bora region of the White Mountains, riddled with elaborate cave complexes. After U.S. bombers pounded the area for days, anti-Taliban forces mounted an assault against a suspected 1,500 al-Qaeda troops on Dec. 10. Six days later Osama's forces surrendered—but there was no sign of the terror kingpin

SPIN BOLDAK
At least 60,000 refugees were living in camps within sight of the Pakistani border

LAGHMAN
Jalalabad
NANGAHAR
Khyber Pass
Tora Bora
PAKISTAN

30 mi.
30 km

FREE AT LAST! Citizens hail the arrival of Alliance troops in Kabul on Nov. 13, after the Taliban withdrew from the capital city

Meanwhile, U.S. Green Berets slipped into rebel-held territory and worked to prepare the Alliance's factions for a coordinated series of assaults.

WAR ON THE GROUND After 29 days of bombing, the Alliance troops mounted an offensive—literally mounted it, for some troops were cavalry who charged the Taliban's leftover Soviet tanks on horseback. On Nov. 4, 3,500 rebels serving under Uzbek warlord Rashid Dostum pushed the Taliban out of Kishindi with a 16-hour assault. To the west, forces loyal to Ustad Atta Mohammed, another Alliance commander, lost 30 men in a barrage of Taliban tank fire but seized the outlying village of Aq Kuprik. From there the Alliance's long-promised and much delayed march on Mazar-i-Sharif gathered an irresistible momentum. Some Taliban soldiers ran and hid; others switched sides. The advancing rebels found a Taliban commander, Mullah Qahir, trying to avoid capture by snipping off his beard. He wasn't alone. "From what I hear," said an Alliance officer, "it's a good time to be a razor salesman in Mazar."

A few days later, it was an even better time to be a barber in Kabul. For once the Taliban began to give ground in the north, their downfall was swift. Mazar-i-Sharif had barely been liberated when Dostum's forces overran the towns of Tashkurghan and Hairatan. Shortly after, the Alliance took control of another Taliban stronghold, Kunduz. Hearing that Taliban troops were moving toward them, Alliance forces marched into battle, only to be met by discouraged soldiers eager to surrender.

Kabul was liberated on Nov. 13, as alliance soldiers entered the capital, meeting only token resistance. Taliban warriors who had promised a fight to the death disappeared in the middle of the night like a long bad dream, and by morning the people were throwing flowers at the tanks as Northern Alliance forces rode victorious into town. "I knew we'd beat the Talibs," said a grinning commander of an armored unit, "but I never thought it'd be this easy." It wasn't: only days later, 300 surrendered Taliban prisoners rioted and took control of Qala-i-Jangi, a sprawling 19th century prison fortress to the west of Mazar-i-Sharif. They were subdued only after a grim, three-day battle that saw the death of a U.S. CIA agent, Johnny Micheal Spann, 32.

Qala-i-Jangi held another surprise: among those who crawled out of a flooded basement in the old fortress was an American, John Walker, 20. A videotape found after the uprising showed a bizarre confrontation: Spann, the U.S. CIA agent, interrogating Walker, the U.S. Taliban soldier. Walker was taken into custody; his future, which may include a trial for treason, was still in doubt in mid-December. (*See p. 47 for profiles of Walker and Spann.*)

Meanwhile, Kabul was rejoicing. With the capital freed from theocracy at last, some men ignored the call to prayer, preferring instead to line up for their first shave in five years. Children climbed to a high, windy point atop the ruins to fly the kites that the mullahs had banned as frivolous. On Tuesday night, the lights of Kabul came on for the first time in weeks, and music was heard for the first time in years. Families and merchants dug out their television sets, their VCRs and tape players; they swapped pictures of movie stars and reveled in irreverence.

And Kabul's women, so long smothered in commandments, shrugged them off. Female faces, shy and bright, emerged from the dark cellars of house arrest. Families went for joy rides through the streets, and a teenage girl with her veil off laughed and waved at the crowds she could at last see without a scrim.

INTO KANDAHAR The liberation of northern Afghanistan left three main objectives of the U.S. campaign unfulfilled: bin Laden was still at large; Mullah Omar and the remnants of his Taliban army were still in control of their southern stronghold, Kandahar; and a new government to ensure Afghanistan's security had yet to be put in place.

On Nov. 27, negotiators gathered under United Nations auspices at the Hotel Petersberg in Bonn, Germany, to create a future for a post-Taliban Afghanistan. After more than a week of acrimonious talks, the negotiators agreed on a plan. An interim Afghan government, composed of 29 members representing a cross section of tribes and interests, would take power on Dec. 22, supported by a multinational corps of peacekeepers. This interim government would be followed by a *loya jirga*, a traditional constituent assembly of Afghan leaders, which would formulate plans for a lasting new constitution and government.

The Bonn conferees selected Hamid Karzai, 43, a Pashtun and an elder of the half-million-member Popolzai tribe in southern Afghanistan, as the nation's interim Prime Minister. Seeking to balance ethnic rivalries, the conferees selected three ethnic Tajiks of the Northern Alliance—Mohammed Fahim (defense), Yonus Qanooni (interior) and Abdullah Abdullah (foreign affairs)—as his chief ministers.

Karzai, who described himself as "a politician, not a fighter," was a promising figure to lead a unified Afghanistan. His father had been a chief tribal leader in Kandahar until July 1999, when the 75-year-old was shot to death on the street in the Pakistani city of Quetta, where father and son had both fled from the Taliban. The killing is presumed to have been carried out by Taliban agents. Educated partly in India, Karzai speaks English fluently, as well as six other languages. His manner is quiet and reassuring. Early in October, he had slipped inside southern Afghanistan, hoping to recruit tribal elders to join an anti-Taliban coalition. It was not long before the Taliban got on his trail. He escaped ambush and certain death by calling in U.S. forces to rescue him by helicopter.

Karzai's foes, Taliban leader Mullah Omar and his remaining forces, were now bottled up in Kandahar. With the U.S. and the Northern Alliance in control of some two-thirds of the country, the Pentagon began sending in the Marines. In early December, 1,000 of them set up a base some 70 miles southwest of Kandahar, christened Camp Rhino. They later took over the main airport outside the city.

■ OVER THERE: BUSH'S TEAM GOES TO WAR

George Bush came into office vowing to concentrate his energies on the national scene: his key goals involved taxation and education. The terrorist attacks starched up his Administration—and shook up the playing field for his team. Colin Powell, previously relegated to the sidelines by the President's more hawkish foreign policy advisers, became a critical figure. And Defense Secretary Donald Rumsfeld emerged as a commanding voice.

COLIN POWELL
A week before 9/11, TIME's cover asked, "Where have you gone, Colin Powell?" The Secretary of State seemed a bit player as Bush focused on a domestic agenda. After the attacks, Powell took on a key role as Bush's alliance builder

DICK CHENEY
The ever cautious Vice President took heat for advising Bush to take cover on Sept. 11, then disappeared from view as he and Bush stayed apart for security reasons. Insiders insisted he was still a pivotal member of Bush's inner circle

CONDOLEEZZA RICE
The tough, opinionated National Security Adviser dominated foreign policy before 9/11, and gave up some ground to Colin Powell's diplomats afterward. But she remained one of Bush's closest advisers and is often with him in Texas or at Camp David

TOMMY FRANKS
As commander in chief of the U.S. Central Command, the lanky four-star general ran Operation Enduring Freedom from his HQ at MacDill Air Force Base in Tampa. No Schwarzkopf, he kept a low public profile but carried a big stick

DONALD RUMSFELD
Before the attacks, the Secretary of Defense was struggling with Pentagon brass over the future of the military. Energized by the war, he emerged as a forceful leader whose candid remarks during briefings earned laughs—and respect

EUREKA! An anti-Taliban fighter finds a deserted cave filled with ammunition

The southern front offered no standing army of rebels to serve as U.S. proxies; most local tribes were ethnic Pashtun, like the Taliban. But now a force emerged: troops loyal to Karzai surrounded the Taliban's spiritual capital.

With the jaws of a vise closing around them, the remaining Taliban within Kandahar began talking surrender terms with Karzai and his aides. But a proposed deal fell through, and on Dec. 7, the Taliban's barbaric, medieval rule unraveled for good as the regime's soldiers fled their last stronghold. Some skulked back to their home villages with the idea of starting new lives. Others, like prime target Mullah Omar, went missing, perhaps with the aid of local warlords; Karzai and his troops failed to nab him.

HUNTING OSAMA As Karzai's men took power in Kandahar, the black turbans and medieval strictures of Taliban rule began to seem like a long nightmare. But in eastern Afghanistan, the manhunt for bin Laden went on. For the terror kingpin and his dwindling legion of lieutenants—an estimated 1,500 fighters—the last sanctuary was thought to be the famously impregnable cave complex called Tora Bora, built by *mujahedin* during the war with the Soviet Union. The caves are cut into the jagged, 13,000-ft. peaks of the White Mountains range 35 miles south of Jalalabad. They make an ideal retreat: a vast honeycomb of tunnels 8 ft. wide, some carved 1,150 ft. deep into the mountains. The warren of entrances, tiny slits in the rock, lead into ventilated chambers that are virtually invisible from the sky.

With the Taliban routed elsewhere, the full fury of the U.S. aerial campaign was now directed on Tora Bora. Sorties by U.S. F-15Es, unmanned Predator drones and commando ground troops in early December killed scores of Taliban and al-Qaeda lieutenants, including key bin Laden deputy Mohammed Atef, the reputed architect of the Sept. 11 attacks. The wife and children of al-Qaeda's strategic mastermind, Ayman al-Zawahiri, the leader of the Egyptian Islamic Jihad, were

KARZAI Can he heal Afghanistan?

also confirmed dead, but al-Zawahiri himself was thought to have survived.

In the second week of December, forces loyal to three U.S.-backed warlords clambered into the mountains to stage assaults on al-Qaeda redoubts, while as many as 40 U.S. commandos called in B-52-delivered bombs and precision-guided missiles. But American leaders were infuriated when a botched "surrender" of al-Qaeda troops arranged by one of the warlords, Haji Zaman, may have given bin Laden's men more time to slip away. For now U.S. military officials thought they were getting close to their prey: after weeks of playing Where's Osama?, they believed they had overheard bin Laden on handheld radio in the White Mountains, giving orders to his dwindling forces. The ferocity of the fighting in Tora Bora also suggested that al-Qaeda was defending more than just snow-covered rocks.

But the mouse escaped the trap: on Sunday, Dec. 16—after weeks of devastating U.S. bombing—the remaining al-Qaeda forces surrendered. Bin Laden was not among them. If he had indeed been in the Tora Bora region, U.S. officials believed he had probably escaped somewhere across the 1,510-mile border with Pakistan. The day before the surrender, there were reports that 50 Arab al-Qaeda fighters had traversed the border in a mule train. Neither technology nor vigilance can secure a border that spans impossibly remote mountain trails.

With the fall of Tora Bora, the first stage of America's war on terrorism came to an end. Afghanistan's Taliban regime had been toppled, in a surprisingly short time and with surprisingly little loss of life among both Afghans and Americans. Al-Qaeda's network of terrorist camps within Afghanistan had been utterly destroyed. And a new, more democratic regime was preparing to take office; on Dec. 22, a multinational force, led by British troops, moved into Kabul as guarantors of the Bonn accord.

But some key goals of the initial stage of the war had not been achieved: Mullah Omar and bin Laden had lost their base of power, but both men remained at large, the subjects of a massive manhunt. Equally troubling, an unknown number of both Taliban and al-Qaeda fighters had escaped capture, perhaps to practice terror again.

The Bush Administration was said to be planning the next stage of the war, which might include strikes against other staging areas for terrorism, including Iraq, Yemen and Somalia. And with Osama bin Laden still at large, there was little joy in America: the accounts in the devastating attacks of Sept. 11 would not be settled until al-Qaeda's leader had been nabbed. As President George Bush declared on Dec. 17: "When the dust clears, we'll find out where he is, and he'll be brought to justice." Americans hoped the dust would clear soon. ■

IN THE CRUCIBLE

The worst of times revealed the best in some people, and led two young Americans to a fateful meeting

JOHN WALKER AND MIKE SPANN

On Nov. 25, two young men met in a bizarre face-off inside the 19th century fortress at Qala-i-Jangi near Mazar-i-Sharif, which had recently fallen to the Northern Alliance. Johnny Micheal Spann, 32, was a CIA agent interrogating Taliban prisoners—one of whom, John Walker (Lindh), 20, was an American, raised in affluent Marin County, Calif.

Walker, a spiritual seeker, converted to Islam at 17 and left the U.S. in 1998 to attend an Arabic-language school in Yemen. He returned at Christmas 1999 but went to Pakistan in November 2000 to attend an Islamic school, or madrasah. His parents last heard from him in May, 2001, just before he joined the Taliban in Afghanistan.

Spann was a small-town boy from Winfield, Ala., a polite kid who dreamed of being a CIA agent. Moments after he spoke to Walker, he was killed when he and a colleague identified only as "Dave" were overpowered by surrendered Taliban prisoners. Spann was buried in Arlington National Cemetery.

MUSLIM AMERICANS

The Sept. 11 attacks put enormous pressure on America's seven million Muslims, who are largely social conservatives. Hundreds of incidents of vandalism, harassment, and assault were reported nationwide, as well as at least one death (of an Arizona Sikh mistaken for a Muslim). But the backlash led to a reappraisal; by early December, a nationwide poll showed more Americans had a favorable view of U.S. Muslims than before the attacks.

TONY BLAIR

After Sept. 11, Britain's Prime Minister—whose Labour Party had cruised to victory in an election three months before—became a roving ambassador, zooming through Europe, India, Pakistan, Russia, the U.S. and the Middle East to invigorate the anti–bin Laden coalition. Sending Foreign Secretary Jack Straw to Tehran to meet with Iran's Mohammed Khatami, Blair made good on his words in a prophetic speech: "This is a

moment to seize. The kaleidoscope has been shaken. Soon [the pieces] will settle again. Before they do, let us reorder this world around us." On Dec. 22, it was a cadre of British troops who led a group of peacekeepers into Kabul to guarantee peace and the Bonn accord.

DAYNA CURRY & HEATHER MERCER

Along with four German colleagues, American aid workers Curry, 30, and Mercer, 24, were arrested by the Taliban early in September and charged with disseminating Christian literature. After 102 days in detention, they were freed by Northern Alliance troops as the Taliban fell. Though prison conditions were grim, they said the Taliban treated them with respect.

F SOWING DEATH WERE THE MEASURE OF one's impact, Osama bin Laden would own the year 2001; America lost more lives on Sept. 11 than it did at Pearl Harbor. And bin Laden did more than kill. To watch his operatives destroy the gigantic Twin Towers of the World Trade Center—embracing their own deaths as they took thousands of innocent civilians with them—was to confront not only the nature of evil but how much we still don't know about it. Yet bin Laden is too small a man to get the credit for all that happened in America in the autumn of 2001. We paint him larger than he is in order to fit his crime; yet those who have studied his work do not elevate him to the company of history's monsters, despite the monstrousness of what he has done. It is easy to turn grievance into violence; that takes no genius, just a lack of scruples and a loaded gun.

It is what followed after bin Laden's men had finished their job that came to define the year. Having raced to the scene at the first news of the attacks, Rudolph Giuliani, the mayor of New York City, was nearly buried alive. In the hours that followed, he had to lock parts of the city down and break others open, create a temporary morgue and a makeshift command center, find a million pairs of gloves and dust masks and respirators, throw up defenses against another attack and persuade the citizens of his city that it had not just been fatally shot through the heart.

There was a test in that moment, and Giuliani was the first to pass it. On that day, for his security and the country's, George Bush was on the move. The rest of us had stopped in our tracks, frozen. It was Giuliani who held off despair long enough for the rest of us to get our balance, find our armor and join in to fight at his side. That day and in the days that followed, he sounded realistic and optimistic at the same time. He drew a line between information and inspiration, never substituting one where the other was needed.

For teaching us that lesson, for having more faith in us than we had in ourselves, for being brave when required and rude where appropriate and tender without being trite, for not sleeping and not quitting and not shrinking from the pain all around him, Rudy Giuliani, Mayor of the World, is TIME's Person of the Year 2001. ■

PERSON OF THE YEAR

RUDOLPH GIULIANI

Photograph for TIME by Gregory Heisler

SIXTEEN LONG HOURS HAD PASSED SINCE THE TWIN Towers crumbled and fell, and people kept telling Rudy Giuliani to get some rest. The indomitable mayor of New York City had spent the day and night holding his town together. He arrived at the World Trade Center just after the second plane hit, watched human beings drop from the sky and—when the south tower imploded—nearly got trapped inside his makeshift command center near the site. Then he led a battered platoon of city officials, reporters and civilians north through the blizzard of ash, and a detective jimmied open the door to a firehouse so the mayor could revive his government there. Giuliani took to the airwaves to calm and reassure his people, made a few hundred rapid-fire decisions about the security and rescue operations, toured hospitals to comfort the families of the missing and made four more visits to the apocalyptic crime scene.

Now, around 2:30 a.m., Giuliani walked into the Upper East Side apartment of Howard Koeppel and his longtime partner, Mark Hsiao. Koeppel, a friend and supporter of Giuliani's, had been lending the mayor a bedroom suite since June, when Giuliani separated from his second wife, Donna Hanover, and moved out of Gracie Mansion. His suit still covered with ash, Giuliani hugged Koeppel, dropped into a chair and turned on the television—actually watching the full, ghastly spectacle for the first time. He left the TV on through the night in case terrorists struck again, and he parked his muddy boots next to the bed in case he needed to head out fast. But he was not going to be doing any sleeping. Lying in bed, with the skyscrapers exploding over and over again on the TV screen, he pulled out a book—*Churchill*, the new biography by Roy Jenkins—turned straight to the chapters on World War II and drank in the Prime Minister's words: "I have nothing to offer but blood, toil, tears and sweat."

There is a bright magic at work when one great leader reaches into the past and finds another waiting to guide him. From midmorning on Sept. 11, when Giuliani and fellow New Yorkers were fleeing for their lives, the mayor had been thinking of Churchill. "I was so proud of the people I saw on the street," he says now. "No chaos, but they were frightened and confused, and it seemed to me that they needed to hear from my heart where I thought we were going. I was trying to think, Where can I go for some comparison to this, some lessons about how to handle it? So I started thinking about Churchill, started thinking that we're going to have to rebuild the spir-it of the city, and what better example than Churchill and the people of London during the Blitz in 1940, who had to keep up their spirit during this sustained bombing? It was a comforting thought."

With the President out of sight for most of that day, Giuliani became the voice of America. Every time he spoke, millions of people felt a little better. His words were full of grief and iron, inspiring New York to inspire the nation. "Tomorrow New York is going to be here," he said. "And we're going to rebuild, and we're going to be stronger than we were before … I want the people of New York to be an example to the rest of the country, and the rest of the world, that terrorism can't stop us."

Sept. 11 was the day that Giuliani was supposed to begin the inevitable slide toward irrelevancy. It was primary-election day in the city, when people would go to the polls to begin choosing his successor. After two terms, his place in history seemed secure: great mayor, not-so-great guy. The first Republican to run the town in a generation, he had restored New York's spirit, cutting crime two-thirds, moving 691,000 people off the welfare rolls, boosting property values and incomes in neighborhoods rich and poor, redeveloping great swaths of the city. Even so, other great swaths of the city were sick of him. People were tired of his Vesuvian temper and constant battles—against his political enemies, against some of his own appointees, against the media and city-funded museums, against black leaders and street vendors and jaywalkers and finally even against his own wife. His marriage to cable-television personality Hanover had become a bitter war: ugly headlines, dueling press conferences. Giuliani's girlfriend, pharmaceutical-sales manager Judith Nathan, had helped him get through a very public battle against prostate cancer, and his struggle touched off a wave of concern and appreciation for him. But most New Yorkers seemed ready for Rudy and Judi to leave the stage together and melt into the crowd.

Fate had another idea. When the day of infamy came, Giuliani seized it as if he had been waiting for it all his life, taking on half a dozen critical roles and performing each with mastery. Improvising on the fly, he became America's homeland-security boss, giving calm, informative briefings about the attacks and the extraordinary response. He was the gutsy decision maker, balancing security against symbolism, overruling those who wanted to keep the city buttoned up tight, pushing key institutions—from the New York Stock Exchange to Major League Baseball—to start up and prove that New Yorkers were getting on with life. He was the crisis manager, bringing together major players from city, state and federal governments for marathon daily meetings that got everyone working together. And he was the consoler in chief, strong enough to let his voice brim with pain, compassion and love. When he said, "The

With Dick Cheney and George Pataki

The Mayor attended close to 200 memorial services

Giuliani: "We're not in a different world"

number of casualties will be more than any of us can bear," he showed a side of himself most people had never seen.

Giuliani's performance ensures that he will be remembered as the greatest mayor in the city's history, eclipsing even his hero, Fiorello La Guardia, who guided Gotham through the Great Depression. Giuliani's eloquence under fire has made him a global symbol of healing and defiance. World leaders from Vladimir Putin to Nelson Mandela to Tony Blair have come to New York to tour ground zero by his side. As Jenkins, author of the biography that inspired Giuliani after Sept. 11, told TIME, "What Giuliani succeeded in doing is what Churchill succeeded in doing in the dreadful summer of 1940: he managed to create an illusion that we were bound to win."

THE GLORIOUS BLUFF

WHEN HE THINKS ABOUT CHURCHILL'S WARtime words, Giuliani now says, "I wonder how much of it was bluff." Three months to the day since the towers fell, he is riding with TIME in his big tan SUV as it steers through the maze of concrete barricades, switchbacks and checkpoints that lead into the heart of ground zero. "A lot of it had to be bluff," he says. "Churchill could not have known England was going to prevail. He hoped it, but there was no way he could know."

He is asked the obvious question: How much of his confidence on Sept. 11 was bluff?

"Some," he says matter-of-factly. "Look, in a crisis you have to be optimistic. When I said the spirit of the city would be stronger, I didn't know that. I just hoped it. There are parts of you that say, Maybe we're not going to get through this." He pauses. "You don't listen to them."

He climbs out of the SUV and looks around. "It's still amazing," he says. From here on West Street, near the Hudson River, inside the high fences and past the tourist throngs, ground zero looks like a huge, patriotic construction site—flags on the cranes, flags on the hard hats, flags on the huge white temporary domes that house the mess hall and the EPA decontamination stalls. But your eye finds the last standing chunk of the north-tower façade (it would be removed in a few days) and the stump of twisted, melted steel that used to be 6 World Trade Center and the pit where corpses are still being found, and then the place looks like what it is: a mass grave. "This is the most emotional spot for me," Giuliani says, waving a hand, "because this is where I was that morning." He points straight overhead, where the north tower used to be. "I looked up and saw a man jump out—above the fire, must

have been at least 100 stories—and my eye followed him, almost transfixed, all the way down. He hit the top of that building," he says, pointing to what's left of 6 WTC. "Over there"—he gestures a few feet down the street—"is where the guys had their command post set up." The guys were the fire department's top brass: Chief of Department Pete Ganci, Commissioner Tom Von Essen, First Deputy Commissioner Bill Feehan and Special Operations Chief Ray Downey. All except Von Essen are now dead.

"'Scuse me, Mayor, would you sign my hat?" The workman is extremely big, extremely dirty and just a little bit awestruck. He holds out a scuffed white hard hat, and Giuliani smiles. "I would love to," the mayor says, and by the time he has done so, 10 more guys with 10 more hats are waiting in line. It was like this everywhere Giuliani went in his last days on the job. The mayor, who would be leaving office Jan. 1, drew one long, loud thank-you from the people of his city. "Rudy, way to go!" calls Dwayne Dent, 37, an African-American ironworker. "You're about the greatest mayor ever, ain'tcha?" Giuliani gives him a melancholy smile. It's nice to be loved, but at times the cost is, as he predicted, more than he can bear.

THE OLD RUDY

YET ALL THE GRIEVING, ALL THE GRATITUDE, ALL THE valedictory warmth that have been showering the mayor cannot obscure his pugilist's heart. The old Rudy resurfaced on Sept. 22, when Giuliani fired a counterterrorism specialist named Jerry Hauer—whom he had recruited just eight days earlier—because Hauer dared to appear at a press conference with a Democratic rival. The old Rudy showed up again when the mayor returned a $10 million relief check from Saudi Prince al-Waleed bin Talal, who had suggested that America should rethink its support for Israel. And he was seen frequently that month as Giuliani made a bid to extend his term as mayor and slapped down those who questioned his motives. If he had found a way to get on the ballot, he would have won in a landslide. That's because Giuliani had saved New York twice: the first time, in the mid-1990s, through sheer toughness—asserting control over a crime-ridden city—and the second time, after Sept. 11, through a mix of toughness and soul. Each time, he gave the city the part of him it needed.

Giuliani has spent his adult life searching for missions impossible enough to suit his extravagant sense of self. A child of Brooklyn who was raised in a family of fire

With Homeland Security chief Tom Ridge

With Russian President Vladimir Putin, right

With Prime Minister Tony Blair

With Kofi Annan, Pataki and U.N. representatives

fighters, cops and criminals—five uncles in the uniformed services, an ex-con father and a Mob-connected uncle who ran a loan-sharking operation—he chose the path of righteousness and turned his life into a war against evil as he saw it. As a U.S. Attorney in New York during the 1980s, Giuliani was perhaps the most effective prosecutor in the country, locking up Mafia bosses, crooked politicians and Wall Street inside traders, though his vindictiveness and thirst for publicity led to excesses. In 1987, for instance, his men arrested two stockbrokers in their offices, then handcuffed and perp-walked them past the TV cameras; later he quietly dropped the charges against them.

Yet by 1993, when Giuliani made his second run for mayor—four years before, he lost to Democrat David Dinkins, the first African American to win the job—a tough prosecutor seemed to be just what the city needed. More than a million New Yorkers were on welfare, violent crime and crack cocaine had ravaged whole neighborhoods, and taxes and unemployment were sky-high. The squeegee pest was the city's mascot. The windows of parked cars were adorned with pathetic little signs that said RADIO HAS ALREADY BEEN STOLEN. It was fashionable to dismiss the place as ungovernable, and when candidate Giuliani gave speeches decrying that notion, he of course used Churchill to do it. Imagine, Giuliani said, if while the bombs were falling on London during the Battle of Britain, Churchill had said, "You know, this is really beyond our control. We can't do much about this." That, he argued, is what New York's leaders were doing: abdicating in the face of grave threats.

Candidate Giuliani eventually dropped the comparison because it seemed too dramatic, even for him. But after he defeated Dinkins, Mayor Giuliani made good on its implied promise. He did away with New York's traditional politics of soft and ineffectual symbolism—empathizing about problems but not fixing them—and got to work. His first police commissioner, William Bratton, came on the scene sounding like Churchill too ("We will fight for every street. We will fight for every borough"). Using computer-mapping techniques to pinpoint crime hot spots, Bratton's N.Y.P.D. reduced serious crime by more than one-third and murder by almost half in just two years. But there was room in town for only one Churchill. Giuliani forced Bratton to resign, in large part because the commissioner hogged too many headlines. Giuliani felt vindicated when the crime rate kept dropping under the loyalists he appointed to succeed Bratton. And the public—delighted that the streets were actually

safer and cleaner—didn't care how it happened. If Giuliani picked fights big and small, if he purged government of those he deemed insufficiently loyal, so be it. "People didn't elect me to be a conciliator. If they just wanted a nice guy, they would have stayed with Dinkins," Giuliani says now. "They wanted someone who was going to change this place. How do you expect me to change it if I don't fight with somebody? You don't change ingrained human behavior without confrontation, turmoil, anger."

He governed by hammering everyone else into submission, but in areas where that strategy was ineffective, such as reform of the city schools, he failed to make improvements. "The Boss," as his aides call him, inspired extraordinary loyalty and repaid it. He elevated a streetwise N.Y.P.D. detective named Bernard Kerik through the ranks of city government, eventually making him corrections commissioner and then police commissioner. Kerik, who compares entering Giuliani's inner circle with becoming "a made man in a Mafia family," reduced violence 95% in the city jails and kept crime on the decline in New York this year even as it spiked around the country.

"Nobody believed Giuliani had a heart," Kerik says. "He's not supposed to have a heart. He's an animal, he's obnoxious, he's arrogant. But you know what? He gets it done. Behind getting it done, he has a tremendously huge heart, but you're not going to succeed in New York City by being a sweetie. Giuliani has no gray areas—good or bad, right or wrong, end of story. That's the way he is. You don't like it, f___ you."

The city's black and Latino leaders did not like it. Focused on enforcing "one standard" for all New Yorkers (and obsessed with marginalizing activists like the outspoken Rev. Al Sharpton, whom Giuliani saw as a racial opportunist), the prickly Giuliani rarely reached out to any minority leaders. They complained that his aggressive cops were practicing racial profiling, stopping and frisking people because of their race. And though police shootings declined 40% under Giuliani, minorities did not take comfort in that because of three awful brutality cases that, for many people, came to define the Giuliani years.

LOSING THE PEACE

I N 1997 A HAITIAN MAN NAMED ABNER LOUIMA WAS savagely sodomized with a mop handle by a cop in a Brooklyn-precinct bathroom. Two years later, an unarmed, uncharged street peddler named Amadou Diallo was killed when police in the Bronx fired 41 shots at him in a dark vestibule. And a year after that, an unarmed security guard named Patrick Dorismond, who had been trying to hail a cab outside a midtown bar, was shot

Showing Bush the damage, with Von Essen and Kerik

The first New York City mayor to address the U.N.

At the Yankee Stadium memorial with Hillary and Bill Clinton

to death after a scuffle with undercover cops. Giuliani denounced the cops who brutalized Louima but defiantly backed those who killed Diallo and Dorismond. (In those cases, juries cleared the officers of wrongdoing.) After Dorismond was killed, Giuliani's instinct to defend the police led him to attack the unarmed victim; the mayor authorized release of Dorismond's juvenile records to "prove" his propensity for violence. The dead, Giuliani argued, waive their right to privacy. Even old friends and supporters were appalled. The man who had saved New York City saw his job-approval rating drop to 32%.

Even as New York City was getting better, its mayor seemed to be getting worse. When *New York* magazine launched an ad campaign calling itself "Possibly the only good thing in New York Rudy hasn't taken credit for," Giuliani had the ads yanked from the sides of city buses. The magazine sued and won. With the criminals on the run, the mayor was again resembling Churchill, a wartime leader too obstreperous to win the peace. Giuliani launched a "civility campaign" against jaywalkers, street vendors and noisy car alarms and a crusade against publicly funded art that offended his moral sensibilities. But the pose seemed hypocritical at best when Giuliani, whose wife had not been seen at City Hall in years, began dating the stylish Judi Nathan. The clash between the mayor's lifestyle and his policies was deftly skewered by *Saturday Night Live* comedian Tina Fey. "New York Mayor Rudy Giuliani is once again expressing his outrage at an art exhibit, this time at a painting in which Jesus is depicted as a naked woman," Fey deadpanned. "Said the mayor: 'This trash is not the sort of thing that I want to look at when I go to the museum with my mistress.'"

In the spring of 2000, Giuliani was edging toward a political move that he did not appear completely interested in making: running against Hillary Rodham Clinton for the Senate seat being vacated by Daniel Patrick Moynihan. That's when his carefully controlled, highly effective life went off the rails. He had been seeing Nathan since at least the previous year, but now the relationship exploded into the headlines. Donna Hanover later won a court order to prevent Nathan from attending city functions held at Gracie Mansion. Giuliani's divorce lawyer, Raoul Felder, counterattacked, calling Hanover an "uncaring mother" with "twisted motives." One of Giuliani's biographers, *Village Voice* reporter Wayne Barrett, broke the news of Giuliani's father's criminal past.

Finally, in April 2000, Giuliani announced that he had been found to have prostate cancer, the disease that had killed his father. He withdrew from the Senate race and pledged to devote his remaining 18 months in office to breaking down "some of the barriers that maybe I placed" between him and minority communities. "I don't know exactly how you do that," he said, "but I'm going to try very hard."

THE BARRIERS FALL

N THE END IT WAS GIULIANI'S PERFORMANCE ON AND after Sept. 11 that broke down those barriers, demonstrating once and for all how much he cared about New Yorkers, even if he had not always been able to show it. After Sept. 11, a good many Rudy watchers assumed he had changed—a rigid, self-righteous man had morphed into a big-hearted empath—but Giuliani's friends and aides say his warm side has always been there. Outsiders just couldn't see it. Countless times in the past eight years, he has sat at the bedside of an injured or dying cop or fire fighter, gently broken the awful news to the family, even remembered a widow's name years later. The public never saw these moments because the press was not there. Giuliani, so famously thirsty for attention, did away with the custom of holding mayoral press conferences at police funerals; he felt it was unseemly.

It is now customary to say Sept. 11 put the central values of life into perspective and swept away the things that don't matter, and that is true for Giuliani. Suddenly the whole world saw the New York City police and fire departments the way Giuliani had always seen them. And the whole world saw Giuliani the way only his closest friends had seen him. "I spent my first 7¾ years as mayor living out my father's advice that it's better to be respected than loved," he says. "But I had forgotten the last part of what he used to say: 'Eventually, you will love me.'"

The mayor has aged in the past year, but it suits him. His hair is grayer, thinner but still defiantly combed over. Small oval eyeglasses have softened his look; cancer and exploding skyscrapers have softened it more. "The whole experience continues to be very strange," he says one afternoon in his office at City Hall, where he is packing up eight years' worth of files, photos, baseball bats and Yankees caps, "because it is very personal, but it's also part of my public duty as mayor to deal with it.

"People ask, 'Have you changed a lot since 9/11?'" Giuliani says. "Actually, I changed more from the prostate cancer. Having to deal with that had a bigger impact and, I think, gave me more wisdom about the importance of life, the lack of control you have over death. It removed some of the fear of death."

Reopening the promenade in Battery Park

In Israel, with a victim of suicide bombing

With Nelson Mandela

His cancer treatment consumed the last six months of 2000. After intense study and consultation—with immeasurable help from Nathan, a trained nurse in her mid-40s—Giuliani chose a course of treatment involving radioactive-seed implantation and radiation rather than surgery. Just hours after the implantation operation on Sept. 19, 2000, Giuliani held a press conference. The next day he marched in a parade. But two weeks later, he felt "as bad as I had ever felt"—the seeds were starting to work. In November he began six weeks of daily external radiation treatments, and they turned out to be "very, very tough weeks"—full of nausea, hot flashes, exhaustion. He concealed his condition as best he could, though he sometimes had to excuse himself from meetings or a press conference. And most days he took a long nap.

Nathan, who is divorced and has a teenage daughter, was at his side through it all. She recently had become managing director of a philanthropic consulting firm called Changing Our World Inc., and she moved easily in Giuliani's supercharged universe. With Donna Hanover and Giuliani's two children, Caroline, 12, and Andrew, 15, still living in Gracie Mansion, Nathan had been functioning as a kind of shadow First Lady—attending memorial services but not sitting with the mayor; keeping a low public profile while playing a significant role behind the scenes. After Sept. 11, she helped organize construction of the Family Center on Pier 94 in New York, leading 3,000 volunteers who, in just 36 hours, turned 125,000 sq. ft. of raw space into what she calls a "warm place where the survivors could grieve in dignity and get the help they needed."

Giuliani is now cancer free, and Nathan believes that God spared him so he would be able to lead on Sept. 11. The timing of his ordeals also makes the mayor think about God's hand. Had the terrorists struck one year earlier, "when I was going through daily radiation, I couldn't have done it." Had he not had the cancer, he probably would have stayed in the Senate race and might have won—and thus would not have been on the scene to help his city get through the crisis. And if not for the cancer, he says, "I would have dealt with Sept. 11 effectively, but not as effectively. I would not have been as peaceful about it."

Yet Giuliani wrestles mightily with his faith, with the question of whether events happen randomly or according to a divine plan. He won't say he was "chosen" to lead the city at this moment. "Whatever my belief in God, I don't believe he enters into politics," he says. But the more he thinks about it, the more he accepts that "there must be some plan in all of it. As for my own personal odyssey, it worked out better for me and better for the city that all those things happened."

Giuliani has attended almost 200 funerals, services and wakes for police officers, fire fighters and emergency workers who died on Sept. 11, and each time he has offered a variation on the theme that "what could have destroyed us made us stronger," thanks to the heroes "who turned the worst attack on American soil into the most successful rescue operation in American history," with some 20,000, perhaps even 25,000, civilian lives saved. Wherever he went, Giuliani took to leading each congregation in a whooping, foot-stomping ovation for its fallen hero.

THE REAL WORLD

WHEN GIULIANI HEARS PEOPLE TALKING ABOUT how Americans have been living in "a different world" since Sept. 11, he disagrees. "We're not in a different world," he says. "It's the same world as before, except now we understand it better. The threat and danger were there, but now we recognize it. So it's probably a safer world now."

Giuliani understood the danger earlier than most. "I assumed from the time I came into office that New York City would be the subject of a terrorist attack," he says. The World Trade Center was bombed by Islamist terrorists in 1993, before he became mayor, and while most New Yorkers pushed the memory aside, Giuliani did not. To ease the long-standing disaster-scene turf battles between fire and police, he created the Office of Emergency Management and built a $13 million emergency command center on the 23rd floor of 7 World Trade Center, a mid-size building in the complex. The place was ridiculed as "Rudy's bunker." (Only the location was a mistake; on Sept. 11 the bunker had to be evacuated, and the entire building collapsed.) He and his staff held drills playing out 10 disaster scenarios, from anthrax attacks to truck bombs to poison-gas scares.

He didn't foresee terrorists' flying airliners into office towers, but the constant drilling ensured that when it happened, everyone in city government knew how to respond. "We used to make fun of those drills," says chief of staff Tony Carbonetti, "but I think they saved lives." In the weeks after Sept. 11—but before spores started getting mailed to media targets around Manhattan—Giuliani convened meetings with the Centers for Disease Control and Prevention and the FBI to discuss the threat of anthrax. As a result, he knew more about anthrax than Homeland Security chief Tom Ridge and Health and Human Services Secretary Tommy

Working the phone in his mobile office, an SUV zooming around town

With Saudi Prince bin Talal—he criticized U.S. policy, so Rudy returned his check

Thompson. While Ridge and Thompson contradicted each other and downplayed the lethal nature of the spores, Giuliani treated the public like grownups, offering unvarnished information and never having to backtrack. When he told people not to panic, they didn't.

A MAN IN FULL

MOST NEW YORK MAYORS LEAVE OFFICE DEFEATed and embittered by the demands of running the city. But when Giuliani handed over the reins to billionaire Mike Bloomberg at a ceremony in Times Square just after midnight on Jan. 1, he left at the peak of his popularity. He had changed the outcome of the race to succeed him, ensuring Bloomberg's victory simply by making a TV commercial endorsing him.

In one sense, his mayoralty ended as it began, with the economy in recession and his aides negotiating painful budget cuts with the city council in the wake of 9/11. The city's schools were little better than he found them, and cops were again rousting the homeless from Fifth Avenue. But so much else had changed that Giuliani had vaulted into the ranks of world leaders. He ignited adulation in the streets of Jerusalem. His Blackberry pager pulled in an e-mail message from the Queen of England, who was available in February to knight him. He had a $3 million, two-book deal. The networks were dangling offers. He would command six-figure speaking fees and open a consulting company with some of his aides (Rudy would not be happy working for someone). His divorce would soon be final, and some of his friends thought he and Nathan would get married, but he wouldn't confirm that. He did look forward to spending more time with his children, though even in the midst of post-9/11 recovery he managed to attend eight of Andrew's nine high-school football games as well as see Caroline's school play and take her to see ground zero.

As long as Giuliani remains healthy, his friends believe, he will sooner or later make his next move and run for higher office. He is keeping his political-action committee up and running, and he will wait for his opening. At 57, he has time. He doesn't want to be Homeland Security boss or run for Governor against fellow Republican George Pataki, but he has always had half-concealed presidential dreams, and it's easy to imagine him trying for the Senate (in New York or New Jersey) or even serving as George W. Bush's running mate if Dick Cheney chooses not to run again. "You never know what you would do if a President asked you," he says. "That's further in the future, which might make a difference. But right now I'm not looking for anything. Even before Sept. 11, I was looking forward to some private time. I need to take a break, reflect on everything that's happened. I could use a vacation."

His last one was 40 minutes long.

It was the night of Sept. 13, and Giuliani was at the police academy command post, where he had been virtually around the clock for almost three days. The 72-hr. wave of adrenaline was wearing off, and he was feeling the strain. The President would be arriving in the morning for his first trip to ground zero. The city was still pretty well closed down. And the casualties were, as Giuliani had predicted, more than anyone could bear. Nobody had been pulled alive from the site since the first night, and the city's medical examiner, Dr. Neil Hirsch, was telling him that additional rescues were extremely unlikely. Giuliani wasn't ready to abandon hope. "These are New Yorkers," he said. "Give 'em another week."

Nathan could see he was near the end of his rope. (She hadn't realized his rope had an end, but here it was.) They retreated to his tiny office—a nook she had commandeered for him near the coffee lounge. "You need a moment," she told him. "I probably need a couple," he said.

"Why don't you go for a walk?"

"I can't do that. How can I?"

Nathan showed him how. She knew the deputy mayors would be hovering outside, so she got his security detail to sneak Rudy out the back door of the office, slip him down the fire escape and into the SUV, and drive him off. Nathan stayed behind. The deputies burst into the room. "Where is he?"

"He went for a walk."

"What? Where?" They were ready to chase him down the street, but he was gone.

When his SUV had made it a block from the command post, Giuliani told the driver to pull over. He got out on First Avenue and walked through Peter Cooper Village, an old brick apartment complex full of middle-class teachers, nurses, cops and office workers—his people. He asked his security team to hang back so he could walk alone. People saw him and did double takes. Some approached hesitantly; every New Yorker feels entitled to fill the mayor's ear, but not this night. This night they simply offered him a quick hug or a few soft words of thanks and let him walk on alone. He headed east, through a tunnel under the F.D.R. Drive, toward the East River. "I wanted to look at it," he says. "I wanted to look at the river. It was still there." He turned from the dark water and stared up at the lights. "I looked at the skyline," he says. "It was still there." Then he walked back to work. ■

Giving the O.K. to laugh on *Saturday Night Live*

He fills in on 9/16, escorting a fallen fire fighter's sister down the aisle

In Far Rockaway after Flight 587 crashed

With Ariel Sharon in Jerusalem

January 20

By the end of the year 2001, this scene had the feel of ancient history. But the record will show that the year began with George Walker Bush being sworn in as America's 43rd President by Chief Justice William Rehnquist, as daughters Jenna and Barbara (obscured) and wife Laura looked on, joined by new Vice President Dick Cheney, his wife Lynne and Bush's erstwhile challenger for the Republican nomination, Steve Forbes. Following the terrorist attacks of Sept. 11, with the nation united as seldom before, another fact seemed forgotten: at the time of Bush's Inauguration, Americans were still divided by the botched election of 2000, which was only resolved by the 5-to-4 vote of the Supreme Court on Dec. 12, 2000, that handed the presidency to the former Texas Governor.

Nation

SEARCHLIGHT **Hunting down toothpaste in a San Rafael drug store**

MARK RICHARDS FOR TIME

Lights Out!

A bungled deregulation plan turns off the juice in the Golden State

CCORDING TO THE LAWS OF MOTHER NATURE, ELEC-tricity follows the path of least resistance. Mother apparently wasn't hanging around California in Jan-uary 2001, when rolling blackouts spread darkness at noon across some of the richest cropland, most complex high-tech factories and busiest streets in America.

The blackouts were the latest and most painful phase of a statewide energy crisis that was years in the making, triggered by a spectacularly twisted and shortsighted deregulation plan. The foul-up enraged consumers and businessmen even as it pushed California's two largest utilities toward bankruptcy. It threatened to undermine the state's $1.3 trillion economy, the sixth largest on earth. It was the most prominent face of 2001's nationwide win-ter of energy discontent, in which natural-gas rates soared to their highest level in 15 years, and that ever lovable car-tel, OPEC, slashed its oil output again to keep prices up.

California's woes tested everyone from Governor Gray Davis, a moderate Democrat seen as presidential timber, to George W. Bush, who in his first week in office stiffed Davis' request for federal aid to the staggering utilities. And the Golden State's plight cast a shadow over ambitious deregulation plans being launched in other states.

The state's largely self-inflicted energy wounds were rich in irony. A deregulation plan that was supposed to cut electric rates instead more than tripled what some Cali-fornia consumers paid, and proved powerless to slow a 10-fold increase in the state's wholesale prices. And instead of pulling regulators out of the utility business, the plan plunged Sacramento and Washington ever more deeply into it. The entire mess was amplified by California's fail-ure to complete the building of a single large power plant over the past 10 years, even as Silicon Valley boomed and the state economy expanded 34%.

Ironically, new construction was one of the aims in 1995 when the state, whose environmental laws make it a utility builder's nemesis, launched the nation's first and most sweeping electric deregulation plan—endorsed by utilities, lawmakers and environmental and consumer-advocate groups. The goal enunciated by Republican Governor Pete Wilson was to bust up the monopolies held by utilities like Pacific Gas & Electric and Southern California Edison (SCE). They in turn would be free to purchase and market power in the state as well as to pursue business elsewhere. Conversely, out-of-state operators were supposed to flock to California, helping bring down electric rates that were among the highest in the country.

In sum, California dismantled its private power-generating industry without securing adequate power supplies. The Big Three utilities, which in addition to PG&E and SCE include San Diego Gas & Electric, sold off plants to outsiders like Duke Energy of Charlotte, N.C., and Reliant Energy of Houston and became middlemen. But the state wouldn't allow these new intermediaries to enter long-term purchasing agreements for fear they would be locked into fixed-price contracts as prices dropped. Their purchases had to be made on the so-called spot—or cash—market, and prices were low at the time. The utilities willingly accepted this limitation, as well as a

GOING UP! The crisis wasn't amusing to Californians like Jesse Sigold, trapped in a suddenly powerless elevator

rate freeze until 2002. But they were gambling that they could wheel and deal their way through the marketplace without exposure to price swings.

They lost. In fact, the utilities rolled snake eyes time and time again. While the state's appetite for electricity was growing fast, its generating capacity was getting no bigger. No one foresaw the spike in rates for natural gas, which fires about half of California's generating plants and can account for more than half of the price of electricity. Then, as the rising demand for power met its restricted supply, the wholesale price of energy jumped from less than 5¢ per kilowatt-hour in January 2000 to nearly 40¢ per kilowatt-hour in December 2000.

The results were catastrophic. Unable to pass along rising costs to homes and businesses, PG&E and SCE piled up losses and owed more than $12 billion to their banks and power providers. The utilities defaulted on some loans and refused to pay bills, creating a showdown with their bankers and power suppliers. Either group, in fact, could have forced the utilities into bankruptcy.

With the California utilities so shaky, some generating companies were reluctant to supply them with more power. To keep the juice flowing, outgoing Energy Secretary Bill Richardson ordered suppliers to keep selling to California—a demand that rankled. Nonetheless, the business was highly profitable. In January 2001 Duke Energy reported a hefty $284 million in fourth-quarter earnings—compared with a $189 million loss in 2000—thanks in no small part to California's soaring wholesale prices.

The gap between demand and supply forced California's Independent System Operator, which manages the power grid, to find some 6,000 megawatts a day outside the state. And when it couldn't—lights out! The crisis finally subsided in June, thanks to factors as diverse as a slowing economy (which deflates energy demand), cooler weather, increased conservation, and a drop in prices for natural gas and oil. But as other Americans watched Californians load up on flashlights and batteries, adjust their thermostats and turn off those needless lights burning in the basement, they learned a basic lesson: a marketplace that is only partly free is a prescription for complete disaster. ■

HOT SEAT The crisis put California governor Gray Davis on the defensive, though it was approved by his predecessor, Pete Wilson

Star Wars

Will the controversial missile-defense shield get off the ground?

TAKE YOUR PICK. THE U.S. NEEDS A new antimissile defense system: a) tomorrow b) like a hole in the head. There seems to be no middle ground: advocates of the system see it as an absolute necessity, while critics view it as a fiasco in the making—an unproved technology, to be deployed at massive expense against a threat that doesn't exist.

The missile-defense system is a cornerstone of George Bush's foreign policy strategy. Critics pointed out after Sept. 11 that such a system would not have stopped the sort of terrorist attack that destroyed the World Trade Center, but Bush still advocated its deployment.

Building the system would require scrapping the Antiballistic Missile Treaty of 1972, which has ensured that the U.S. and the Soviet Union (now Russia) would remain naked to the other's atomic wrath. While the logic of such mutual assured destruction was ghoulish, it worked. Bush tried hard to convince Russian President Vladimir Putin that the end of the cold war made the ABM treaty obsolete. At the Asian economic summit in Shanghai in October, Putin said that the U.S. and Russia could find common ground, but an expected deal did not emerge after Bush and Putin huddled on Bush's Crawford, Texas, ranch a few weeks later.

Four systems are being studied. A ground-based system is nearly ready, but failed some early tests. An orbiting network of killer satellites won't be ready until 2020. So the Pentagon is modifying two systems now in progress. The Navy's ship-based missiles and the Air Force's plane-based lasers were designed to take out shorter-range missiles. But they are being retooled to defend against ocean-crossing ICBMs. ∎

BIG-BUCKS BLUEPRINT

A multilayered system—high-tech satellites, ships, planes and "kill vehicles"—offers the best chance of destroying incoming missiles. But the latticework of national missile defense poses daunting technological challenges. Experts say even the cheapest layered system will start at $100 billion and that systems deploying space-based lasers could cost double that. And, not surprisingly, each branch of the military wants in on the action. Here's how the different layers would work:

TIME Graphic by Joe Lertola

BOOST PHASE

EARLY-WARNING SATELLITE

SPACE-BASED LASER

ENEMY MISSILE LAUNCH

1 SPACE BASED

AVAILABLE: 2020, if then
COST: $50 billion to $100 billion, for starters

The crown jewel for any missile-defense system, advocates say, is constellation of satellites armed wi lasers. They would scour the skies their own—no need for mere humans—detecting and blasting enemy rockets during the "boost phase," shortly after launch.

HOW IT WORKS — Space-based heat detectors would s a launch and cue the lasers to track destroy enemy missiles early in flight Each satellite could down as many a 100 enemy missiles up to 2,500 mi away without refueling.

UPSIDE — Protection for all, from all. The Penta predicts that 12 satellites could dest 94% of incoming missiles, while a 2 satellite system could eliminate virtu all threats.

DOWNSIDE — These extremely complex Air Force satellites must be small enough to b launched into orbit. Packing such a punch into a small package won't be easy.

SEA BASED

[AVA]ILABLE: 2010

[COS]T: $15 billion on top of $50 billion [alre]ady spent on Aegis ships

[Bas]ed aboard existing warships, this [syste]r would be built by the Navy using [imp]roved versions of its Aegis radar [and] Standard missile. A fleet could [prot]ect wide sections of the globe.

③ AIR BASED

AVAILABLE: 2006

COST: $6.4 billion for a seven-plane laser fleet

The Air Force is also developing another boost-phase system, designed to shoot down missiles as they climb into space. In order to shoot down, say, an Iraqi or a North Korean missile, the Pentagon would probably base the planes as close to those countries as possible.

④ GROUND BASED

AVAILABLE: By 2004, a small number of interceptors could be standing guard

COST: $60 billion over 15 years

This has been the Pentagon's missile defense of choice for the past decade, which is why it is the most ready to be built. Current plans call for about 200 missiles based in Alaska and North Dakota.

[W]ARHEAD

KILL VEHICLE

USA

INTERCEPTOR MISSILE

UNITED STATES

AIRBORNE LASER

Additional facilities and equipment would be needed to support these systems

COMMAND AND CONTROL

[United] States

NAVAL INTERCEPTOR MISSILE

United States

HIGH-RESOLUTION RADAR

United States

U

[Tie]d to space and ground radar, [ship]board missiles would be fired at [enem]y missiles in midflight. Navy [plan]ners believe a modified Aegis radar [syste]m, originally designed to shoot [dow]n enemy airplanes and cruise [missi]les, could also detect and destroy [long-]range ballistic missiles.

A sophisticated oxygen-iodine laser is crammed into the nose of a 747. Targeting a laser through many miles of air is challenging, so 324 quarter-inch pistons, each pulsating up to 1,000 times per sec., control the laser's focus and allow it to kill the enemy missile.

The interceptors, cued by satellites and long-range radar, would destroy enemy warheads as they streaked toward targets in the U.S.

[Se]a-based system has mobility that a [land]-based system lacks, and is capable [of qu]ickly moving to troubled areas.

Destroying missiles early in flight—before they have disgorged their warheads and decoys—dramatically simplifies the defender's task.

Even though it has failed two of its three tests, this is the Pentagon's ripest option.

[The] Antiballistic Missile Treaty bars sea-[base]d systems. There's also concern [insid]e the Pentagon that the planned [non]explosive kill vehicle—which weighs [less] than 40 lbs.—will be too small to [destr]oy the enemy's warheads.

Beyond the amazing technology involved, a fleet of laser-wielding 747s would be costly—and a tempting and vulnerable target.

Because the 120-lb. interceptor carries no explosives—it destroys a missile simply by colliding with it—it must be extremely accurate. What's more, it must discriminate between warheads and decoys, which is no easy feat. And say goodbye to Europe and Japan. Only the U.S. and Canada would be protected.

HANNSEN AND MCVEIGH Two black eyes for the bureau

MUELLER The terrorists struck in his first week on the job

Federal Bureau Of Aggravation

New leaders shoulder old burdens—
even as they confront drastic new ones

HISTORY REPEATS ITSELF: FORMER ATTORNEY GENERAL Janet Reno had to contend with cult leader David Koresh in her first months in office. Her successor, former Missouri Senator John Ashcroft, came into office with a mandate from George W. Bush to restore confidence in the Justice Department and the FBI—only to run smack into a pair of crises he didn't create in his first weeks on the job. First came the arrest of agent Robert Hanssen, charged with spying for the Russians inside the FBI for 15 years. Then came the discovery of thousands of pages of undisclosed documents in the case of Oklahoma City bomber Timothy McVeigh, which delayed the confessed mass murderer's execution for six weeks. In the middle of putting out those fires, Ashcroft and Bush had to select a new FBI Director to replace the retiring Louis Freeh.

Their choice: Robert Mueller, a decorated Marine and the former head of the Justice Department's criminal division. The tough Mueller, 56, is a Princeton graduate who enlisted in the Marines in 1967 and earned a rack of medals for his Vietnam service. After law school at the University of Virginia and a stint in private practice, he became a federal prosecutor and then U.S. Attorney in Boston. At Justice, he handled cases ranging from the bombing of Pan Am Flight 103 to the prosecution of Panamanian strongman Manuel Noriega; Mueller left in 1993 and later became the U.S. Attorney in San Francisco.

History repeats itself: Mueller was sworn in on Sept. 4. One week later, he was up against the greatest crimes the FBI had ever tackled, the terrorist attacks on the World Trade Center and the Pentagon. The FBI faced a two-front war: investigating the four hijackings, while tracking down leads to fend off future attacks. That was enough to stretch the bureau to its limits. But then came the anthrax scare and the new responsibility of finding out who sent the contaminated letters and where they got the bacteria.

Within a few days of the first anthrax letter, the overwhelmed FBI had received more than 400,000 leads and tips—for 11,143 agents to cover. Almost immediately, the FBI was tangling with federal health officials over the extent and nature of the threat. Meanwhile, local law-enforcement authorities around the country raised a perennial charge: the bureau's agents wouldn't share intelligence with them. "I wish I could say the FBI is doing a better job of communicating with us," said a state official in the South. "It's frustrating because I can't tell my people what to look out for." And George Bush's creation of a Office of Homeland Security meant the FBI would have to learn to work more closely with a host of agencies and people across the nation. Good luck, Mr. Mueller. ∎

ASHCROFT A Pentecostal, he leads daily prayers at work

Run Silent, Run Deep, Run Amuck

In a deadly blunder, a U.S. submarine sinks a Japanese trawler, killing nine

MOURNING Families of the Japanese lost from the *Ehime Maru* sprinkle flowers over the site of the collision, off Hawaii

T HE U.S.S. *GREENEVILLE* ROCKETED BLINDLY FROM THE deep like a black torpedo in the rapid-ascent drill known as a "ballast blow," spewing ocean foam as its bow rose more than 100 ft. out of the Pacific and crushed the Japanese fishing boat *Ehime Maru.* "Jesus!" exclaimed Commander Scott Waddle from the attack sub's control room. "What the hell was that?" Some 30 sailors and civilians watched in horror as Waddle brought the periscope around to reveal what the sub had just done: a TV screen displaying the periscope's view suddenly filled with the sickening image of a rapidly sinking trawler.

There was even more terror aboard the 190-ft. *Ehime Maru,* which was taking students from the Uwajima Fisheries High School in southwest Japan on a training voyage nine miles south of Hawaii's Diamond Head. For the next few minutes, the Americans—unable to render aid because of roiling 6-ft. waves—watched helplessly as the 25 Japanese aboard struggled to board a trio of lifeboats. Nine Japanese, most of them teenagers, did not survive.

The Feb. 9 crash occurred with 16 U.S. civilians aboard the *Greeneville;* the Navy routinely invites dignitaries aboard its vessels to bolster public support for its missions. During the rapid-ascent drill a pair of landlubbers, closely overseen by sailors, had their hands on the sub's controls. When the 6,900-ton *Greeneville* shot to the surface, the *Ehime Maru*—half as long as the 360-ft. sub and only 7% of its weight—didn't stand a chance.

Had Waddle, 41, taken the necessary precautions before ordering the rapid ascent? Five weeks later, crew members testifying at a 12-day Navy court of inquiry left the clear impression that he had not. Testifying in his own behalf, Waddle said, "As commanding officer, I am solely responsible for this truly tragic accident, and for the rest of my life I will have to live with the horrible consequences." The court ruled that Waddle had breached proper procedure, but decided against a court-martial. Waddle resigned his commission, but to the disgust of many Japanese, he was allowed to retain his full rank and pension.

The collision shook relations between the U.S. and Japan. And it proved a knockout punch for Japanese Prime Minister Yoshiro Mori—who made the mistake of continuing a round of golf after getting the news. He was replaced by Junichiro Koizumi. By the fall, a $60 million U.S. recovery effort had retrieved eight of the nine bodies of the dead. Recovering the vanished mutual respect between the U.S. and Japan may take longer. ∎

SUB FLUB Waddle, inset, commanded the *Greeneville*

People

The Fog of War

Former Senator Bob Kerrey is a public figure respected for his candor, a certified Vietnam war hero who survived grievous wounds, a man who once sought and may again seek the presidency. But a single deed from the war haunted him with shame and remorse for more than three decades. In April, when a fellow Navy SEAL who lived through the same nightmare came forward with an even more damning chain of events than Kerrey would admit to, the former Senator revealed his secret: one night in Vietnam in 1969, he and a squad of six SEALs under his command killed a score of unarmed civilians, mainly

KERREY Facing ghosts of Vietnam

women and children, during a raid as they sought Viet Cong in the small village of Thanh Phong.

The story was uncovered by investigative reporter Gregory Vistica and was published in the New York *Times* Magazine and aired on *60 Minutes II*. Both these accounts condemned the raid, strongly suggesting that Kerrey was wrong when he said the civilian deaths were the tragic result of the "fog of war," and that the former squad mate, Gerhard Klann, was right when he said the killings were a deliberate execution.

Kerrey gathered the five other veterans of the mission, who conferred and then released a statement saying Klann's version of the event "is simply not true." The statement continues, "We took fire, and we returned fire." Three decades after he served in Vietnam, Bob Kerrey is still taking fire.

LOST Roni Bowers and Charity

A Mission Interrupted

Roni and Jim Bowers, an American Baptist missionary couple, lived in Peru with their two adopted children, Cory, 7, and newborn Charity, on a 55-ft. houseboat with two bedrooms and a solar-powered refrigerator. They collected rainwater in tanks on the roof, then filtered it for drinking. From their home base in Iquitos, they motored along a lush 200-mile stretch of the Amazon, stopping at some 50 villages to visit and preach. In April, as the Bowers were flying home by air, a Peruvian army jet shot down their small seaplane: a mistaken tip led drug agents to believe the plane harbored smugglers. Both Roni and Charity were killed.

Clinton's Last Daze

Bill Clinton weathered impeachment but tarnished his last days in office: in a last-minute flurry, he ordered up 177 presidential pardons—including one for fugitive financier Marc Rich that former President Jimmy Carter dubbed "disgraceful." Then it turned out Hillary Clinton's brother Hugh Rodham had made $400,000 for helping broker a commutation for a Los Angeles drug dealer and a pardon for a Florida swindler. The Clintons' image was further soiled when $28,000 worth of furniture they had shipped to their new home in Chappaqua, N.Y., had to be returned to the capital after it was deemed White House property.

LINKED The politician and the intern

Disappearing Act

Chandra Levy, 24, was enjoying her work as an intern with the Department of Justice. She was also—secretly—romantically involved with a married Congressman, California Democrat Bill Condit. Then, late in April, Levy simply disappeared without a trace. Frustrated when police failed to make progress in the case, her parents pointed the finger at Condit. A

HOMEBOY Excited neighbors welcome Bill Clinton to his new office in Harlem

Images

CINCINNATI BURNS After Timothy Thomas, an unarmed 19-year-old African-American man, was killed by a white police officer in April, Cincinnati erupted in ferocious racial riots and protests. Thomas, wanted on several slight misdemeanor charges, had run from the police. Surrounded by 12 officers, he was killed by a single bullet. The officer who fired it, Steven Roach, said he thought that Thomas had a gun. Since 1995, 15 black men have died at the hands of Cincinnati police.

three-month media frenzy ensued: by September, Condit had had his apartment ransacked by police, his DNA tested, his evasions questioned by Connie Chung on TV, his picture spattered across tabloid covers, his other extramarital affairs revealed and his guilt presumed by endless hours of cable talkers. Yet no one ever found a firm connection between Levy's disappearance and Condit. At press time, Chandra Levy remained missing.

CHAD ALERT Harris and Reno will run

They're Back!

Faulkner could have told Floridians, The past isn't dead; it isn't even past. Just as weary voters were doing their best to put hanging chads and butterfly ballots behind them, two key figures of the great presidential election fiasco of 2000 announced they were interested in running for office in the Sunshine State. Following months of speculation, former Attorney General Janet Reno firmly declared she would run for Governor in September, while Florida Secretary of State Katherine Harris played cagey, teasing voters for months until finally announcing in October she would run for Congress from the state's 13th district.

Gaudeamus Igitur, Girl!

Jenna Bush, one of the President's twin daughters, had an eventful freshman year at the University of Texas. First her father was elected (more or less) President. Then she used the Secret Service to bail a drunken male buddy out of a Fort Worth, Texas, jail. In April, Bush, 19, was cited at about 1 a.m. for drinking from a glass of beer in Cheers' Shot Bar in Austin; the drinking age in Texas is 21. A month later, she and sister Barbara (the more diffident twin, who attends Yale) were in trouble again, for ordering margaritas in another Austin bar. Said America's First Grandmother, Barbara Bush, whose son's early years were not distinguished for restraint: "George is getting back some of his own."

PARTY! Jenna and Dad: soulmates?

Photograph by Sherwin Crasto—AP/Wide World

World

February 1

January 26 is Republic Day in India, the holiday that honors the nation's constitution. Shortly before 9 a.m., just as many Indians turned on their TVs to watch the annual military parade, the ground began to shake in the western state of Gujarat, near the Pakistan border. A temblor measuring 7.9 on the Richter scale had struck the region; by day's end more than 14,000 people were dead—including 400 schoolchildren buried alive as they marched in a Republic Day parade. Among the survivors: Daksaben Pantaki, left, who picks her way through the ruins of her house in the town of Rapar a few days after the quake.

"REVENGE!" Mourners bear the body of a Palestinian, one of some 1,000 killed in the first 11 months of 2001

THE AVENGERS

Entangled in a deadly web of punch and counterpunch, Israelis and Palestinians practice the diplomacy of revenge as hopes for peace fade

EVEN BY THE STANDARDS OF A REGION THAT TAKES perverse pride in living without illusions, the Middle East endured an unrelentingly grim year in 2001. In January, Bill Clinton, with three weeks left as President, tried for the last time to jump-start the stalled peace process. Israeli Prime Minister Ehud Barak agreed to begin negotiations, but P.L.O. Chairman Yasser Arafat hedged. Ever since the Camp David talks had broken down in July 2000 and a new, violent uprising had begun among Arabs within Israel's borders, Arafat increasingly had the sense that both time and world public opinion were working on his side.

DEAD Hamas' Mansour and Salim

The Palestinian leader would soon have reason to wish he had taken Clinton's deal. He failed to reckon with how weary Israeli voters had become with a stalemated peace process and seemingly endless violence. In this mood, they turned to the man who could fairly be described as the P.L.O.'s worst nightmare: Ariel Sharon. The hardline ex-general took office in February, and the region was soon engulfed in an escalating cycle of violence and reprisal.

In the first month after Sharon took office, a Palestinian bus driver plowed into a bus stop at high speed, killing eight people (seven of them Israeli soldiers) and injuring 20 others. Sharon didn't hesitate to strike back. In March, Israeli army helicopters rained missiles on targets in the West Bank and Gaza. In April, militant Islamic Jihad leader Iyad Hardan was killed by a phone booth that had been rigged to explode. On June 1, Israel suffered its worst terrorist attack in more than five years when a suicide bomber walked into a Tel Aviv nightclub popular with Israeli teenagers. Eighteen people died, and more than 100 others were injured.

A string of cease-fires failed: most lasted less than 24 hours. Between the pauses, the dying continued. In July, Israeli helicopters killed Hamas leader Omar Sa'adeh. This

"REVENGE!" Israelis carry the body of a settler killed in a raid near the divided West Bank city of Hebron in July

led Hamas to shell Gilo, a Jewish suburb of Jerusalem. In response, Israeli tanks moved on Bethlehem and Jenin.

Israeli anti-tank rockets killed two top Hamas leaders, Jamal Mansour and Jamal Salim, on July 31 in the West Bank town of Nablus. When another militant leader, Mustafa Zibri, was killed in September, his faction, the Popular Front for the Liberation of Palestine, assassinated Israeli Tourism Minister Rehavam Ze'evi. The next day, Israeli tanks were rolling deep into Ramallah, Bethlehem and Beit Jala. They would not pull out for six weeks.

The spiral of reprisals was interrupted by the Sept. 11 terrorist attacks on the U.S. Suddenly, a Bush Administration that had seemed willing to walk away from the region found that attention must be paid. The Israelis feared that the U.S., in its zeal to build an Arab coalition against terror, might soften its commitment to their security. In October, Sharon blurted out that "Israel will not be Czechoslovakia," the nation that was sacrificed by appeasement before World War II. This brought a sharp rebuke from the White House, an apology from Sharon and a new low point in U.S.-Israeli relations. Meanwhile, Palestinians took heart when Secretary of State Colin Powell asserted that the U.S. backed an eventual Palestinian state.

In late November, a new U.S. envoy—former Marine general Anthony Zinni—arrived in the region. His task: broker a lasting cease-fire, fast. On the day he walked

HORROR An August suicide bombing in Jerusalem killed 13 and wounded 70

off his plane in Jerusalem, a suicide bomber killed three Israelis on a bus in northern Israel. Days later, as Sharon was in the U.S., Israel was shaken by a double suicide bombing in Jerusalem that killed ten; another bombing on a Haifa bus killed 15. The Israelis responded by shelling both Arafat's headquarters on the West Bank and his home in Gaza City, destroying three helicopters. Sharon accused Arafat of waging a "war of terror" and demanded he arrest the leaders of Hamas and Islamic Jihad and dismantle the militant groups—or pay a heavy price. As this story for the TIME Annual closed in early December, ongoing upheaval—if not outright war—seemed assured. ∎

A MIDAIR COLLISION ...

THE U.S. AND CHINA WEATHERED A MAJOR crisis in April, following the collision of a U.S. spy plane and a Chinese fighter jet. Both countries agreed that two Chinese fighters were tracking a U.S. EP-3 Aries II plane when the collision occurred and Chinese pilot Wang Wei, above, was killed. The EP-3 dropped 8,000 ft. before the pilot regained control and flew to Lingshui air base on Chinese soil, where the U.S. crew was taken into custody. The two nations disputed the cause of the crash.

■ THE U.S. SCENARIO

Judging from damage to the EP-3, experts believe Wang was flying directly **underneath** its left wing. He was apparently known to the U.S. as a maverick pilot who had been photographed flashing his e-mail address from his F-8 cockpit. Some Pentagon experts believe Wang was a victim of the **Venturi effect**—shrinking air pressure between two craft flying parallel and too close to each other caused the EP-3's wing to dip onto the F-8. Once it issued a Mayday call, the EP-3, under international law, was allowed to land at the nearest airport without permission.

❝ The faster, more maneuverable aircraft has the obligation to stay out of the way ... It's pretty obvious who bumped into whom. ❞

—Admiral Dennis C. Blair, commander in chief, U.S. Pacific Command

... STRANDS A SPY PLANE

The lumbering EP-3, dubbed the "flying pig" by its crews, is a "signal intelligence" gatherer. It is packed with highly sensitive equipment that collects electronic emissions by radar, airport control, weather devices, military commands and more—from coastlines to deep within foreign territory. Its mission is dangerous but essential: the EP-3 intercepts information that spy satellites cannot.

THE EP-3E ARIES II

Maximum range	2,380 nautical miles (4,408 km)
Maximum speed	403 m.p.h. (648 km/h)
Cost	$36 million
Hourly running cost	$2,100
Ceiling	28,300 ft. (8,626 m)

THE CREW

The EP-3 carries 24 people, who fill 20 designated positions and provide a relief team of four. In addition to the flight crew, two teams—known as ELINT and COMINT—work on intercepting and interpreting various types of electronic and communications intelligence.

Sources: U.S. Navy; U.S. Pacific Command; Xinhua News Agency; Embassy of the People's Republic of China; *Aviation Week*; *Jane's*; GlobalSecurity.org; CNN; Federation of American Scientists; TIME reporting. Illustration based on 1996 interior photographs of a similar EP-3.

TIME Graphic by Ed Gabel and Amanda Bower

Antenna arrays

Communications station

Thought to house "Big Look" radar

①

① ELECTRONIC-INTELLIGENCE TEAM
This team identifies and locates radar using the extremely accurate antennas on the outside of the plane. The staff is believed to perform four main duties.

■ Manual operators: Identifies characteris[tics] of radar, such as the frequency of pulses a[nd] the intervals between them. Generally this [is] the newest crew mem[ber]

■ Low-band signal collector: Watches f[or] signals associated w[ith] air-traffic control, ea[rly] warning, fire-control a[nd] meteorological radars

■ THE CHINESE SCENARIO

The surviving Chinese pilot said he and Wang Wei were flying to the left of the EP-3 when the American plane veered **left,** crashing into the tail of Wang's plane with its nose and left wing. (An earlier account had the Chinese planes flanking the U.S. aircraft.) The encounter took place beyond China's territorial limits, 12 miles (19 km) from the coast, that is recognized as **international airspace.** The EP-3, however, then violated China's national security by landing at Lingshui without permission. That illegal entry gave China the right to "investigate" the plane and hold its crew, and to negotiate with the U.S. about the losses incurred by China.

❝ It was directly caused by the U.S. plane veering at a wide angle toward our plane, making it impossible for our plane to avoid it. ❞

—Zhao Yu, pilot of the second Chinese jet

② COMMUNICATIONS-INTELLIGENCE TEAM

Cryptologists collect, analyze and interpret communications. Their duties are highly classified, and their equipment is always off during observer flights. However, the team is believed to intercept aircraft-to-aircraft and control-tower radio communications, as well as telephone calls.

■ **Cryptologists** rarely speak a foreign language fluently, but they know key words associated with military activity, equipment and logistics. Using them, they annotate tapes made during a mission and send them to other intelligence agencies—such as the National Security Agency, which has headquarters in Fort Meade, Md.—for full analysis.

■ **Communications teams** are also believed to be trained in a system that intercepts an enemy radio transmission, alters its meaning and retransmits the communication in the original operator's voice. The Pentagon asserts that such "spoofing" is used rarely and cautiously.

HOMEWARD BOUND

The landing of a U.S. Navy EP-3 reconnaissance plane on Chinese soil following a collision with a Chinese fighter jet handed George Bush his first foreign policy crisis. The President was at Camp David on Sunday, April 1, when he first got word that 24 U.S. service-men and -women were being held on Hainan Island. When Chinese President Jiang Zemin claimed the U.S. was responsible for the crash and owed China an apology, Bush called the collision an accident and offered no apology. When China refused to budge, Bush demanded, "It is time for our [personnel] to return home." With tensions ratcheting up, quiet diplomacy finally prevailed: both parties dialed back the rhetoric, the U.S. declared it was "very sorry" about the incident, and the crew returned to its home base on Whidbey Island in Wash-ington State on April 14.

Canoe fairings house signal receivers and transmitters

Scientific/ technical operator

Modified tail cone houses electronic equipment

enna arrays

High-band analyzer: Conducts rapid alysis of higher-band radar signals cally used by fighter planes and for ssile guidance. Within 30 seconds, operator can determine whether a ar has locked onto a target, and ss along the information.

Big Look" operator: s the longest-range ipment to see signals and assign them to relevant team mber.

Antenna arrays

③ SUPERVISORS
The two team supervisors flank the **combat coordinator,** who integrates and sends data to other aircraft, operations headquarters and intelligence agencies.

NIGHTMARE IN NEPAL

Infuriated by his parents' rejection of his choice of bride, the Crown Prince of Nepal massacres his own family in their innermost sanctum

SANDWICHED BETWEEN SUBCONTINENTAL SUPERPOWER India and Chinese-occupied media darling Tibet, Nepal has developed such a muddled identity that it now comes across as merely a staging ground for Everest expeditions and a destination where bliss-seeking Western stoners can score killer brownies. Nepalese, particularly those who live in the capital city Kathmandu, have wondered how the bewildering influx of Westerners and their values will affect the formerly elder-respecting, ancestor-worshipping, opposite-sex-avoiding youth of the nation—especially such young leaders as the huffy Crown Prince Dipendra, 29, and his cousin Prince Paras, 27.

When the stylish duo arrived at the palace for the royal family's regular Friday dinner on June 1, they were dressed casually in khaki slacks and polo shirts and had already had a few drinks. The two were notorious prowlers

FAREWELL The bodies of the King, Queen and other royals are cremated on the banks of the Bagmati River in Kathmandu

several incidents of discharging firearms in public places. Despite a public outcry in 2000, King Birendra had refused to revoke Paras' royal immunity.

At about 8:30 p.m., the mustachioed Crown Prince Dipendra took his place at the teak dining table. After pouring himself another drink, he began arguing with his parents, shouting at his mother Queen Aiswarya, who didn't approve of his romance with longtime paramour Devyani Rana, 23, the daughter of a former Foreign Minister of Nepal. Prince Dipendra's parents wanted him to marry Priyanka Shaha, a princess of royal blood. Furious, Dipendra then retired to his sleeping quarters, where he changed into camouflage fatigues and equipped himself with an American M-16 rifle and a revolver. Taking a private corridor to the dining room, he barged in and fired a burst that killed his parents. Twelve others in the room were shot. Among those fatally injured were the Crown Prince's younger brother Nirajan and his sister Shruti. He then turned the revolver on himself, firing a .38-cal. slug up through his temple, the bullet exiting the other side. The shooting spree took less than three minutes.

TIM GRAHAM—CORBIS SYGMA (2)

ROYAL INTRIGUE King Birendra and Queen Aiswarya in happier days in 1986. In 1990 the King agreed to serve Nepal as a constitutional monarch. At right, Prince Dipendra

When palace aides dashed into the room, they found that the King's head had been blown nearly in half, and the Queen's body was unrecognizable, save for the sari she had been wearing. Eight of the victims, including the King, were declared dead on arrival at the Royal Nepal Army Hospital. A ninth victim died later.

Incredibly, royal protocol was followed in the wake of the massacre: the next morning, in a coma and sustained by life-support systems and respirators, the Prince, who had killed the King, was enthroned as King. The Privy Council declared that his uncle, the King's brother Prince Gyanendra, the father of Prince Paras, would serve as regent. When the Crown Prince died three days later, Gyanendra was crowned the new King; however, in a break with tradition, Prince Paras was not named Crown Prince and thus may not be his successor. The Shah dynasty, representing a 250-year lineage, had been virtually eradicated in three minutes of gunfire. And the Nepalese people's question—Into what kind of society is our mountain kingdom evolving?—had been answered by an M-16. ■

of the Kathmandu night-life circuit, where they were at the center of a swirl of hip kids and young adults whose favored form of transportation is a Lexus SUV and whose favored intoxicant is locally processed hashish. The Crown Prince and Paras had become increasingly close in the past few months, and the two shared a disregard for what they saw as plebeian laws. Nicknamed the Killer Prince, Paras had been involved in at least four hit-and-run fatalities and

RAISING THE KURSK

A risky operation recovers a sub, its two nuclear
reactors, 22 missiles and an ill-fated crew

A YEAR AFTER THE RUSSIAN NUCLEAR SUBMARINE
Kursk mysteriously exploded and sank with 118 sailors
aboard, an international team succeeded in raising
the submarine from the bottom of the Barents Sea
and bringing it home to Russia. Search teams
retrieved more than 50 bodies from the wreck,
as well as notes indicating many crewmen
stayed alive for hours after the explosion.

Lifting jac[k]

Giant 4 barge

Mooring
line

Saddle

THE SCENE BELOW

The *Kursk* was 377 ft. below the surface. Salvagers
calculated that the submerged vessel weighed more than
21 million lbs. The water termperature hovered just above
freezing. While the salvage concept was simple—attach
cables and pull up the sub—the challenges were formidable

❶ DRILLING HOLES
Divers using high-pressure hoses cut 26
holes through the outer and inner hulls
of the sub and attached cones and wires
to guide the cables. The holes were
27.5 in. wide

Holes
for lifting
anchors

Periscopes
and antenna
were sawed off
and removed

Control
line

❸ INSERTING PLUGS
Specially designed
plugs were lowered
from the barge and
inserted into each
hole in the sub. The
plugs worked like
giant toggle bolts,
expanding once
they passed through
the holes in the hull.
Each plug was shaped
for its specific spot
along the sub

Saw
cuts at
a 10°
angle

❷ REMOVING FRONT COMPARTMENT
A remote-control device—sort of a giant chainsaw—sliced
down through the sub, severing the 65-ft. front
compartment

❹ FREEING THE SUB
The sub had sunk
several feet into the
silty bottom. Salvagers
lifted the tail of the
sub first to break
the suction

THE SCENE ABOVE
A 459-ft. barge from the Netherlands, the *Giant 4*, anchored over the sub. The barge was fitted with lifting equipment and underwater "saddles" to hold the sub in place

Cable spool

Lifting jack

Movement-compensation system

Hull was reshaped to accommodate sub's sail

Each strand was made up of 54 individual cables 0.7 in. in diameter. Each of those cables contained seven twisted steel strings

⑤ LIFTING JACKS
The 26 lifting jacks on the *Giant 4* were controlled by computer to keep them operating in unison. Their frames could move vertically to compensate for rolling seas. Each jack pulled in a small section of cable at a time, for a total of about 33 ft. an hour. Lifting the sub took about 11 hours

Giant 4

Side pontoon

Kursk

Dry dock

⑥ GETTING INTO DRY DOCK
With the *Kursk* held fast to the *Giant 4*, a tugboat pulled the two vessels to dry dock in Ryslyakovo, Russia, where engineers used a system of pontoons and dry docks to separate the two. Below, the *Kursk* at rest in dry dock; the main body of the ship is below the waterline

The *Kursk* still held 22 long-range cruise missiles

The Russians say they will recover the front in 2002

NUCLEAR DANGER
The two nuclear reactors on the *Kursk* were shut down, and Russian officials said no radiation leaks have occurred

Graphic by Joe Lertola

s: Mammoet Smit
ional, Bellona
ion, DSND, Central
Bureau for Marine
ring, Strana

Images

WALK OF SHAME
To reach their school in North Belfast in September, Roman Catholic girls as young as four, none older than 11, had to run a gauntlet of abuse from their Protestant neighbors that began with insults and spit and escalated within days to bricks and bomb blasts. Scores of police and soldiers were injured trying to protect the children. As the chaos spread through Northern Ireland's capital, a Protestant school bus was stoned, and a Catholic motorist, apparently reacting to stone-throwing attacks, killed a Protestant teenager.

PAUL MCERLANE—REUTERS—CORBIS

Death in Genoa

A wave of riots has touched three continents since the "Battle in Seattle" stunned conferees at the meeting of the World Trade Organization in Washington State in 1999. And the level of violence has gradually increased. At the annual conference of the World Bank and International Monetary Fund in Prague in September 2000, protesters hurled Molotov cocktails and chunks of pavement into the faces of Czech police officers. At a summit of the European Union in Göteborg, Sweden, in June 2001, live rounds were fired by the police, and three protesters were injured, one seriously. When the WTO met in Genoa a month later, the protests claimed their first victim: police battling demonstrators shot and killed Carlo Giuliani, 23, the son of a labor union official from Rome.

While the police fought to restrain the protests, eight world leaders, including President George W. Bush and Russian President Vladimir Putin, were safely sequestered in a medieval palace a mile away. They released a statement saying, "We recognize and praise the role that peaceful protest [has] played in putting issues like debt relief on the international agenda."

DYLAN MARTINEZ—REUTERS—TIMEPIX

FALLEN Carlo Giuliani's body lies in a Genoa street

Iconoclasts of the Taliban

Months before the U.S. sent forces into Afghanistan to topple the Taliban, the fanatical Islamist mullahs inflamed world opinion when they destroyed historic religious figures that had stood for more than 1,000 years. In a valley at Bamiyan, about 100 miles northwest of Kabul, Taliban soldiers destroyed two gigantic standing figures of Buddha, recessed into the cliffs, that were created sometime between the 3rd and 6th centuries. The larger of them was 175 ft. high—purportedly the biggest standing Buddha in the world. "The statues are no big issue," said the Taliban's Minister of Information and Culture, Qadratullah Jamal. "They are only objects made of mud or stone."

MUZAMMIL PASHE—REUTERS—TIMEPIX

GONE Buddha's smile

"I'm Going to Disneyland"

North Korea's ruling dynasty is known to be partial to Western goods: dictator Kim Jong Il is said to have a taste for French cognac and Seville oranges. From his trove of 20,000 videotapes, the dictator is known to favor Daffy Duck over Mickey Mouse. His son is the Mickey fan: in May Kim Jong Nam, 29, North Korea's heir apparent, was deported from Japan after trying to sneak into the country with two women and a four-year-old boy he wanted to take to Tokyo Disneyland. Nam was traveling with a Dominican passport under the name Pang Xiong.

SHIZUO KAMBAYASHI—AP/WIDE WORLD

Kim Jong Nam

MILOSEVIC **He defied the tribunal**

Milosevic in the Dock

Now for some good news, in a year that badly needed some. On June 28, Slobodan Milosevic, the former President of Yugoslavia and the man whose policies had ignited a decade of brutal Balkan wars, was whisked from a jail cell in Belgrade to a cell in the Netherlands, where he will stand trial before the United Nations war-crimes tribunal.

Characteristically, Milosevic refused to participate in the proceedings, blasting the trial as a "farce." Prosecutors for the tribunal filed three indictments against him: one for atrocities and murders in Croatia in 1991, another for crimes committed in the Serbian province of Kosovo in 1999 and a third—and perhaps most damaging—for genocide against the Muslims of Bosnia and Herzegovina from 1992-95. The trial is planned for early 2002.

MACEDONIA **Again, the smoke of war**

The Balkans Still Burn

Slobodan Milosevic might be facing justice at last, but turmoil still ravaged the Balkans. This time the battleground was Macedonia,

where rebel ethnic Albanians have been battling the nation's ethnic Slav majority. In September a force of 4,500 soldiers from 19 NATO nations entered Macedonia to disarm the rebels. Though new rights for Albanians were written into the constitution in November, violence again flared. Prime Minister Ljubco Georgievski asked NATO to send more troops to preserve peace.

New Bosses, Old Bosses

Who will lead? By popular vote, by resignation and even by assassination, nations answered the most basic question in 2001.

INDONESIA: MEGAWATI
After the President, Abdurrahman Wahid, was ousted in a coup, ex-leader Sukarno's daughter took over

PHILIPPINES GLORIA ARROYO
Impeached and facing trial, President Joseph Estrada resigned in January. His V.P. (and archrival) ascended

BRITAIN TONY BLAIR
The charismatic PM and his Labour Party kept their strong grip on Parliament in an early June election

CONGO LAURENT KABILA
The ruler who ousted Mobutu Seso Seko in 1997 was assassinated in January; his son Joseph succeeded him

IRAN MOHAMMED KHATAMI
The moderate cleric beat nine challengers to win re-election in June but still battles conservative mullahs

ISRAEL ARIEL SHARON
The hard-line former general led his Likud Party to victory over Ehud Barak's Labor Party in February

People

KOIZUMI **A jolt of energy for Japan**

Koizumi Rocks Japan

In the second richest nation on earth, Mother Teresa's nuns have set up a soup kitchen. Japan's economy continues to shrink, and the official unemployment rate has risen to 5%, the highest in a generation. The blue-chip stars of the country's manufacturing sector—the makers of computer chips, TVs and PCs, such as Toshiba, Fujitsu and NEC— announced they will shed tens of thousands of jobs.

Amid this gloom, the Japanese are placing their hopes on a Prime Minister who comes across like a rock star. Junichiro Koizumi is a 59-year-old career foot soldier of the Liberal Democratic Party, which, except for one brief period, has ruled Japan for the past 46 years. But Koizumi has shrewdly positioned himself as an outsider. His revolutionary program promises a systematic unraveling of Japan's hidebound political and financial institutions. He appointed a free-wheeling Cabinet that is younger, more female and includes more outsiders than any seen before. For a few months after he took power in May, 2001, Koizumi electrified his downcast nation. A record label released a CD of his favorite Elvis hits. Also available: mint-flavored Koizumi chewing gum and a coffee-table book with snapshots of Koizumi in a bathrobe, Koizumi reading, Koizumi playing baseball, Koizumi eating noodles.

Though he plays the maverick, Koizumi was born into a political family. His marriage ended in divorce; he has custody of two of his sons; and he has never met his third son, who was born following the divorce and lives with his mother.

Business

September 17

Before the horrific events of Sept. 11, 2001, few of us could have imagined that the everyday routine of getting out of bed in the morning, donning business attire and heading for the office would ever qualify as acts of quiet bravery and patriotism. But when these flag-waving businesspeople returned to New York City's devastated financial district six days after the terrorist attack on the nearby World Trade Center—arriving by commuter launch—they were soldiers in a frightening new kind of warfare for Americans, a war whose front lines were office buildings, airports and post offices. The attack mangled the city's economy: New York City comptroller Alan Hevesi estimated the total losses could reach $90 to $105 billion by the middle of 2003.

THE NEW MODEL FORD

FORD A devoted family man, he has been satirized as Ford's No. 1 "soccer mom"

A green revolutionary fires the CEO of Ford Motor Co.—and decides to take charge of the shop himself. It helps that his last name is Ford

WILLIAM CLAY FORD JR. KNOWS IT WOULD HAVE been easier to take the money and run. He's a fourth-generation favored son of America's first family of industry, a clan so ludicrously wealthy the members have their own accounting firm to manage their allowances. Life could easily have been a dividend-enriched affair of multiple parties, multiple mansions and multiple marriages, the big challenges being to avoid alcoholism and choose the right charity boards.

Instead, Bill Ford insisted on having a career at the family shop, Ford Motor Co.—a tough sell. Any number of times since the 1920s, the carmaker's professional managers have had to take the keys away from actual Fords before they did irreparable harm to the business. Ford, 44, became chairman in 1999 only after parrying the objec-

tion of his predecessor, Alex Trotman, who didn't care to see another Ford in the driver's seat—particularly this one.

Too late. Having grabbed the wheel, Ford the rich kid is driving Ford Motor down a radical path. Though he grew up in tony Grosse Pointe, Michigan, went to prep school Hotchkiss and graduated from Princeton, he still comes across as an approachable guy, more comfortable in a union hall than at headquarters. He is so devoted to wife Lisa and their four kids that he's been dubbed Ford's No. 1 "soccer mom." A fiercely principled environmentalist, he is leading a charge to transform the family firm—now a worldwide industrial monster with $170 billion in annual sales—into a corporation that cares as much for consumers and the air they breathe as it does for its bottom line. Ford believes that by reconfiguring Ford Motor, he has a shot at rearranging the entire 21st century industrial landscape. "We have the ability to transform a great old-line company into a vital, global model of sustainable manufacturing," he told TIME in his office, gazing over the sprawling River Rouge factory complex that his great-grandfather Henry established in 1917.

WHAT FORD PROPOSES IS FORD MOTOR'S SECOND revolution. His great-grandfather Henry Ford pioneered the assembly line, the service station and, above all, the then heretical notion of a working wage. Bill Ford wants to go Henry one better by embracing the notion of sustainability, or the idea that you can make things without damaging people and planets. This means creating worker-friendly, environmentally pure factories that make emissions-free cars. He hopes to kill off the carbon monoxide-spewing internal-combustion engine by the end of his reign.

If he fails, Bill Ford won't have anyone to blame but himself: in November he took the keys of the company away from CEO Jacques Nasser, becoming the first family member to be CEO since his uncle Henry Ford II relinquished the post in 1979. He then enlisted esteemed financial whiz Carl Reichardt, 70, a longtime director and former head of Well Fargo Bank, as his new vice chairman.

Although not paralyzed, Ford Motor is in great need of an overhaul, and the question is whether that can be accomplished by the man whose family owns 40% of the voting shares. The knock is that Bill Ford has neither the experience nor the mettle to make the tough decisions—on everything from plant closings to new-car programs—required to pull Ford Motor out of the ditch. Ford's much broader legion of admirers, who range from union bosses to the president of the Sierra Club, say his savvy and his rare blend of guts and grace point to success.

Whatever the case, Ford faces a real challenge. Although the company has been exonerated by federal regulators in the death of 271 people in its Explorers whose Firestone tires failed, the company is beset by a garageful of problems. Its dividend has been halved. Its vehicles have been dogged by quality issues. The company's relations with its unions, dealers and suppliers turned poisonous during Nasser's tenure. And many white-collar managers were angered by the Australian-born CEO's crusade for diversity among their ranks. Ford has also blown through an estimated $15 billion in cash since 1999. It is

HULTON DEUTCH COLLECTION—CORBIS

FIRST · CAR

FOUNDER Henry Ford's first car was this 1896 "Quadricycle"

remarkable that a company hailed in the 1990s as a symbol of American competitiveness has sunk so low, so fast.

Bill Ford's biggest triumph to date is the company's commitment to a $2 billion plan to transform the vast River Rouge complex outside Detroit into a global showcase of sustainable manufacturing. The Rouge was an Industrial Revolution icon, embodying Henry Ford's vision of massive vertical integration, with iron ore being unloaded at one end and cars and trucks rolling off assembly lines at the other. But it had fallen into obsolescence. Now Ford plans to retool it as a 1,100-acre monument to sustainability, with a vast, wide-open gallery of a factory and a 454,000-sq.-ft. "natural habitat" for a roof.

In October Ford Motor announced it would join with environmental groups (and Toyota and Honda) in a call for consumer tax credits to help subsidize sales of high-mileage hybrid-fuel vehicles, which are still costly to produce. In any case, Ford will begin selling a hybrid-fuel version of its small SUV, the Escape, in 2003. Not to be outdone, General Motors says it will have its fleet of zero-emissions buses on the roads soon.

So the William Clay Ford Jr. Industrial Revolution No. 2 moves forward, hitting second gear. If it succeeds, a man named Ford will have changed the auto industry once again. The worst that can happen is that the driving public will get better mileage and much cleaner air from their cars. And that's a mighty positive legacy for a rich kid. ■

THUNDERBIRD Ford kept that cool porthole you may recall from the '50s, but cooling-fan glitches keep delaying the rollout of this long-anticipated car

EXPECT TURBULENCE

Already reeling from higher energy bills, airlines around the world are battered when the terrorist hijackings keep travelers grounded

HERE'S A TRICK QUESTION: YOU'RE A CONTESTANT ON *The Price Is Right*, and Bob Barker offers you a choice between the prize sitting in front of you and the one behind the curtain. What's sitting in front of you is a bright, shiny quarter. Behind the curtain: a stack of the profits made by all the major airlines in the world, combined, in 2001.

If you chose to take the quarter and run, congratulations. Hiding behind that curtain was a net loss of between $10 billion and $12 billion. That's how much the Interna-

SwissAir
Switzerland's national airline filed for bankruptcy and briefly suspended operations in October, but a bailout cobbled together by the Swiss government and a former subsidiary—cut-rate regional carrier CrossAir—kept it flying. For now.

tional Air Transport Association, an industry trade group, estimated in November 2001 that the world's major carriers would have lost by year's end.

Fasten your seat belts. The airline industry is notoriously cyclical, subject to buffeting by successive cycles of boom and bust. The big carriers soared through the booming '90s, but as the nation touched down from the longest stretch of prosperity in U.S. history, they had farther to fall than almost any other sector of the economy, outside the dotcom bubble. By year's end, the major U.S. airlines were poised on the brink of their most radical restructuring in more than 20 years, since the Federal Government deregulated the industry in 1978.

The year 2001 began on a turbulent note as oil prices began a steep climb. Airlines are more sensitive than any other industry to fluctuations in the price of fuel. As re-

TWA
As of Dec. 2, American Airlines replaced TWA signs, uniforms, and flight numbers with its own. After 71 years, one of America's most recognized brands ceased to exist, except on the fuselage of a handful of planes as they awaited repainting.

cently as 2000, promising start-up National Airlines was forced into bankruptcy almost entirely owing to a short-term jump in jet fuel prices. That began a march toward insolvency for undercapitalized carriers that didn't have sufficient cash on hand to ride out the storm. TWA was first

to go under: it declared bankruptcy and was absorbed into American Airlines; the grand old brand was retired at the end of the year. TWA's demise set off a furious minuet, as other cash-poor carriers sought merger partners. But even this solution proved tenuous: in July, the Justice Department scotched, on antitrust grounds, a planned merger between United and U.S. Airways.

By summer, the weakening U.S. economy was cutting sharply into business travel, whose high-margin tickets account for nearly 80% of industry profits. Cushy contracts that had purchased labor peace when times were flush were now burning through cash. The bad news wasn't confined to the U.S. By mid-year, several European airlines were on the ropes, no fewer than 34 of Latin America's 40

United
In November, Chairman and CEO James Goodwin abruptly departed after the carrier announced a $1.1 billion loss for the third quarter. Incoming boss John Creighton sought concessions from unions to keep the airline flying.

carriers were facing bankruptcy, and Pacific carriers from Japan to Australia were warning that without government aid they would soon have to shut down.

Then came Sept. 11. "People simply stopped flying," is how an executive described the aftermath of the hijackings that turned into deadly attacks on the World Trade Center and the Pentagon. With bookings off by as much as 70% at several large carriers, some airlines realized that they were weeks away—perhaps a month or two at most—from having to shut down. Within three weeks, U.S. airlines had laid off more than 100,000 workers. But even this was not enough. By the first week in October, the Federal Government had stepped in with a $15 billion bailout package (two-thirds in loan guarantees and the remaining $5 billion in outright grants) to keep the airlines aloft.

However essential, the package had the effect of putting the Federal Government, for the first time in 23 years, back into the business of doling out public largesse to airlines and looking over the shoulders of corporate management. In some cases, President Bush's new Air Transportation Stabilization Board may decide, in effect, which airlines among those seeking federal aid will survive the crunch and which will not.

But while a Republican Administration might find itself squirming in the uncomfortable, unwanted role of effectively reregulating the airlines (at least in the short term), government money soon proved to be more of a temporary reprieve than a miracle cure. By the beginning of November, the airline industry was petitioning the Treasury Department to defer tax payments (already rescheduled once in the wake of the Sept. 11 attacks) amounting to several hundred million dollars, while warning that, without additional assistance, the industry would begin sinking once again.

This is not to say that the picture is uniformly grim. A small handful of American carriers managed to get through

JetBlue
The startup, which has a fleet of just 18 aircraft, reported third quarter profits of $10.5 million at a time when most other carriers were fighting for their lives and predicted that it would turn a profit in the fourth quarter as well.

this most difficult of years with only a few bruises and quite a few more passengers. Two good examples: the consistently profitable Southwest Air, which has a market capitalization equal to all of the other major American carriers combined, and the innovative start-up JetBlue. Even in Europe, as venerable old brands like Sabena

AerLingus
After no investor came forward in response to an Irish government offer to sell a minority stake in the national airline, AerLingus management told workers in October that givebacks were the only course to stave off bankruptcy.

(which ceased operations in October) and Swiss Air (which is facing bankruptcy) struggle, a spunky start-up like RyanAir (Europe's largest low-fare carrier) weathered the year with its bottom line hurt not at all.

But the flight path back to pre-2001 good times may be a long one. Only days after the industry cheered when the Concorde fleet returned to service after an 18-month hiatus following the deadly August 2000 crash in France, an American Airlines jet bound for the Dominican Republic suffered a mechanical failure less than three minutes after taking off from New York City's Kennedy Airport and crashed. All 260 people aboard and five more on the ground were killed. The grim news left airline executives with only one comforting thought: 2002 had to be a better year—for those who were still around to enjoy it. ∎

People

New General at Electric

For a guy taking over the reins from Jack Welch, one of the most famed CEOs of the 20th century, General Electric's incoming chief, Jeffrey Immelt, 45, wasn't fazed. "Believe it or not, I know, operationally, how to do this job," said the towering, affable Immelt. He knows how to do a lot of jobs, having spent almost 20 years at GE. Most recently he ran its medical-systems business.

Following a successful CEO is never easy. Consider such casualties as Coca-Cola's Doug Ivester and Xerox's Rick Thoman, who followed high-profile bosses—Roberto Goizueta and Paul Allaire—and barely got a chance to make a mark before the long knives came out. It doesn't help that Immelt is starting his tenure at the end of an unprecedented bull market and in

BIG SHOES Immelt says he can fill 'em

the midst of a global economic slowdown, when GE businesses from lighting and appliances to NBC are slumping, and cash cows like power systems and aircraft engines are wavering. Meanwhile, European regulators scotched Welch's dream of a final coup: GE's proposed $43 billion takeover of Honeywell.

Welch moved on to plugging his new biz-bio *Jack: Straight from the Gut,* for which he received a $7 million advance. But his debut as autobiographer proved star-crossed: his book tour began on NBC's *Today* show on Sept. 11.

DREAMIN' Disney's new park is a celebration of the lore of the Golden State

The Mouse's New House

Looking for thrills? The world of Disney has always been a good place for them. Take that scream-inducing roller-coaster ride, replete with stomach-churning falls from on high—and that's just the stock price. In 2000 the company shut down its Go.com website, laid off 400 of its 2,000 Internet employees and wrote off more than $800 million in losses stemming from its slumping online operations. Boss Michael Eisner's antidote: the new California Adventure theme park, which opened in February in Anaheim, across the street from the original Disneyland. Theme parks are something Disney has always done well: in 2000 the parks accounted for about 27% of the company's $25.4 billion in sales and nearly 50% of its $3.2 billion in operating profits. California Adventure will advance Disney's latest theme-park strategy, which seeks to offer as much for parents as for kids. Inside,

there's a giant Ferris wheel, a soggy river-rafting ride and the usual characters. Outside lies Downtown Disney, an admission-free shopping and dining esplanade designed to separate adults from their dollars.

NEW BAG Mad for Dad's old plaid

Grandpa's Raincoat? Cool!

Believe it or not, there was once a time when Prada and Gucci were considered dull, cheesy or both. And not so long ago, the distinctive tan-red-white-and-black plaid of

Images

SINKING FEELING
Meet the leaning tower of crude. In March the world's largest oil rig, 78 miles off the coast of Brazil, was ripped by three mysterious explosions that left 10 people dead; 160 workers were safely evacuated. When the 40-story rig sank, it dumped some 1.5 million gal. of crude oil and diesel fuel into the Atlantic Ocean. The massive installation was the pride of Petrobras, Brazil's state-operated oil company, pumping 80,000 bbl. of petroleum a day, about 5% of Brazil's total production.

Burberry was thought to be appropriate only for the lining of Granddad's raincoat. But in 1998 Burberry underwent radical image surgery and made a plaid raid on everything from bikinis to bags to little doggy coats—and became a must-have for the cool crowd. Now such sensible old-timers as Coach, Dunhill and even the venerable Swiss shoe company Bally are going through a similar process of fust removal, hoping to mimic the Burberry magic. The formula: find an unsung young designer to create a new line of products, or conceive of a new store that will catch the eye of the fashion press and stylists.

Encourage those stylists to nudge some free stuff toward a celebrity or two. Create unfathomable but cool ad campaigns. Get rid of all the dowdier stores and licensees. And presto! Your dog of a luxury label just became desirable to three times as many people without losing any of its snob appeal.

Boeing, Boeing, Gone

All together now: Cincinnati is Procter & Gamble, Seattle is Microsoft, and Chicago is … Boeing? Dealing a major blow to its longtime hometown, CEO Phil Condit announced he would move

WILLIAM MERCER MCLEOD

BOEING Still will build in Seattle

the headquarters of the nation's largest airplane builder from Seattle to a more central city, and held a bake-off among Dallas, Denver and Chicago. The winner: the city of big shoulders—and now, wide bodies.

DAIMLERSAURUS WRECKS That's what the spoilsports at the Sierra Club dubbed the latest entry in the auto industry's ongoing attempt to strangle the planet with oversize SUVs, DaimlerChrysler's gigantic new Unimog. The $84,000 behemoth gets 10 m.p.g. and runs roughshod over quaint notions like a recession or an energy crisis. And as these pictures show, the "Mog" can be customized with accessories. Dude!

Technology

June 11

A new generation of high-powered surveillance technologies is helping authorities see through clothing, homes and vehicles—and has some privacy advocates seeing red. Among the new devices: a truck-based X-ray inspection system made by American Science and Engineering Inc. of Billerica, Mass. Using a technique in which images are made from X rays scattered back from objects (rather than passing through them), the system can spot guns, drugs, explosives and other contraband—like the 37 illegal immigrants, some of them visible at left, caught being smuggled out of Chiapas, Mexico, in a shipment of bananas. In June, the U.S. Supreme Court ruled that the use of one such device—a heat-sensing infrared gun—amounted to an illegal search, putting the future use of these gizmos by lawmen in doubt.

A DIGITAL DOGFIGHT

Wily newcomer Microsoft takes on crafty veteran Nintendo in video gaming's Battle of Seattle

THINKING INSIDE THE BOX Bill Gates unveils Microsoft's nifty new Xbox design at the Consumer Electronics Show

THERE'S SOMETHING ABOUT THE NINTENDO CAMPUS that just heaves with secrecy. Its whitewashed buildings with black-tinted windows, closely shrouded by trees, seem more like Langley, Va., than suburban Seattle. A visitor couldn't find Nintendo's powerful new video-game console, the GameCube, in any of the display cases before its mid-November release. Nor would you hear the staff speak the names of the games that would be released for it. "We've said the right amount on Game-Cube, which is nothing," chuckled Nintendo's sagelike executive vice president, Peter Main. "We've got our friends across the road saying, 'What are they doing?'"

If your friends across the road were Microsoft, you'd try to fly under the radar too. Just a five-minute drive down Highway 520, Bill Gates' guys were beavering away on their own powerful new video-game console, the Xbox.

In part because Microsoft is the new kid on this particular block, its approach to launching a new product—like dropping $500 million in 2001 on the roll-out Xbox advertising—was a little different. The Microsofties couldn't wait to thrust a green-and-black Xbox into your hands, show off its cool games—and loudly taunt the game geeks up the road. "Let's face it. Nintendo's system is for kids," said Robbie Bach, Xbox's gruff-voiced team leader. "We're for sophisticated gamers. I don't know any 30-year-olds who want a GameCube."

Welcome to the new battle of Seattle. Its D-day was the Christmas season of 2001, when the $5 billion Mario Bros. gang and the $23 billion Windows heavyweights, neighbors who never before had occasion to compete, began waging a mighty battle for the hearts, minds and $15 billion annual global sales of the video-game industry. It was an even contest: Nintendo had more than a century of arcade experience, but Microsoft had its bruised post-antitrust

PIXEL POWER Both the systems reach new levels in game display, producing far more realistic visuals. Left, Nintendo's Rogue Squadron II; above, Microsoft's Oddworld

trial pride at stake—and nobody ever went broke overestimating Gates' ability to break into a new market. In the long run, the winner of the war could easily oust Sony's PlayStation 2 from the top of the charts, whereas the loser could just as easily go the way of Sega's defunct Dreamcast.

Which digital colossus would prevail? On the Nintendo side, Luigi's Mansion is one of several new works from Shigeru Miyamoto, the man behind Mario, Zelda and Donkey Kong and an inductee of the game designers' Hall of Fame. Great game play aside, it is an excuse to show off the GameCube's spectacularly realistic lighting effects. Probably the most potent example of GameCube's capabilities is LucasArts' Rogue Squadron II. Replicating the climactic shoot-out sequence in *Star Wars,* designers created a Death Star that looks embarrassingly more realistic than the 1977 movie model.

developers can practically forget programming altogether and let their imagination run riot. In both of these cases, however, the claim turned out to be true. Developers say the standards and software in both GameCube and Xbox have chopped in half the time it takes to program a game— at least compared with the PlayStation 2, whose so-called "emotion engine" system is so arcane that it left a lot of developers badly burned. Watch your back, Sony.

For the first time, Nintendo is enlisting outside designers; previously the company subsisted almost entirely on its own games. Now popular sports games like Electronic Arts' Madden NFL will be on the roster. This is part of Nintendo's bid to lose the kids-only label and grab a chunk of the elusive twentysomething market. Microsoft came at it the other way around: let Dad buy the Xbox in the first place, partly because he wants to play

START YOUR ENGINES The Xbox, near right, will compete against reigning champ Sony's PlayStation, center, and Nintendo's GameCube system, far right

But Xbox matched GameCube's visuals. If anything, the Microsoft games are even more cinematically realistic and detail obsessed. Just take a walk through the space station in Halo, an action game based on Larry Niven's classic sci-fi novel *Ringworld,* and you will notice fingerprint marks on triple-glazed windows.

The key goal of any nascent game console is to make your machine easier to program than the other guy's—so

DVDs on it (GameCube runs on 3-in. mini-CDs), and then buy a couple of cartoonish multiplayer games (like the Marioesque Fuzion Frenzy) for the kids. Both strategies could work. So, from the retailer's point of view, "it's like having a ticket on every horse in the race," said Joe Firestone, CEO of Electronics Boutique. Long before the dust settled, it looked as if we already had one winner. ■

ON A ROLL

Forget the lever: inventor Jeff Kamen says he can move the world with two wheels

SCIENCE FICTION WRITER ARTHUR C. CLARKE ONCE OBSERVED that "any sufficiently advanced technology is indistinguishable from magic." By that standard, Jeff Kamen's latest invention is advanced indeed—so advanced, Kamen hopes his newfangled personal transportation device may change the way we live and design our cities. Unlikely as it seems, he just may be right. There is no denying that Kamen's machine is an engineering marvel. Developed at a cost of more than $100 million, this one-person vehicle—the Segway Human Transporter, also known by its skunk works moniker, Ginger—is a complex bundle of hardware and software that mimics the human body's ability to maintain its balance. Not only does the battery-powered gizmo have no brakes, it also has no engine, no throttle, no gearshift and no steering wheel. Best of all, it has no gas tank. And yet it can carry the average rider for a full day, nonstop, on only 5¢ worth of electricity.

The commercial ambitions of Kamen and his team are as advanced as their technical virtuosity. They have erected a 77,000-sq.-ft. factory a few miles from their Manchester, N.H., headquarters that will be capable of churning out 40,000 Segways a month by the end of 2002. Kamen maintains that the Segway "will be to the car what the car was to the horse and buggy." He believes it will change the world by changing how cities are organized. To Kamen's way of thinking, the problem is the automobile. "Cities need cars like fish need bicycles," he says. Unlike cars, Segways are cheap, clean, efficient, maneuverable. Unlike bicycles, they are designed specifically to be pedestrian friendly. By traveling at three or four times walking speed, and thus turning what would have been a 30-min. walk into a 10-min. ride, Kamen contends, Segways will in effect shrink cities to the point where cars "will not only be undesirable, but unnecessary."

Kamen's dream of a Segway-saturated world won't come true overnight. In fact, ordinary folks won't be able to buy one until late 2002, when a consumer model is expected to go on sale for about $3,000. For now, the first customers to test the Segway will be such deep-pocketed institutions as the U.S. Postal Service, General Electric and Amazon.com—outfits that can shell out about $8,000 apiece for industrial-strength models. And Kamen's dream world won't arrive at all unless he and his team can navigate the obstacles that are sure to be thrown up by competitors and government regulators.

The world of technology has never been short of eccentrics and obsessives, of rich, brilliant oddballs. But even in this crowd, Dean Kamen stands out. The 50-year-old son of a comic-book artist, he is a college dropout, a self-taught physicist and mechanical engineer with a handful of honorary doctorates, a multimillionaire who wears the same outfit for every occasion: blue jeans, a blue work shirt and a pair of Timberland boots.

While he was still struggling in college, Kamen invented the first drug-infusion pump, which enabled doctors to deliver steady, reliable doses to patients. In the years that followed, he invented the first portable insulin pump, the first portable dialysis machine and an array of heart stents. This string of successes made him wealthy and turned DEKA Research, his R.-and-D. lab, into a kind of Mecca for medical-device design.

The seeds of Ginger were planted by what had previously been Kamen's most widely-known project: the IBOT wheelchair. The IBOT is his bid to "give the disabled the same kind of mobility the rest of us take for granted"—a six-wheel machine that goes up and down curbs, cruises effortlessly through sand or gravel and even climbs stairs. In its standing mode, an IBOT rises right up on its wheels and lifts its occupant to eye level while keeping balance with such stability that it can't be knocked over even by a violent shove.

As Kamen and his team were working on the IBOT, it dawned on them that they were onto something larger: "The big idea," he said, "is to put a human being into a system where the machine acts as an extension of your body."

Pulling off this trick requires an unholy amount of computer power. In every Segway there are 10 microprocessors cranking out three PCs' worth of juice. Also a cluster of aviation-grade gyros, an accelerometer, a bevy of sensors, two batteries and software so sophisticated it puts Microsoft to shame. Yet it is so compact that to many, the Segway may not look like a revolution. It may look … well, sorta like a scooter. Kamen gets irked when the IBOT is called a wheelchair, so imagine his pique if his magical mover becomes regarded as only a souped-up scooter. "If all we end up with are a few billion-dollar niche markets, that would be a disappointment," he told TIME. Jeff Kamen may build his devices small, but no one doubts he thinks big. ∎

INSIDE THE SEGWAY

How does Dean Kamen's self-balancing "human transporter" achieve its magic? Using the latest advances in gyros, tilt sensors and high-performance motors. Here's how it works:

Kill switch

Intelligent key A digital security code thwarts would-be thieves. Also sets speed limits

User interface Tells you the machine is on, what mode it's in and how much battery life is left

UNDER THE HOOD

"Sisterboards" A pair of circuit boards sends commands to the motors based on input from sensors. If one fails, the other can function by itself

Turning control A single axle gives Segway something no other vehicle has: a turning radius of zero

Control shaft Die-cast aluminum, height adjustable

Motors Two of them drive each wheel independently. Emission free and fully redundant; if one fails, the other takes over

Balance sensors Gyroscopes and tilt sensors work together to pick up tiny shifts of body weight and changes in terrain. The five gyros operate by committee, voting among themselves to eliminate errant readings

Batteries Two types available; NiCd and NiMH; rechargeable by plugging into any outlet

Chassis Houses Segway's electronic innards. Tested to withstand 7 tons of force—the weight of three SUVs

Rubber diaphragms Hidden beneath the rider's platform, they engage the machine's self-balancing systems. Step off; and the Segway stops

Tires Tubeless and resistant to flats. Treated for enhanced traction on wet surfaces and to leave no marks indoors

Source: Segway
TIME Graphic
by Lon Tweeten

FUTURE SHOCK

Today's coolest gear—and a peek at tomorrow's

MOVE OVER, DICK TRACY. YOU MAY HAVE HAD A two-way wrist radio, but we bet your Timex couldn't take a licking—and then connect to the Internet. Nor could you download 1,000 songs off your computer and onto a nifty little battery-operated thingamajig that fits in your hand. On the other hand, Dick, you lived before the great dotcom bubble burst—so clear-domed cars won't remind you of your losses.

Avant Headset
$149

In New York State it's now illegal to use a handheld phone while driving. One solution: the earpiece of this elegant Avant headset acts as a cordless phone linked by radio to a base that plugs into your cell phone's earphone jack. At recharge time, a built-in speakerphone kicks in.

iPod $399

This tiny gem from Apple redefines the market for portable music players. It holds 1,000 songs in MP3 format, uses a FireWire link to swap them with your Mac quickly—and can tell when you've downloaded new songs onto your computer.

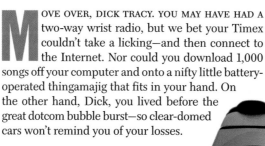

Timex Internet Messenger
$99

This watch is capable of receiving (but not sending) e-mail and pages, plus news, sports and weather headlines fresh from the Internet. Oh, yeah—it also keeps time.

Sony Clié PDA
$500

The Clié PEG-N710C is an upgrade of Sony's first (feeble) foray into the Palm-clone market. Its brilliant color screen makes the Palm m505's look putrid. And it's the first Palm clone to feature a headphone jack and the ability to play MP3 files.

Scoot
Not available

Coming in 2003: Scoot, the world's first hydrogen-fuel-cell-powered scooter, with a wide, scooped-out footrest and rugged, over-size wheels. Scoot folds in half so that the tires and grimy underside are neatly tucked away. Visit *fuseproject.com* for a quick sneak preview.

MARCUS HANSCHEN—FUSEPROJECT (2)

Mercedes Bubble Car
Not available

O.K., we cheated: this concept car from Mercedes, half convertible and half George Jetson, isn't on the market yet. The goal is to determine how best to minimize blind spots in real cars, thus reducing accidents. The roof of this bubbly little number is made entirely of Plexiglas.

The Last *Standard* Issue

Call it the final nail in the coffin of the dotcom bubble: the *Industry Standard*, the irreverent weekly chronicle of digital business, folded in August. The shutdown came as a shock: compared with the frothy content plays of the era, the *Standard* stood on a solid foundation, pulling in $158 million in ad revenue in 2000—and actually turning a profit, albeit briefly. The problem: like dotcom flameouts Kozmo.com and Webvan, the *Standard* followed the mantra—first popularized by Amazon.com founder Jeff Bezos—of Get Big Fast. Hundreds of reporters were hired. A New York City office opened. So when dotcom-driven ads dried up, the overcommitted *Standard* gave up the ghost.

NO ESCAPE Beach ads have true grit

When Gizmos Collide

Ask Arnold Schwarzenegger: you'll never go broke overestimating a boy's yen to see stuff get smashed to hell. Cousins Trey Roski, 35, and Greg Munson, 34, knew this desire as kids. "Whatever we built Legos, Lincoln Logs—the end result would be destroying it," Munson recalled. They also collected remote-controlled helicopters, and those twin lusts— for remote control and destruction— explain why their TV show *Battle-Bots* become a surprise hit for Comedy Central in 2001. Putting homemade, remote-controlled robots with WWF-style names like Mauler and Vlad the Impaler in a Plexiglas cage and letting them hammer, buzz-saw and ram the

BOTS These remotes are feeling their oats

motor oil out of each other, our heroes created a brave new art form. Or maybe they simply had fun and made a lot of money.

Fighting the Ad Deficit

The average American sees an estimated 3,000 advertisements a day. And he's seeing them in increasingly odd places—at gas pumps, on stickers on apples and bananas, on sidewalks and rooftops, even in full-color, full-sound commercials at ATM machines. So-called ambient advertising is exploding as companies attempt to get at jaded consumers where they work, shop and play. New Jersey–based Beach 'n Billboard, for example, imprints ads on sand, while New York City taxis are topped with digital ads.

FIORINA Hold 'em or fold 'em?

The Chips Are Down

Hewlett-Packard CEO Carly Fiorina, 47, is one of the most powerful women in American business, a steely-nerved visionary who once compared the computer business to a game of blackjack. She proved she was a gambler in September, when she announced that H-P would link up with one of its key rivals, Compaq.

The two companies are vastly different: Hewlett-Packard is an invention factory that has created hundreds of products, things like the handheld calculator, over its 64-year history. Compaq hasn't really invented anything. It sprang to life as an IBM-clone maker in 1982 and shot into the FORTUNE 500 in record time on the basis of its ability to give consumers low-priced machines built with mostly off-the-shelf parts. The proposed stock deal was initially valued by the companies at $25 billion; the combined company would rival IBM in size and revenue, and theoretically could leapfrog Dell in sales of PCs and midrange servers, the machines that act as the Internet's traffic cops.

But plenty of people were skeptical. Wall Street sent H-P stock plunging 22% within days of the announcement, while Compaq sank 14%, wiping more than $3 billion off the value of the proposed takeover. The planned takeover took a stronger hit in November, when heirs of the Hewlett family declared they would oppose it. As the TIME Annual closed, the fate of Fiorina's bet was unresolved.

Photograph by Douglas C. Pizac—AP/Wide World

Society

May 18

With the Winter Olympics coming to Utah, the state cracked down on polygamists like Tom Green, shown at left with his five wives, Hannah, Lee Ann, Shirley, Linda and Cari. Unlike most religious polygamists, who live discreetly, Green openly boasted about his plural marriage, long banned by the Church of Jesus Christ of Latter-day Saints, the state's dominant religion. In May, after this picture was taken, Green was found guilty of bigamy and criminal failure to pay child support; he was later sentenced to serve up to five years in jail and ordered to repay $78,000 in welfare money fraudulently obtained from the state. The pater-familias (he has sired 30 children) still faces a charge of child rape—wife Linda was 13 when he impregnated her in 1986. His other four wives are two pairs of sisters; he was previously married to two of his present wives' mothers. Green had once boasted: "We thought we could even set up a polygamy booth at the airport and sell T shirts with pictures of my wives inside the five Olympic rings."

WELCOME TO AMEXICA!

BORDER TOWNS Above, Melissa Juarez, 11, shoots hoops in Laredo, Texas, after her first Holy Communion. At right, four Mexican towns.

Along the 2,000-mile border between America and Mexico, a rich new hybrid culture takes shape—a piñata bursting with paradoxes

O N AN AVERAGE WEEKDAY, THIS IS WHAT CROSSES the border that separates the U.S. and Mexico: a million bbl. of crude oil, 432 tons of bell peppers, 238,000 light bulbs, 166 brand-new Volkswagen Beetles, 16,250 toasters, $51 million worth of auto parts. It all comes in trucks and boxcars and panel vans, and that's just the stuff that Customs can keep track of. There is also the vast shadow market—not just co-caine and heroin and freshly laundered money but also cut-price Claritin, banned bug killers and boots made from the flippers of endangered sea turtles.

And then there are the people, more than 800,000 crisscrossing legally every day, some walking, more driv-ing, not to mention the 4,600 or so who hop the fence and get caught a few minutes or hours later. The ones who make it are on their way to jobs as meat packers in Iowa and carpetmakers in Georgia and gardeners in Pennsylva-nia. They want to be in the U.S. so badly they will risk the scorpions and rattlesnakes, the surveillance cameras and underground sensors; they will fold into hidden compart-ments behind the dashboard of a car or in the belly of a tanker truck. They know they can get a job no one else wants, save some money, send some home, maybe find a way to bring their family—because someday this border may not look anything like what it does now: a barbed-wire paradox, half pried open, half bolted closed.

So, how much has to cross a border before it might as well not be here at all? There is no Customs station for cus-toms—for ideas and tastes, stories and songs, values and attitudes—and none of those stop in El Paso or San Diego anymore. The Old World fades away—salsa is more popu-lar than catsup—and the border is everywhere.

ockwise from top left: a woman in Tanque de Guadalupe; U.S. retirees in San Felipe; a boy in Juárez; an Aztec festival in Neuvo Laredo

One day soon it may seem a little backward for someone in the U.S. not to speak some Spanish, even the hybrid Spanglish of the Southwest: "¿*Como se llama* your dog?" Signs appear in the store windows of Garden City, Kans., that say SE HABLA ESPAÑOL, and you can buy extremely fresh mangoes at bodegas all over that town. Dalton, Ga. (pop. 27,900), has three Spanish-language newspapers. Said longtime resident Edwin Mitchell, 77: "We're a border community—1,000 miles away from the border." Already we are living in a whole new world: Welcome to Amexica!

Sometime in the next few years, Mexico will pass Canada as the U.S.'s top trading partner. Hispanics have overtaken African Americans as the country's largest minority, the swing vote to woo, the constituency to grab. Yet many Americans fear an unbridled influx of Mexican immigrants. Prior to Sept. 11, 2001, America's 4,000-mile border with Canada was basically defended by a couple of fire trucks, and most Americans thought that was sufficient. The Southern border is half as long, has the equivalent of an Army division patrolling it, and many Americans say it

should be buttoned down even tighter. Terrorist outlaws aside, there may be no country on earth with as much potential as Mexico to destabilize the U.S.—and to preserve its standard of living. No wonder people can't decide how much the border should be a barrier, how much a bridge.

From the moment you set foot in the boomtowns of the Rio Grande Valley, you sense you are watching a gold rush, headlong and free-spirited and corrupt and ingenious. Stand on a corner some morning in Laredo, Texas, and watch the first of 8,000 trucks a day hauling the global economy north and south, 18-wheelers full of bulldozer claws and baby cribs, all passing through a town that once didn't bother to pave the streets. Now it can't pour concrete fast enough. The banks are open 7 to 7, seven days a week; the pager shops are everywhere. Yet much of the border is still desperately poor. McAllen, Texas, at the heart of the fourth fastest-growing metro area in the U.S., is America's poorest city: its average per capita income is $13,339 a year.

Here, where boom and bust coexist, people on both sides of the border are helping one another do the deals, cut the corners, take a region that was forever left behind and turn it into the New Frontier. The NAFTA (North America Free Trade Agreement) gold-rush gang saw in the opening of the border a chance to make a killing by taking factories that would otherwise head to Malaysia and plunking them down right across the border.

RESULT: JUÁREZ, ONCE A DUSTY BORDER MOUNTAIN pass, is now Mexico's fourth largest city, with a population of 1.3 million and 50,000 more arriving each year. Huge clusters of tiny workers' houses rise out of the sand and stretch in every direction. Juárez and its outskirts are dotted with enormous new plants, but these are not your padre's *maquiladoras:* some resemble

teachers and technicians and surgeons and Senators. If they all put down their tools tomorrow, the U.S. economy would take a serious siesta.

It is often said that Amexica is its own country, neither Mexican nor American. Both sides regard their sovereign governments as distant and dysfunctional. They are proud of their ability to take care of themselves, solve their problems faster and cheaper than any faraway bureaucrat. "The only way the cities in this region can make it," said Juárez Mayor Gustavo Elizondo, "is to forget that a line and a river exist here."

Yet for all the frontier pioneer spirit, local leaders do draw a line. Why should the whole country benefit from the blessings of free trade if the border region pays the

DIVIDED WE STAND Above, a boy and his father remaining on the U.S. side part with their family on the Mexican side; right, the fence runs

Italianate palaces (Johnson & Johnson) or works of modern art (Thomson electronics). Still, life hasn't been upgraded for everyone here: hourly pay remains about $1.25.

The countries are growing more interdependent every day. There are now four or five cities the size of Cleveland, Ohio, sitting right next door, and by 2026 as much as 40% of the entire Mexican population may be living on the border. The region is Mexico's economic engine, a huge commercial classroom where the unskilled workers who were making gauze eye patches in 1980 now make ATMs and modems and the most popular Sony TV sold in the U.S.

As for the U.S., it imports not just the gizmos and gadgets but also a way of life, thanks to a shadow labor force that works for sub-minimum wage. The U.S. depends on the maids and gardeners and carpenters and home-health-care workers whose children will probably become

price? To enforce immigration policies over which they have no control, border counties lay out $108 million a year in law enforcement and medical expenses associated with illegal crossings, money they can't afford to spend.

There is a shortage of judges to hear all the drug and smuggling cases. Schools are poor, overcrowded and growing. Good health care has always been scarce here, but the border boom makes it worse. The poor on both sides are united by a struggle just to survive what most Americans can barely imagine. Mothers in the rural El Paso outpost of Revolución cross into Juárez to buy methyl parathion, a pesticide so lethal it is banned in the U.S. They sprinkle it around their shanties, and it kills the roaches and tarantulas for a year. But their children play in the dust and dirt, and when they get sick, their parents take them to Juárez doctors, who are cheaper. If the children die, they are buried in Mexico, where it costs about $150 instead of the $2,000 for an American grave.

The hemisphere's economic future may depend on whether the U.S. and Mexico can fix what is broken here. But that day won't come until Mexico goes straight, cleans up its justice and banking systems. Some American borderlanders who cheer integration in public go off record to talk about what's wrong, admit they rarely visit the other side or whisper quietly that they haven't felt the same about the place since a friend had his car hijacked a few years ago and they never saw him again.

Here in Amexica, police and Customs people pay for their government jobs so they can get in on the *mordida*, the payoff system. Mexicans call it Article No. 20, as in

m the land into the sea on the beach at Playa de Tijuana, Baja California

Which of the $20 is for me? Midwives in Brownsville have sold thousands of birth certificates to be used as proof of U.S. citizenship. The Arelano Felíx brothers, Tijuana drug kingpins known for torturing, roasting and carving up their rivals, are paying $4 million a month in bribes in Baja California alone, just as the cost of doing business. The people-smuggling cartels are prospering as well. No matter how many surveillance cameras and motion detectors the U.S. installs, the immigrants still come.

Across this 2,000-mile border, two countries that need each other but don't exactly trust each other must create a vision of the future both can agree on. If Presidents George W. Bush and Vicente Fox manage to solve the problems of Amexica, the American Century could give way to the Century of the Americas, and the border might as well have disappeared altogether. ■

THE TWO AMIGOS

A pair of ranchers from the border country—George Bush and Vicente Fox—aim to reform immigration

The last time Mexico tried invading the U.S., in 1916, Pancho Villa led a doomed horseback adventure that was quickly snuffed out by Uncle Sam. So you had to admire the stealthy 21st century raid Mexicans launched in 2001: they came not to conquer but to lobby—and all with the tacit encouragement of the American President. As the Mexican Foreign Minister and three of his country's leading Senators traveled the U.S. in July recruiting allies, it fell to Mexican President Vicente Fox to disclose what he and George W. Bush had been discussing in secret for months: the most sweeping change in U.S.-Mexican relations in nearly a century and the biggest overhaul of U.S. immigration law in 15 years. The goal: a graduated amnesty program for Mexicans who are living illegally in the U.S. When Fox paid a state visit to Bush in early September he upped the ante, apparently surprising his host by declaring, "We must, and we can, reach an agreement on migration before the end of this very year." Bush hedged his response—and a week later, dreams of immigration reform were put on hold by the terrorist attack.

The proposed plan would take three giant steps. First, it would pave a road toward legal status for some 4.5 million Mexicans who are already living and working—in the shadows—in the U.S. Both sides envision a new system in which Mexicans would spend several years in the amnesty program before getting their green cards.

The second step is arcane but crucial: remove the annual U.S. ceiling on immigration from Mexico and Canada. The third and perhaps most controversial part of the plan is a proposal to revise the U.S. "guest worker" program and allow as many as 300,000 Mexicans to work in industries like meat packing, construction and landscaping—and then go home. That's a sweetener for the Republicans' big-business financial backers. But labor unions and Democrats are sure to fight any guest-worker arrangement that lacks full labor protections.

Both men see an upside in reform. Fox's goal is to make Mexico more like Canada: an economically healthy neighbor whose citizens aren't eager to leave. In the short term, he would ship excess workers abroad to earn money and send it home. In the long run, he's praying that the cash would create new jobs so people don't have to migrate. Bush's goal is to change his party's course on immigration. To be re-elected in an increasingly Latino America, he needs to win more of the Hispanic vote than the 35% he collected in 2000. Fox and Bush, veteran politicians, know that an amigo in need is an amigo indeed.

RANCHERS Two Amexicans meet in the Oval Office

Tiki bars! Action figures! Felt? Even chocolate milk was back, as Americans dressed up faded fads in today's brighter colors

BUZZ BAROMETER

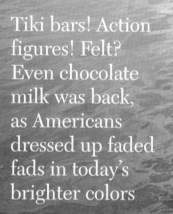

Dinner in Bed
At eateries from Hollywood to Miami, tables and chairs were replaced with comfy, oversize beds, on which diners nibbled their lamb chops or salmon

Felt as Furniture
Humble old felt popped up in clothes, furniture and even as vases. Because it's not woven, its edges don't fray, so a soft object can have a sharp profile

Iceland
It may be the marketing coup of the century: take a frozen lava field on the edge of the Arctic Circle, where the skiing is not great, the food is overpriced and the capital city is a windswept collection of multicolored concrete boxes, and turn it into one of the world's hottest winter vacation spots. Iceland did it by promoting its swinging nightclubs, soothing hot tubs, comely natives (like cool singer Bjork), unspoiled natural wonders—and cheap airfares

Chocolate Milk

You know you love it. Now here's proof: sales of flavored milks, more than 90% of them chocolate, rose 18% in 2000. Much of the growth is coming from calcium-conscious, diet-conscious, Coke-kicking adults

Ballroom Dancing

As tens of thousands of young people embraced ballroom dancing, its fast-growing competitive dance-sport community began lobbying to include ballroom as a sport at the 2008 Olympic Games

Labyrinths

Ten years ago, there were only a few labyrinths in the U.S., but seekers can now walk more than 1,500. Mazes are designed to confuse, but labyrinths have only one continuous path to the center—and are often used as physical metaphors for spiritual centering

Action Figures of the 1980s

Vintage superheroes from the '80s, like Voltron, He-Man and the Transformers, were hot items in toy stores again. They had been popular for years on eBay, where nostalgic adults buy old heroes for eight times their original value. That got toymakers' attention, and the boys were back in town

Tiki Bars

Bali Hai was calling—again—as tiki bars, those hula-hut hangouts made popular in postwar America by G.I.s returning from the South Pacific, made a comeback from Seattle to Santiago. Aficionados swapped reviews and mugs on websites like *www.tikinews.com*

People

Climb Every Mountain

Mount Everest eats the unready and the unlucky. Almost 90% of Everest climbers fail to reach the summit. Many—at least 165 since 1953, when the peak was first conquered—never come home at all, their bodies lying uncollected where they fell. Four climbers died in May 2001.

But Eric Weihenmayer prevailed—and became the first blind person to climb the world's highest mountain. Weihenmayer, 33, was born sighted but became blind at 13, the victim of a rare hereditary disease of the retina. The gifted athlete and former champion wrestler began attacking mountains in his early 20s. Though he had summited Denali, Kilimanjaro in Africa and Aconcagua in Argentina,

WEIHENMAYER One word: Excelsior!

among other peaks, he viewed Everest as insurmountable, until veteran climber Pasquale Scaturro persuaded him to make the attempt and helped find sponsors.

On May 24, Weihenmayer and teammate Jeff Evans defied a fierce storm and made their way to the top of Everest. "Look around, dude," Evans recalled telling his blind friend when they were standing on top of the world. "Just take a second and look around."

ENSLAVED A shelter in Port-au-Prince provides aid for these young *restaveks*

Up from Slavery

Child slavery is an entrenched tradition in Haiti: the government estimates that 300,000 youngsters there are *restaveks,* or child slaves. Like malaria and political violence, the scourge was thought to have been left behind as more Haitians emigrated to America. Not so: the plight of U.S. *restaveks* began to emerge in 1999, when Florida officials removed a 12-year-old Haitian girl—filthy, unkempt and in acute abdominal pain from repeated rape—from the affluent suburban home of middle-class Haitian-American merchants in Pembroke Pines. The girl said she had been forced to have sex with the family's 20-year-old son since she was nine.

Officials vowed to fight the practice: "We are not going to let Haitian traditions like *restavek* flourish here because we know now that America is the great equalizer among us," said attorney Phillip Brutus, Florida's first Haitian-American state legislator.

Europe Goes to Pot

Holland used to be Western Europe's only tokers' paradise, courtesy of 900 cannabis cafés where adults can legally buy five grams of marijuana or hashish. But now all over the Continent the weed has won a new level of social acceptance: a European Union drug-monitoring report says at least 45 million of its citizens—18% of those ages 15 to 64—have tried marijuana at least once. Result: politicians are easing up on criminality. Most are trying variants on what the Dutch call *gedogen*—turning a blind eye. The authorities keep pot-possession statutes on the books to avoid the political controversy of changing the law. But they opt for quite lenient enforcement. Still, surveys show many Europeans don't approve of decriminalizing the wacky weed.

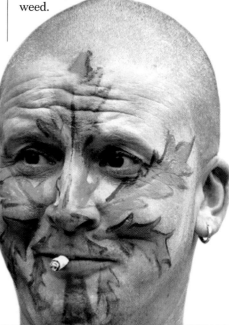

Images

SMOKE SIGNALS
Pope John Paul II is one of the longest-serving Pontiffs in history. But as he is a mortal being who must be succeeded, Vatican insiders are increasingly abuzz with the names of *papabili* (Italian for "Popables"). Among the favored are two Latin Americans: Colombian Cardinal Dario Castrillon Hoyos and Cardinal Oscar Andres Rodriguez Maradiaga of Honduras. But most observers suspect that an Italian will be chosen: after all, John Paul is the first non-Italian Pope since the 1500s.

Well, Bless My Success!

After decades of willful ignorance, the publishing world has learned that titles by and for Evangelical Christians can sell angelically. Case in point: a slim inspirational text

called *The Prayer of Jabez*, written by an evangelist based in Atlanta, Bruce Wilkinson, and published by a tiny firm in Sisters, Ore. By November it had sold a whomping 7 million copies and had spent 28 weeks atop the New York *Times* Advice, How-To & Miscellaneous best-sellers list—even though the *Times* does not count books sold in religious bookstores.

Reading the volume's back-cover blurb ("Do you want to be extravagantly blessed by God?"), one might suspect that Wilkinson is selling Prosperity Theology, a wide-spread if superficial gospel that amounts to praying for dollars. This turns out not to be the case. The riches he has in mind are the wealth of God's spirit; the more one has, he argues, the more one wants to spread it. It appears Wilkinson's prayer has been answered.

Dead Man Talking

Fad of the year? For many, it was *Crossing Over with John Edward*, the cable-TV show starring a fast-talking former ballroom-dancing instructor. Edward worked rating magic via his proclaimed ability "to connect with energies of people who have crossed over." Died, that is. Indeed, his nightly necrobabble was the highest-rated show on the Sci Fi network. But skeptics like professional debunker James "the Amazing" Randi argued that Edward was more adept at chicanery than channeling. Call it a lively debate.

MEDIUM WELL Edward's nightly séance is smash success for the Sci Fi network

Photograph by John Biever—Sports Illustrated

Sport

October 4

Going ... going ... gone! At Pac Bell Park, San Francisco Giants slugger Barry Bonds smacks home run No. 70, tying the single-season record set by St. Louis Cardinals great Mark McGwire only three years before. Bonds, who went on to finish the season with 73 dingers, was in the home-run groove all season, notching 39 of them before the All-Star Game break, a record clip. The only problem: Bonds, 36 in the 2001 season, has a reputation for being aloof and arrogant. The son of three time All-Star Bobby Bonds and the godson of diamond legend Willie Mays has had 14 major-league seasons to become popular, but at that task, he's still batting in the low .200s.

CHAMPS!

They pedaled, served, dunked, birdied, hoofed and otherwise fought their way to first place

DOUG PENSINGER—ALLSPORT

Venus Williams

Though she let Jennifer Capriati take two majors, Venus, 21, topped Justine Henine to defend her Wimbledon crown, then beat little sis Serena, 19, in the U.S. Open—their first Grand Slam final

Lance Armstrong

Feigning agony to fool his foes on one of the Tour de France's toughest climbs, and slowing down when chief rival Jan Ullrich took a fall, Armstrong sped to his third straight victory in cycling's greatest event

Marian Jones

Her string of 42 straight wins in the 100-m dash was broken by Zhanna Pintusevich-Block of Ukraine at the world meet, but Jones beat her rival in their next three races

David Duval

Putting like a dream, Duval overcame a 73 on the second round at the gorse-heavy Royal Lytham course to finally win his first major—the claret jug of the British Open

Lisa Leslie

The 6-ft. 5-in. center became the dominant player in women's pro basketball, leading her Los Angeles Sparks to their first championship crown—and ending the four-year reign of the Houston Comets

Kobe Bryant and Shaquille O'Neill

Coach Phil Jackson's two Lakers superstars fought like cats and dogs in the early days of the season but buried the hatchet—and then Allen Iverson's Philadelphia 76ers—to win two NBA titles in a row

DEATH IN THE FAST LANE

NASCAR racing great Dale Earnhardt is killed at Daytona—but his son carries on the family trade

JACOB LANGSTON-ORLANDO SENTINEL-CORBIS SYGMA

FOR DALE EARNHARDT, THE RACE WAS NEVER OVER. Back when he was winning everything in sight—11 races one year, nine in another—he would come home some nights mad as hell about something that somebody had done to him on the track. Squeezed him, bumped him, as if he would never do such things himself. And this was after a victory. Earnhardt had been a wild-child teenager, as reckless as they come and headed for nowhere, but he grew up to be his sport's father figure and a corporate titan to boot. He could

regale a crowd of GM dealers with war stories for an hour—Mr. Charm—then shift gears in a heartbeat, chiding drivers who wanted to slow the cars down as "candy asses." He made tens of millions of dollars in racing, but even at 49, a man of considerable responsibilities and with nothing left to prove, he would never take his foot off the gas. That is why they loved him. Ironhead, the Intimidator, Earnhardt: he had massive, irresistible appeal—the rebel soul of a sport that had gone corporate.

Dale was his father's son. Born in Kannapolis, N.C., in

SADDLE UP! Dale Earnhardt strides to his car at Daytona with only hours left to live. The popular seven-time Winston Cup champion was the first NASCAR driver on a Wheaties box

1951, he didn't take naturally to school—he would drop out in the ninth grade—but loved being around cars. Ralph Earnhardt, known as Ironheart, was a short-track racing god and taught his son to wrangle a stock car. Dale married at 17, and he and his first wife had a son, Kerry. By the time he began his pro racing career at age 24, Earnhardt had a young family to support and, more than most other drivers, was all business and no fooling. When strapped for cash, he would borrow from fellow racers, betting that he would win enough in Sunday's race for payback on Mon-

day. That's pressure, and it made Earnhardt bear down. He was NASCAR's rookie of the year in 1979 and won the season-long title in 1980. Even critics of his aggressive tactics acknowledged that in Earnhardt, NASCAR had as talented a driver as it had ever seen.

He married a second time, and then a third; his family grew to include Kelley and Dale Jr., with second wife Brenda; and Taylor Nicole, with third wife Teresa. He got into the business of racing, using the money from his on-track success, which would eventually burgeon to an all-

VICTORY! Dale Sr. celebrates his win at Daytona in 1998

GRIEF Generations of fans mourn the legendary Intimidator

time record $41.6 million, to start Dale Earnhardt Inc., an auto-racing company that today employs 200 in Moores-ville, N.C. and fields three cars on NASCAR's major circuit.

But as Earnhardt thrived, two elements of his driving career—his readiness to mix it up and his regular place at the center of crashes—continued to make him controver-sial. His great rival of the 1980s, Darrell Waltrip, once spoke for the field when he said, "You ought to get 10 bonus points for taking Earnhardt out of a race." But as Earnhardt's legend grew, so did NASCAR's popularity, and in recent years both took on a nuanced appearance. Earn-hardt settled down with Teresa, and by all accounts settled down a bit on the oval too. He came to be seen as a grand, grizzled gentleman of the game, the kind of athlete you take your kid to see, so that one day he can say he once saw Dale Earnhardt drive. Another change: Dale Jr. joined him on the circuit. "These past two years, having Junior on the track, we've all seen a marked change in Dale," said David Allen, his longtime p.r. manager.

But if Earnhardt was slowing down, his sport was speeding up. In the past five years, NASCAR's races have been electric, and its reach has been growing. With a

brand-new $2.4 billion network TV contract, the last thing NASCAR officials wanted at the Daytona 500, their show-case event, was a repeat of the boring 2000 race, which fea-tured only nine lead changes. In the fall of 2000 they ex-perimented at the circuit's other superspeedway course, Talladega, with ways of slowing down the cars to make for bunched, exciting racing. Some of the drivers had come out of that Talladega race looking ashen, but there had been 49 lead changes and no big wrecks, so it was deter-mined to go with restrictor plates on the carburetors (to reduce horsepower) and aerodynamic spoilers on the cars' surfaces (to increase drag) at Daytona too.

Earnhardt, who won that race at Talladega, had opin-ions on slowing down cars, as you might imagine. "If you're not a race driver, stay the hell home. Get the hell out of the race car if you've got feathers on your legs or butt," he had said in 2000, addressing the chicken-hearted. He had opinions about some of the proposed safety measures too. He wasn't wearing the new Head and Neck Support, or HANS, system, which fights whiplash in a crash.

So with new rules in place, new controversies in the air and TV cameras ready to roll, the gentlemen started

VICTORY! Dale Jr. exults after winning at Talladega in October 2001

their engines. It was going to be a triumphal afternoon, with a huge network audience watching, the ultimate proof, as if anyone needed it, that NASCAR was nationwide. An early crash looked like an Armageddon of a wreck: 19 cars careering around, smashing into one another, Tony Stewart's Pontiac soaring through the air, ripping the hood off another car, metal clanging, a 16-minute red flag to clean up the mess—and only a bum shoulder, Stewart's, as a result. Constant jockeying eventually produced 40 more lead changes than in 2000.

Earnhardt, for his part, was having a decent day. Some dings to the Monte Carlo changed the car's aerodynamic shape and let him know before the endgame that he wouldn't be the winner. But up ahead, there was a good chance that someone else from Dale Earnhardt Inc. would be, as Michael Waltrip and Dale Jr. were leading the pack. Talking with his pit crew over the radio, Earnhardt started coaching his teammates. Waltrip screeched home with the victory, his first in 463 NASCAR races.

Behind Waltrip, Earnhardt was seconds from the finish line when the first contact was made—with Sterling Marlin's car. It didn't seem a big thing, although Marlin

would receive death threats in the week ahead. Dale's car veered right, plowed into the wall and slid back just as Ken Schrader's car broadsided it. The crash was undramatic. Ironhead had survived much worse.

The track hounds knew better. They knew that when a car isn't coming apart, the energy isn't dissipating. The sheet metal in these cars is designed to shred and fly away so that a driver isn't crushed or sliced. Earnhardt's car was still more or less intact. "Talk to us, Dale!" The plea from the pit crackled in the earphones of a driver—a champion, a legend—who was, in all probability, already dead.

It was learned later that Earnhardt's left lap seat belt had torn apart, and he may have been thrown into the steering column. No one could ever recall a seat belt failing that way. In September, NASCAR announced new, tightened rules for the placement and configuration of seat belts. But in the immediate aftermath, NASCAR determined that the next week's race, in Rockingham, N.C., would be held as scheduled. Incredibly, or possibly not, Dale Jr. announced he would race his Earnhardt Inc. car. Incredibly, or possibly not, when the checkered flag came down at Rockingham, it waved over Dale Jr.'s car. ■

WE GOT GAME
Women athletes keep getting buffer—and tougher

Jennifer Capriati
Tennis' prodigal daughter, now 25, fought her way back to the top, whipping Martina Hingis to win the Australian Open, then nuking the young Belgian Kim Clijsters to take the French Open title as well

Naoko Takahashi
A year after winning the women's marathon at the Sydney Games, Takahashi, 29, became the first woman to run 26.2 miles in under 2 hr., 20 min., winning the Berlin Marathon in 2:19:46

Karrie Webb
The Australian star, 26, became the first woman golfer to notch a career Grand Slam, taking both the U.S. Open and LPGA titles. But frequent foe Annika Sorenstam teamed with Tiger Woods to beat Webb and David Duval in TV's *Battle of Bighorn*

Ellen MacArthur
The gutsy Briton, 24, became Europe's heroine by spending 100 days alone at sea in the Vendee Globe round-the-world yacht race; 200,000 fans hailed her arrival in France—in second place!

Tiffany Milbrett

The stars of the U.S. women's World Cup soccer team made good on their promise to take their game to the pro level, forming the eight-team Women's United Soccer Association. Playing for the New York Power, the 5-ft. 2-in. Milbrett, 28, led the league in scoring, but the Bay Area CyberRays topped the Atlanta Beat to become the WUSA's first champs

Michelle Kwan

The brilliant 20-year-old added new jewels to her crown, taking the U.S. figure-skating championship for the fifth time and out-dueling Russia's Irina Slutskaya in Vancouver to win the world championship for the fourth time. But Kwan stunned the skating world when she summarily dismissed her longtime coach, Frank Carroll, in October

Images

Mario Returns to the Rink

Picasso painted daily into his 80s. Monet underwent eye surgery at 83 so he could continue painting his gardens at Giverny. But athletes face a death-in-miniature—the end of their playing days—when their bodies wear out.

But why fill your days with handshakes and commercials when you still have a few good games left in you? That was the thinking behind the comeback of two of professional sport's greatest stars of the '90s, Mario Lemieux and Michael Jordan. Actually, it was Lemieux's comeback that inspired Jordan to return to the hardwood. The former Pittsburgh Penguin star—and current Penguin owner—put on his mitts at age 36 after 3½ years of retirement. Lemieux had promised he wouldn't come back unless his skills were still sharp; in his first game he proved they were, notching a goal and two assists. His return transformed his struggling franchise into a sold-out smash—and golf buddy Michael paid heed.

Say It Ain't So, Cal!

Baseball said goodbye to a full roster of heroes in 2001. Among the things we'll miss: the long doubles to left field stroked by one of the game's sweetest hitters, Tony Gwynn of the San Diego Padres. Also hanging up his spikes was the

LEMIEUX Still explosive on blades

IRONMAN Ripken was named All-Star MVP

giant redhead of the St. Louis Cardinals—and erstwhile single-season home-run champ—Mark McGwire. And finally bidding farewell to the game was the man who broke Lou Gehrig's legendary record for most games played in a row, Cal Ripken Jr., the sturdy infielder for the Baltimore Orioles. Cal went out in style: he was hailed in American League parks around the nation, and delighted fans when he smacked a homer in his last All-Star game in Seattle.

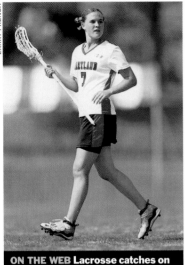

ON THE WEB **Lacrosse catches on**

Make Tracks—Lax Attacks!

Little girls who used to dress up like soccer star Mia Hamm have a new athlete role model: Jen Adams, star of the University of Maryland's women's lacrosse team, which won its seventh-straight NCAA championship on May 20. Adams spearheaded the fast-rising popularity of lacrosse, especially among girls and young women. Since 1995, more than 40 new varsity women's programs have been established at U.S. colleges. The sport is growing in high schools as well: more than two-thirds of the nation's several hundred thousand lacrosse players are under age 17.

Reputedly America's oldest athletic game, "lax" is played by two teams of 10, each athlete using a long stick with a webbed pouch to maneuver a ball into the opponents' goal. The sport got another boost in June, when the Fox Sports Net began televising the inaugural season of Major League Lacrosse, made up of six teams in the Northeast. It's men only—for now.

Bronx Bummer

Well, it seemed too good to be true—and it was. Danny Angelo, a 12-year-old immigrant from the Dominican Republic, retired 18 batters in a row in a first-round victory in the Little League World Series; won the other three games he pitched; and helped his Rolando Paulinho All-Stars from

DANNY **Ringer!**

the Bronx finish third out of 16 teams. Trouble was, he wasn't 12, as his father said; he was 14. His wins were forfeited. We can't even say, Wait till next year.

People

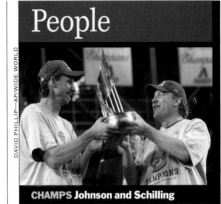

CHAMPS **Johnson and Schilling**

Winning Ugly

Capping a seven-game classic that was hailed as one of the greatest World Series ever, Arizona Diamondback hurlers Randy Johnson and Curt Schilling celebrated their triumph over baseball's most recent great dynasty: the New York Yankees, champs in '98, '99 and '00.

Catching the resolute mood of terror-scarred New York City, the veteran Yankee lineup (Paul O'Neill, Derek Jeter, Bernie Williams, Roger Clemens) relied on last-gasp heroics, salvaging two games in a row on two-out, ninth-inning homers. But the bats of the Bombers were finally subdued by Arizona's sizzling pitching duo, Johnson and Schilling, who accounted for all four Diamondback Series wins—and who justly shared the title of Series MVPs.

TANKED **If this story on the XFL, or Extreme Football League, seems heavy on sexual display and light on football—well, that was the idea. The league, developed by World Wrestling Federation guru Vince McMahon and NBC, was ... a bust**

Science

April 30

"I'm flying!" California millionaire Dennis Tito, 60, became the first tourist in outer space when he lifted off atop a Russian rocket from the Baikonur Cosmodrome in Kazakhstan on April 28 and successfully linked up with the International Space Station two days later. Here he cavorts with his fellow travelers, Russian cosmonauts Yuri Usachev, left, the station commander, and Talgat Musabayev. A modern-day Peter Pan, Tito fulfilled his longtime dream of venturing into space by sprinkling a little fairy dust— a reported $20 million worth—on the capital-poor Russian space program. The top brass at NASA strongly opposed the visit, but the Russians held their ground— so that Tito could leave it.

SUMMER OF
THE SHARK

A series of vicious attacks—some deadly—bring back
memories of *Jaws* and send swimmers and surfers ashore

SHARKS COME SILENTLY, WITHOUT WARNING, STRIKing in one of three ways: the hit-and-run, the bump and-bite and the sneak attack. The hit-and-run is the most common. The shark may see the sole of a swimmer's foot, think it's a fish and take a bite before realizing this isn't its usual prey. It swims away, leaving the bleeding victim in need of stitches. The bump-and-bite is far more serious. In 2000 Chuck Anderson was training for a triathlon off Gulf Shores, Ala., when he was bumped by a bull shark, testing whether he was preyworthy. The shark apparently decided that he was and then repeatedly attacked Anderson. He lost an arm.

Then there's the sneak attack. The shark is in the right place to find its prey, it is the right time to feed, and the target is the right size. At sunset on July 6, 2001, off Pensacola, Fla., Jessie Arbogast, 8, fit the needs of a bull shark. Dusk is one of the shark's feeding periods; the boy was in the shallow water where the bull prowls; and splashing about, Jessie may have seemed to be a large fish. The shark pounced. The ensuing attack revived our fascination—part fancy, part dread—with nature's sleekest predator.

Suddenly reports of shark attacks—or what people thought were shark attacks—began to come in from all around the U.S. On July 15 a surfer was apparently bitten on the leg a few miles from the site of Jessie's attack. The next day another surfer was attacked off San Diego. On July 18 a 12-ft. tiger shark chased spear fishers in Hawaii. On Labor Day two people were attacked off Avon, N.C.; Sergei Zaloukaev was killed.

Shark attacks have been on the rise in recent years. But for all the terror they stir, the numbers remain minuscule. Worldwide, sharks killed only 10 people in 2000. There were 79 unprovoked attacks, compared with 58 in 1999 and 54 the year before. Two-thirds were in U.S. waters. The higher numbers may reflect more surfers, boogie-boarders and open-water swimmers—more people splashing around, hence more attacks.

For sharks, which tend to end up in soup or medicine, it's the humans who are dangerous. Fishing nets tangle and drown some 100 million sharks each year. In contrast, in California there is only one shark attack for every 1 million surfing days, according to the Surfrider Foundation. You are 30 times as likely to be killed by lightning. Poorly wired Christmas trees claim more victims than sharks, according to Australian researchers. And dogs—man's best friends—bite many thousands more people than sharks do.

But these are terrestrial and mundane risks. Sharks lurk in the vast, mysterious ocean, an element that still stirs mythic fear. Science is shedding light on why sharks behave the way they do. Researchers are coming closer to understanding why they attack humans. The three large sharks that account for most attacks on people—the great whites, the tigers and the bull sharks—have been studied extensively. We now know that great white sharks keep their blood warmer than the surrounding water, that tiger sharks are not territorial, and that bull sharks have the highest levels of testosterone measured in any creature, land or sea. Each has a different diet, a different behavior pattern, a different mode of attack.

Scientists ultimately hope to de-mythologize sharks, to erase their images as rogue man eaters like the great white shark that figures in *Jaws*, the Peter Benchley novel turned Steven Spielberg movie classic. Benchley told TIME, "I couldn't write *Jaws* today." After 25 years of research, the demonization of sharks doesn't hold, he says. "It used to be believed that great white sharks did target humans; now we know that except in the rarest of instances, great white shark attacks are mistakes." Robert Lea, a marine biologist working for the state of California, goes further: "I used to call them shark attacks—now I call them incidents. It is not a case of sharks preying on humans. It is just humans sharing a spot in the ocean with sharks—at the wrong time."

Sharks are one of nature's ultimate designs, tested over 400 million years—confident, sleek and lethal. Studies show some sharks can measure changes in electric currents as tiny as five-billionths of a volt. They use this ability to hunt for prey hidden under the sand and to navigate according to the earth's magnetic field. When they do attack a human, the weight of evidence now suggests, they have mistaken a person for a seal or some other prey, and most often will spit out human flesh after the first bite. The problem is, of course, that the one bite comes from jaws that are up to 3 ft. across and lined with hundreds of knives.

THE GREAT WHITE Scott Yerby never saw the great white shark before it attacked him as he surfed off Clam Beach near Eureka, Calif. "This thing jumped me—it had enough force to lift me right out of the water. It was on my leg, I could see my femur, there was blood in the water—I knew then it was pretty serious," says Yerby, who was 29 at the time of the August 1997 attack. He hit the shark on the nose (the prescribed last-ditch defense, along with ripping at its gills), managed to get back on his board and, with his surfing buddy, paddled back to shore. By the time he got to the hospital he had lost almost half the blood in his body and was close to death. Later, he was asked if he hoped to hunt

---

ATTACKS IN 2001

Aug. 4, Bahamas
Wall Street banker Krishna Thompson is attacked by a shark while celebrating his 10th wedding anniversary with his wife on Grand Bahama Island. He survives, but one leg is amputated just above the knee.

Aug. 16-18, Florida
A surfing competition at New Smyrna Beach (near Daytona) turns into a running series of attacks. Four surfers and two swimmers suffer minor injuries from a series of shark bites, mostly to the hands and feet.

Sept. 1, Virginia
David Peltier, 10, of Richmond, Va., bleeds to death after a shark severs a major artery in his leg in an attack at Virginia Beach—the area's first attack in 30 years.

Sept. 3, North Carolina
Two Russians living in Washington, Sergei Zaloukaev and Natalia Slobodskaya, are attacked off Avon. Zaloukaev dies; Slobodskaya loses her left foot.

NOT A MOVIE It's no myth: great white sharks do leap out of the water—as high as 15 ft.—as they attack their prey

C & M FALLOWS—SEAPICS.COM

pushed him off his board. The shark's nose struck Spencer's head, then its jaws locked onto his arm. "I could almost see the whole shark. My elbow was down his throat." The shark ripped muscles, tendons and blood vessels, then chomped down on the surfboard before disappearing. Spencer made it to shore, and today his arm is recovering. His mistake? Surfing at sundown. The tiger shark generally hunts at night.

Scientists believe tigers, usually found in tropical waters, are not territorial. Because they are slower swimmers than great whites, humans often see the shark before it closes in to attack. But tigers, if not territorial, are persistent. "If you are bitten by a tiger, you have a good chance of being chewed up. They come back," says John Mc-Cosker, a scientist at the California Academy of Sciences.

BULL SHARK When Dawn Schauman was attacked by an 8-to-10-ft. bull shark in October 1993, she said, "it felt like a truck had slammed into me, then I felt a compacting squeeze and an acute burning in my left hand and my left leg." The shark spun her around, leaving her disoriented as she hemorrhaged blood into the water. The shark left, and willpower alone got Schauman—more than 6 months pregnant—back to shore. Her baby was later born prematurely but safely. For months Schauman woke at 3 a.m. replaying the attack in her head.

The bull shark usually grows no longer than 10 ft. and weighs up to 500 lbs., but what it lacks in size it makes up for in aggressiveness. Experts regard it as the most pugnacious of sharks. It has the highest level of testosterone in any animal, including lions and elephants. Its lower spiked teeth are designed to hold prey while the upper triangular serrated teeth gouge out flesh.

A unique feature of bull sharks is their ability to live in both salt- and fresh water; they have attacked people in Lake Nicaragua in Central America and have been seen above St. Louis, Mo., in the Mississippi River. Those born in the Mississippi delta usually spend about six months in the brackish water before migrating along the coast to Florida to winter in the Keys. The bull is the only shark that prowls regularly in water shallow enough for humans to walk in—and it may be territorial.

Human shark victims almost always seem to be inadvertent intruders rather than targeted prey. Scientists who work with sharks know how dangerous they can be, and many are critical of the guided shark-feeding tours that are proliferating in Florida and the Bahamas. Sharks there have begun to associate the sound of an outboard motor with food, and there have been attacks by sharks apparently impatient to be fed, according to George Burgess, head of the International Shark Attack File. Shark feeding is illegal in two Florida cities, and a campaign to ban it statewide is under way. "When you are training animals, you are changing their basic behavior and their respect for human beings," says Burgess.

That would be a strange development: the ocean's fearsome hunters lured unnaturally into the company of humans—then learning to bite the hands that feed them. Nature has its bounds. ∎

down the shark that attacked him. "I said I had no reason to—he was in his element," says Yerby.

The great white is perfectly adapted to that element. Sometimes growing to more than 20 ft. in length and up to 4,000 lbs., it keeps its body temperature 5°F to 10°F higher than that of the surrounding water by recycling heat from its swimming muscles. This allows great whites to hunt in cooler seas. They have enormous livers to store energy, and can go for months without eating.

Great whites are the most lethal to humans. Since 1876 there have been 254 confirmed unprovoked attacks on humans by great whites, 67 of which were fatal, according to statistics compiled by the International Shark Attack File at the Florida Museum of Natural History. Over the same period, tiger sharks have attacked 83 times with 29 fatalities, and bull sharks have attacked 69 times with 17 fatalities. Great white attacks on humans generally involve just one bite. Researchers are not sure, but most think the shark's sensory organs quickly differentiate between humans and the blubber-rich seals it prefers, so it effectively bites and spits out humans. Unlike tigers and bulls, great whites hunt mostly during the day, and their preferred method of attack is to shoot up vertically from 30 ft. down, knocking their prey right out of the water with the impact.

TIGER SHARK Jesse Spencer, now 18, from the Big Island of Hawaii, was surfing near Kona in October 1999 when a 10-ft. tiger shark came halfway out of the water and

The Ordeal of Jessie Arbogast

"He's got me!" A day at the beach turns into a nightmare for an 8-year-old boy

AT DUSK, TWO DAYS AFTER THE FOURTH OF JULY, JESSIE Arbogast was having a Kodak moment on the beach in Pensacola, Fla. The Gulf waves were mild, so his sister and some other girls had ventured out into them, but Jessie, 8, his brothers and some cousins stayed only 15 ft. from shore. Then, one brother felt something swish by his leg, and Jessie saw the sharp fins of a bull shark protruding 2 ft. above the water. The shark took an exploratory bite of his arm and a chunk of his thigh. "He's got me!" Jessie yelled. "Get him off! Get him off me!"

Onshore, his uncle Vance Flosenzier turned toward the screaming children and saw blood coloring the ocean. He and another man sprinted into the surf and found the 7.4-ft., 200-lb. shark about to roll away, its jaw on Jessie's arm. Vance, who trains for triathlons, grabbed the shark by its sandpapery tail and tried to pull, but it would not budge. He yanked again, and Jessie fell away, his arm ripping, as the shark clamped down. With Jessie's arm only partly swallowed, the shark tried to wiggle free from Vance's barehanded grasp. But Vance, at 6 ft. 1 in. and 200 lbs., held on and dragged it to shore, where his wife Diana and others had laid Jessie on the sand.

"Shark! My brother's been bitten by a shark!" a boy yelled as he ran down the beach. Tourists Trina Casagrande and Susanne Werton of St. Louis, Mo., thought it was a prank and kept walking. Then they saw the chaos and the crowd gathered around the unmoving body of a boy, the red muscle of his thigh exposed and looking like a "bite [had been taken] out of a drumstick." The women could not see much blood. Most of it had drained from the boy into the Gulf. Jessie's lips were whiter than his face and body. His eyes were open but rolled back.

The shark attack had severed Jessie's arm 4 in. below the shoulder. Vance Flosenzier tied towels into tourniquets and used T shirts to cover the bone sticking out from the stump, slowing the loss of what little blood was left in the boy's body. While Werton took over CPR compressions from Vance, he called the 911 dispatcher. Jessie had basically been drained of blood, the worst situation in a trauma. In such situations, fewer than 1% of victims survive. No medication can help the heart. When the helicopter landed, the medics could have declared Jessie dead. Instead, with Vance, they carried the boy to the chopper.

The shark was still thrashing on the beach. Jared Klein, a National Park Service ranger, wondered whether the arm was in the water or in the shark's mouth. He took his expandable baton and pried apart the bull shark's jaws. There it was. He asked the crowd to step back and shot the shark four times in the head. Then he opened its mouth with the baton, while Tony Thomas, a lifeguard and volunteer fire fighter, reached in with hemostats and extracted the limb. He covered it with a towel and packed it in ice to be rushed to a waiting ambulance.

At the hospital, Jessie was pumped full of blood but was slow to regain a pulse. "As soon as his limb came through the door, we got a heartbeat," said Nurse Sandi Miller. After 12 hours of surgery, Jessie was wheeled into a recovery room, his arm reattached. On Nov. 1, 2001, he was released from the hospital following his third stay since the surgery. While the loss of blood has damaged his brain, doctors report that he continues to look more alert and seems to follow people's movements with his eyes. ∎

TONY GILBERSON—PENSACOLA NEWS JOURNAL; GULF PINE CATHOLIC NEWSPAPER/ JESSIE DAVID ARBOGAST MEDICAL FUND; CARLSENKBEIL—HUNTSVILLE TRACK CLUB

IN HARM'S WAY
Jessie, left, in orange shirt, at his First Communion party; Uncle Vance, above; Thomas, in red trunks, reached into the shark to retrieve Jessie's missing arm

TIPPING THE BALANCE

Pisa's famous tower has been heading south for more than 800 years. Here's how today's engineers stopped the slide

IN 1989 ALMOST A MILLION VISITORS CLAMBERED UP THE 294 steps and peered out over its vertiginous tilt—about 13 ft. off plumb and still growing by an alarming four one-hundredths to eight one-hundredths of an inch each year. Pisa's historic Leaning Tower, the experts warned, had leaned too far and could topple at any time in the next decade or two. So the 800-year-old white marble structure, one of Italy's most famous monuments, was closed for nearly 12 years to allow for $25 million of ingenious engineering work to set it a little straighter. Not, of course, entirely straight—*Dio mio!*—that would have destroyed its tourist appeal. But straight enough to keep it stable for an estimated 300 more years.

In June, timed to the Feast of San Ranieri, Pisa's patron saint (and just in time for the summer season), the plaza beneath the tower was reopened to the public. The tower itself reopened in the fall—but only to 30 visitors at a time, accompanied by a guide. And no leaning out!

La Torre Pendente, the Leaning Tower, is the bell tower for the cathedral in Pisa's Campo dei Miracoli, or Field of Miracles

Pisa

BELFRY
1360-1370

Galileo is said to have performed his famous falling-object experiment from this level, though no proof exists.

4 to 7
c. 1230s–1278

In an attempt to straighten the tower, builders try using thicker stones on the downward side.

War with Genoa—and Pisa's defeat in 1284—suspends building for nearly a century.

The tower is a hollow cylinder with a 3-ft.-wide (1 m) spiral staircase inside the walls.

Sensitive electronics in the walls monitor the slightest movements.

About 1198, documents show, a bell ringer worked at the tower, which was about this high at the time.

1990 5.5°

1817 5.1°

1350 2.5°

Vertical 0°

Baptistry

Counterweights

Cathedral

Bell tower

WHY DOES IT LEAN?

The tower is built directly on an ancient riverbed of soft, sandy soil, and the foundation is shallow for a structure that weighs 32 million lbs. (14,500 metric tons).

Various efforts over the centuries to stabilize the 192-ft. (58.4-m) tower had the opposite effect—increasing the tilt until the tower was on the verge of collapse.

MAKING THE TOWER LEAN BACK

In recent decades, forces pulling the tower askew began to compound. Soil continued to give way underneath, while stress increased on the stones on the downward side at the base of the second level. A panel studied several ideas before selecting a low-tech but effective solution.

1 Giant weights stop the tower's tilt ...

Beginning in 1993, nearly 2 million lbs. (870 metric tons) of lead weights were placed on the north side of the tower. Not only did the tower stop tilting, but it moved—very slightly—back toward straight.

to large counterweights

2 ... belts and cables keep it from collapsing ...

Fearing that restoration work would topple the tower, a giant belt was looped around the building and connected to large weights a block away. Thinner steel bands were wrapped around the first level for added support.

3 ...and an array of drills slowly removes soil, allowing the structure to settle

Engineers then sank 41 parallel tubes diagonally under the foundation. A specially designed auger—a giant drill bit—was inserted into each tube. A machine turned the augers one at a time to remove small amounts of soil over several months.

The drilling created small cavities all along the high side of the foundation, allowing engineers to "steer" the settling of the tower.

⟵ 41 parallel tubes

Depth on north: 6.1 ft. (1.86 m)

1173-1178

Very little documentation on the building exists, but the date construction began—Aug. 9, 1173—is part of a carving to the right of the entrance.

The building actually leaned slightly in the other direction—to the north—until more levels were added during the 13th century.

THE LEAN YEARS

The tower began leaning almost from the beginning, in 1173. Over the course of the tower's 200-year construction, builders tried to compensate for the list, resulting in a slightly banana-shaped structure.

The tower now leans at 5°—slightly straighter than the angle it stood at 200 years ago. Engineers once calculated that the tower would fall when it reached 5.4°—yet it continued to stand at 5.5°.

Depth on south: 12.3 ft. (3.75 m)

Sources: Coordination Committee for the Safeguard of the Tower of Pisa; University of Pisa; CS Informatica, Pisa; *Eyewitness Guide to Italy*; Associated Press

IN THE END, THE TOWER SETTLED BACK 15.6 in. (39.6 cm) — LESS THAN THE LENGTH OF THE OPEN BOOK YOU ARE HOLDING

TIME Graphic by Lon Tweeten, Ed Gabel and Jackson Dykman

ME AND MY BIG MOUTH Paul Sereno
might make an attractive snack in the
6-ft. jaws of *Sarcosuchus imperator.*
Based on the new finds, Sereno posits
the long-extinct croc would have taken
up to 40 to 50 years to reach its full
size of 40 ft. in length

CROC OF AGES

Scientists unearth the remains of a stupendous crocodile in Niger, filling in the fossil record on nature's experiment with gigantism

POOR *TYRANNOSAURUS REX*. FIRST THE VELOCIRAPTORS snitched the climactic scenes in *Jurassic Park*. Now *T. rex's* position atop the totem pole of antediluvian antiheroes may be eclipsed by a creature that doesn't walk upright on two legs, but crawls on the ground like a crocodile. In fact, it is a crocodile—on steroids. In October,

ON LOCATION Sereno at the dig, above. He found the fossils on his fourth trip to the deserts of Niger. Below, Sereno with fossilized teeth: "This thing could have easily pulled down a good-sized dinosaur. A small sauropod, 20 or 30 feet in length, would have been no problem"

a team led by paleontologist Paul Sereno and funded by the National Geographic Society announced they had found the remains of a prehistoric crocodile that was 40 ft. long (about the size of a city bus), had more than 100 teeth (the better to chew up small dinosaurs) and weighed 100 tons (give or take a pound).

Sereno and his team found 6-ft. fossilized jawbones and other remains of the giant croc during a 2000 expedition to the windswept Ténéré Desert in central Niger, home to Tuareg nomads and the richest dinosaur beds in Africa. The first fragmentary remains of the animal, which lived about 110 million years ago, were discovered by French paleontologist Albert-Félix de Lapparent and named *Sarcosuchus imperator* ("flesh crocodile emperor") in 1966 by France de Broin and fellow paleontologist Philippe Taquet. But the fossil record of *Sarcosuchus* was very incomplete. The new finds—bones from several creatures totaling some 50% of a complete skeleton—will provide a much richer look at its world. "*Sarcosuchus* was part of nature's experiment with gigantism," Sereno said, noting that supersized species were commonplace in the middle Cretaceous period, when the huge croc thrived. Though similar to the alligators and crocodiles of today, *Sarcosuchus* belongs to a different, extinct line.

A bulbous protrusion at the front of the croc's snout covered a huge cavity, indicating that the animal may have had a highly developed sense of smell and an unusual call. The eyes of *Sarcosuchus* were set at an upward angle, suggesting it probably submerged itself in water as it awaited its prey, which scientists think included smaller dinosaurs—assuming your idea of small is a 30-ft. sauropod. ∎

6 ft.

A SPACE LEGEND ...

The Mir space station spent 15 years in orbit, circling the planet more than 87,600 times at a cruising speed of 17,885 m.p.h. The 143-ton complex was assembled in space and was composed of six permanent modules. It also had docking ports to accommodate cargo ships and crew vehicles

KVANT-2
December 1989

Used for biological research and Earth observation

PRIRODA
April 1996

Remote sensing module monitored Earth's ozone

CORE
February 1986

A 49-ft. module with pastel living quarters, a 400-book library and an exercise bike

PROGRESS M-15
January 2001

Earlier models transported waste and supplies. This one was to guide Mir to its demise

KVANT-1
April 1987

A pressurized lab in the 19-ft. module was used for astrophysics research

KRISTALL
August 1990

Contains researc equipment and a docking port for U.S. space shut

SPEKTR
June 1995

Remote sensing modu equipment supplied b Russia and the U.S.

... FINALLY COMES CRASHING DOWN

Mir re-entered the atmosphere in a planned death-plunge on March 23, the biggest man-made object ever to do so. Up to 50 tons of debris rained down on the Pacific at near sonic speeds

① MIR puts on the brakes ...

When Mir was 137 miles above Earth, Progress M-15 fired its thrusters several times to orient and decelerate the station. A final burn, starting over Russia, sent the station down in just 30 to 45 min.

② ... and hits the atmosphere ...

Mir began to spin out of control when the atmosphere's drag force overwhelmed its thrusters. The 108-ft.-long, 90-ft.-wide station began tumbling, causing solar panels and masts to start breaking up

No, It Didn't Hit Anything

Computer glitches, power problems and Mir's irregular shape could have affected its descent path. Russia took out a $200 million insurance policy; Japan urged its southernmost residents to stay inside; and New Zealand issued warnings to aircraft and ships. Russia's Aerospace Agency director likened a $6,500-per-head observation flight to a suicide mission

MIR'S FINAL LAP

ASIA
Japan
AFRICA
Indian Ocean
Australia
Pacific Ocean
New Zealand
SOUTH AMERICA

DROP ZONE
3,726 miles long and 124 miles wide

HERE'S TO THE MIR!

After 15 years in orbit, Russia's "little station that could" finally comes down to Earth in a fiery shower of debris—but its stories will live on

I F YOU EVER FLEW ABOARD THE MIR SPACE STATION, YOU would know how important it was to urinate on the barbed wire surrounding the launch pad before you went up. If you were especially thorough, you might want to douse the wheels of the bus that carried you to the pad too.

Nobody called this prelaunch ritual by anything like its proper name. What people called it was "checking the laces"—a reference to the practice early cosmonauts had of tightening their spacesuits' laces before flight. When laces disappeared from modern suits, the checking did too, but superstitious crews needed something to take its place, and ceremonial voiding worked fine.

Such incidental rituals will now linger only in memory, for the Mir space station is no more: on March 23, the 143-ton ship re-entered the atmosphere in a flaming arc over the South Pacific, delighting observers on Fiji with a stunning fireworks show, then hitting the ocean far east of Australia. Planned to last only three years in space, Mir proved to be the little station that could. It kept going for 15 years, and in its final day, its biographers began toting up the station's achievements: the 16,500 experiments conducted in its labs, the 600 industrial technologies it helped create and the 104 crew members who called the ship home (one for a record 438 consecutive days).

But Mir's history is more than a sum of scientific accomplishments. It is also a quietly told collection of decidedly unheroic tales—tales of ordinary people living and working in the most extraordinary of places. As Mir began its valedictory laps, the stories begin to surface.

Holidays could be a dreary time aboard Mir, especially for those from the officially atheist U.S.S.R., which had eliminated many religious observances. On New Year's Eve, crews were permitted to set up a small, nonsectarian tree, which did little to improve the *Das Boot* ambience. To lift their mood further, they would break out the ship's vacuum cleaner and take turns riding it around the tree—the poor man's jet pack.

Karl Marx may have nixed Christmas, but he said nothing about April Fools' Day, and at least one Mir crew member took advantage of the oversight. On April 1, 1988, cosmonaut Musa Manarov alerted the ground that—Eureka!—he had found a mysterious string of numbers written inexplicably, on the outside of the station. His call was received by Vladimir Bezyaev, a mission-control radio commentator who had been chatting with the cosmonauts and was in on the joke. Bezyaev played it straight, relaying the news to the rest of the control room. "Mission control completely believed [Manarov]," he says. "They even asked him to film the numbers."

As time went by and the station aged, crews no longer had the luxury of such pranks. The world remembers Mir for its hair-raising string of crises in the late 1990s—culminating in a collision with an unmanned cargo ship in 1997—but there were other, less publicized near misses. Cosmonaut Alexander Serebrov almost became a satellite himself when his safety tether came loose during a spacewalk. Luckily, he managed to grab hold of the station. In 1994, Mir lost its orientation, causing most of its onboard systems to sputter out, including the fans that keep oxygen circulating. To stay alive, the cosmonauts had to wave their hands in front of their faces to gather in breathable air and flap away carbon dioxide until Mir could power up again. "No one knew how torturous it was for the cosmonauts," says Bezyaev. "They spoke absolutely coolly."

Eventually, no amount of rocket-jock calm could hide the fact that Mir had become a deathtrap. Once parts of the glinting International Space Station went aloft, it was clear there was no need to keep the old outpost in orbit. The "little station that could" is history, but its legend grows.

3 ... the fireworks start ...
A single streak appeared over the horizon, becoming white-hot and beginning to fragment. The pressurized modules, some as big as railroad cars, ruptured and exploded at an altitude of about 31 miles

4 ... and 1,500 pieces land in the Pacific
The heaviest pieces of Mir, some weighing more than 1,000 lbs., survived the heat of re-entry and crashed to a watery grave 3,600 miles off the eastern coast of Australia

Sources: Mission Control Center, Russian Aviation and Space Agency; U.N. International Space Information Service; NASA; MirReentry.com; Ian Bryce

TIME Graphic by Lon Tweeten and Amanda Bower

People

The Iceman Goeth

Murder will out—even after 5,300 years. In July the coldest of cold cases was cracked when scientists announced that they had determined what killed the Iceman, the Stone Age hunter whose remains were unearthed in the Alps in 1991. The verdict? Murder.

For years investigators assumed that the Iceman had died

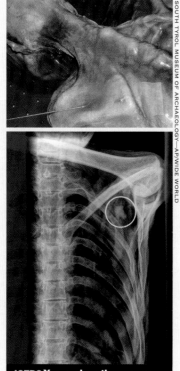

ICED? X rays show the weapon

in a fall or had fallen asleep and succumbed to the cold. But the end was nastier than that. When the body was extensively X-rayed, researchers noticed a suspicious shadow under his left shoulder. Only recently was a CT scan used as well, and it confirmed that the shadow was an arrowhead. Its position made scientists wince. The Iceman, they concluded, was shot from below. The arrow entered his body and paralyzed his arm. Though major organs were spared, major vessels were not; the Iceman bled to death. The identity of the killer remains a mystery; no charges were filed.

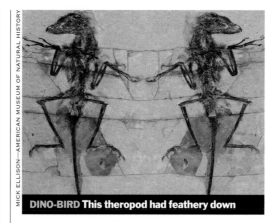

DINO-BIRD This theropod had feathery down

The Thing with Feathers

The once radical notion that birds descended from dinosaurs—or may even be dinosaurs, the only living branch of the family that ruled the earth eons ago—has got stronger in recent years. Remarkable similarities in bone structure between dinos and birds were the first clue. Then came evidence, thanks to a series of astonishing discoveries in China's Liaoning province over the past five years, that some dinosaurs may have borne feathers. But a few scientists still argued that the link was weak.

Not anymore. A spectacularly preserved fossil of a juvenile theropod—a duck-size relative of *Tyrannosaurus rex*—dating from 124 million to 147 million years ago and found in Liaoning, has three different types of feathers. Said co-finder Mark Norell of the American Museum of Natural History: "When this thing was alive, it looked like a Persian cat with feathers."

Move Over, Jupiter

Starting with the 1995 discovery of the first extrasolar planet, each new find of such planets has seemed stranger than the last. The latest mystery: in January, Geoffrey Marcy of the University of California, Berkeley, announced his team had found a solar system 123 light-years away, in the constellation Serpens, that harbors one "ordinary" planet and another object so huge—17 times as massive as Jupiter—that Marcy and his team can't classify it.

Conventional theory suggests that the monster object must have formed like a star, from a collapsing cloud of interstellar gas. Its smaller companion, "only" eight times Jupiter's mass, is certainly a planet, formed by the buildup of gas and dust left over from a star's formation. Yet the fact that these two orbs are so close together suggests to some theorists that they must have formed together—so maybe the bigger one is a planet after all. Or maybe it's time to redefine just what we mean by a planet.

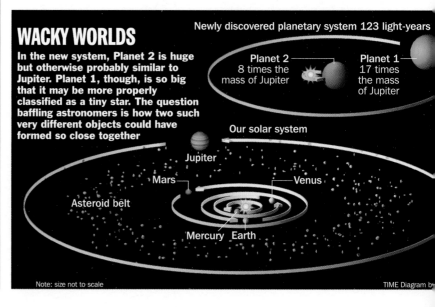

WACKY WORLDS

Newly discovered planetary system 123 light-years

In the new system, Planet 2 is huge but otherwise probably similar to Jupiter. Planet 1, though, is so big that it may be more properly classified as a tiny star. The question baffling astronomers is how two such very different objects could have formed so close together

Planet 2
8 times the
mass of Jupiter

Planet 1
17 times
the mass
of Jupiter

Our solar system

Jupiter

Mars

Venus

Asteroid belt

Mercury Earth

Note: size not to scale

TIME Diagram by

Images

COSMIC COLLISION
In sites ranging from Europe to Asia, scientists extracted buckyballs—soccer-ball-shaped carbon molecules—from 250 million-year-old rock. The buckyballs had trapped traces of extraterrestrial gases. Their conclusion: a comet smacked into our planet at that time, causing the Great Dying that wiped out 90% of Earth's ocean species and about 70% of those that lived on land—much like the impact they believe killed off the dinosaurs 65 million years ago.

Here Come Old Flat-Face

Tracing man's prehistory, paleontologists have generally agreed that there was just one hominid line. It begins with a small, upright-walking species known as *Australopithecus afarensis*, most famously represented by "Lucy," a remarkably complete skeleton found in Ethiopia in 1974. But in March, Meave Leakey—wife and daughter-in-law, respectively, of Richard and Louis Leakey and renowned in her own right—announced a find that roiled the picture. In 1999 her team dug up the fossil skull of a new species, which they call *Kenyanthropus platyops*, or "flat-faced man of Kenya," and dates to 3.5 million to 3.2 million years old—right in Lucy's time. The find reignited one of paleontology's greatest debates: Did we evolve in direct steps from a common apelike

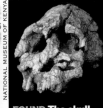

FOUND **The skull**

ancestor between 6 million and 4 million years ago? Or did the human family tree sprout several branches, some of which died off?

New Hope for the Hudson

Finally addressing a problem that had festered for years, in August the Environmental Protection Agency ordered General Electric to begin a much debated dredging of the Hudson River to remove polychlorinated biphenyls (PCBS), probable carcinogens whose removal may end up costing GE stockholders $460 million. GE, which dumped the toxins in the river for decades, had fought dredging for 20 years, arguing that since dumping stopped in 1977, PCB levels in fish have fallen 90%. No sale, GE.

COMING CLEAN **A GE plant on the Hudson, where PCBs were dumped for years**

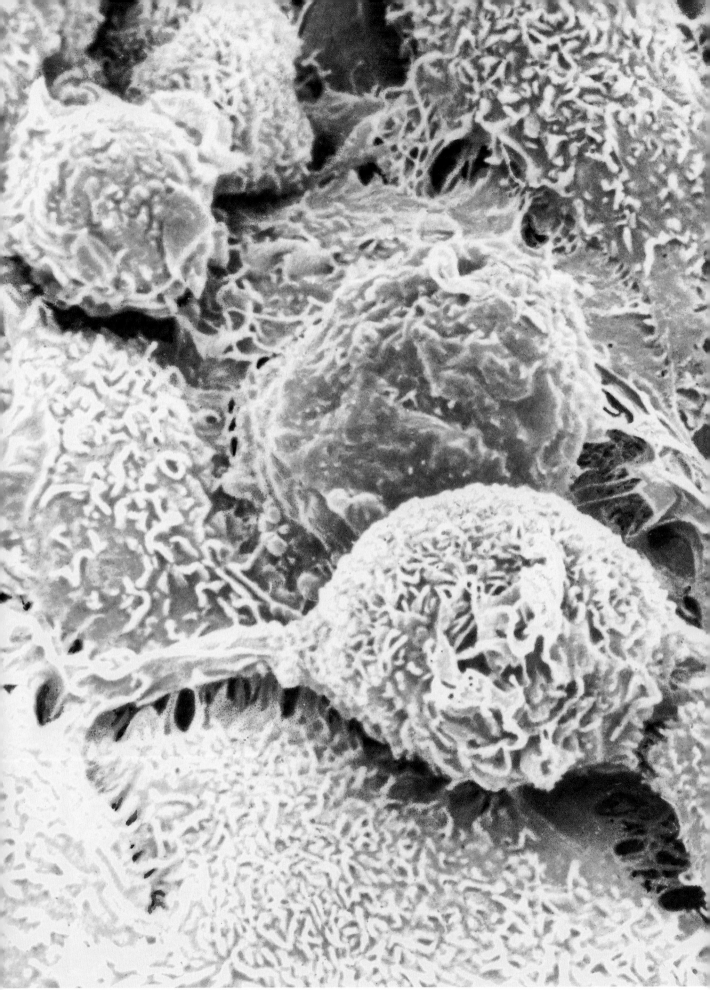

Photograph by Dr. Yorgos Nikas—SPL—Photo Researchers

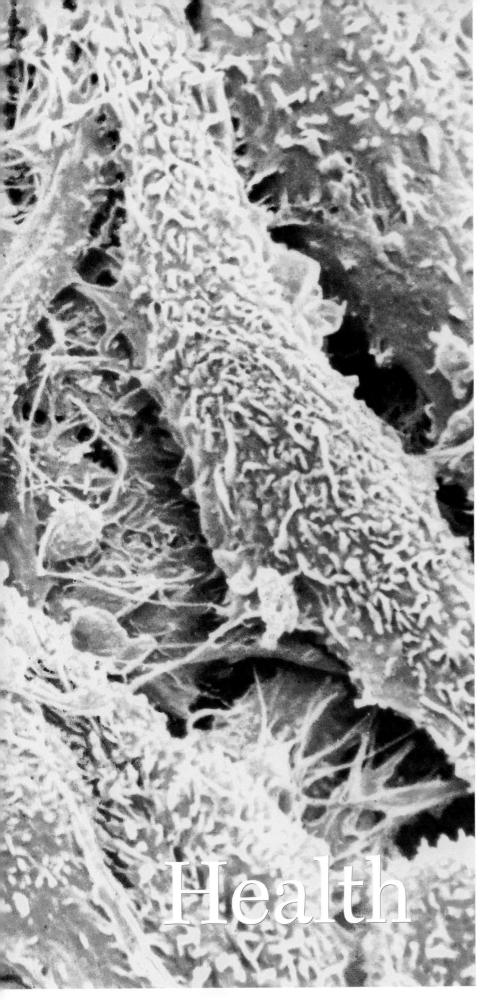

Health

August 9

Taking a cue from William Blake, who urged us to "see a world in a grain of sand," medical researchers believe that a world of benefits may flow from the sort of miniscule landscape seen at left, a cluster of a few dozen cells smaller than a pinhead: mammalian stem cells. Since these undifferentiated cells can grow into any of the 200 or so cell types that make up a human being, scientists believe they can be used as replacement cells for malfunctioning pancreases, injured spinal cords and plaque-clogged brains. But the research has strong foes, including the Pope, who charge that the use of such cells, which are taken from "surplus" embryos created at fertility clinics, is murder. On August 9, President Bush approved further stem-cell research, but restricted such studies to a limited number of existing "lines" of them.

STEM-CELL QUANDARY

Undifferentiated cells offer new ways to heal—but raise ethical questions

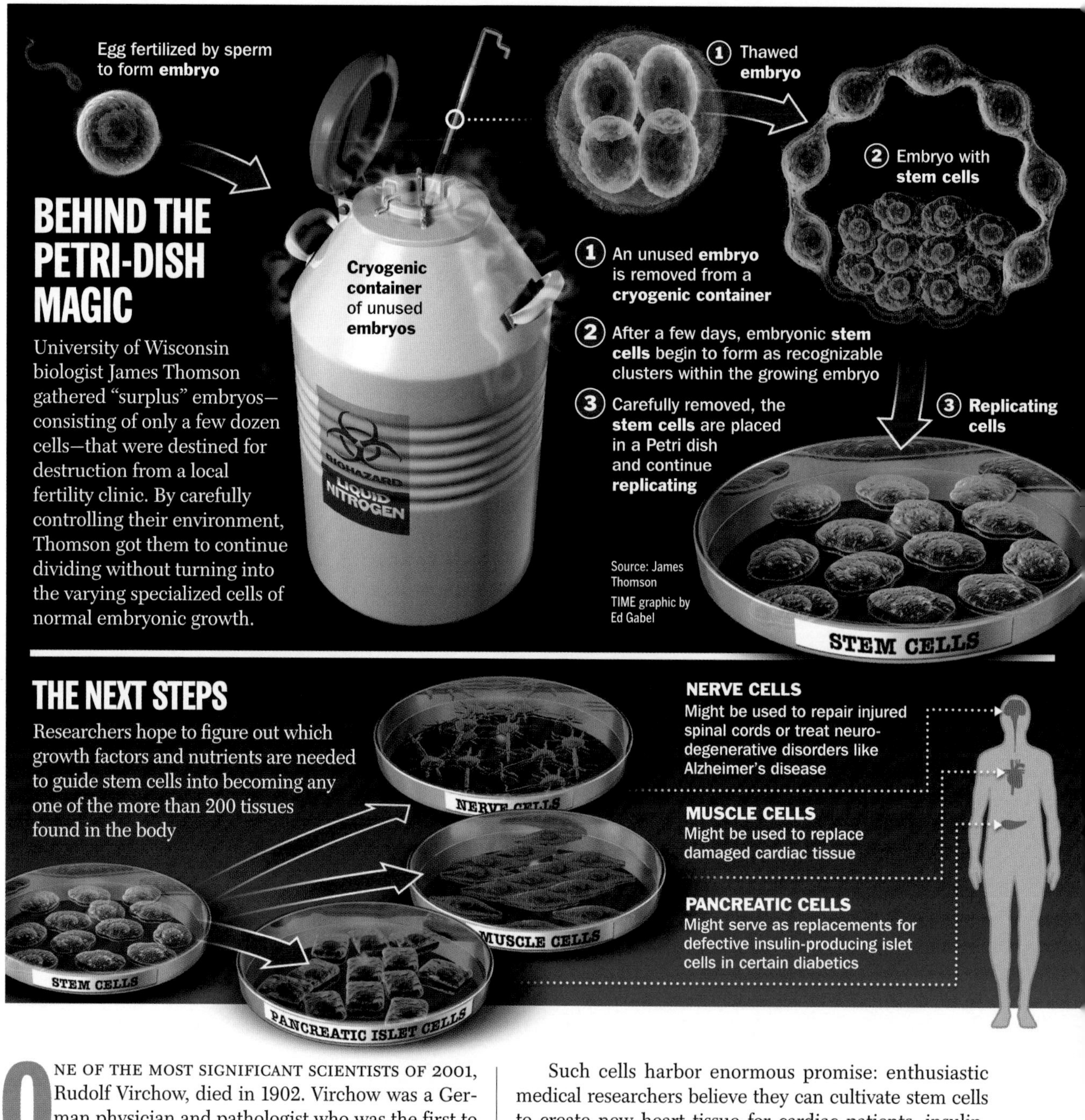

Egg fertilized by sperm to form **embryo**

① Thawed embryo

② Embryo with stem cells

BEHIND THE PETRI-DISH MAGIC

University of Wisconsin biologist James Thomson gathered "surplus" embryos—consisting of only a few dozen cells—that were destined for destruction from a local fertility clinic. By carefully controlling their environment, Thomson got them to continue dividing without turning into the varying specialized cells of normal embryonic growth.

Cryogenic container of unused **embryos**

BIOHAZARD
LIQUID NITROGEN

① An unused **embryo** is removed from a **cryogenic container**

② After a few days, embryonic **stem cells** begin to form as recognizable clusters within the growing embryo

③ Carefully removed, the **stem cells** are placed in a Petri dish and continue **replicating**

③ Replicating cells

Source: James Thomson
TIME graphic by Ed Gabel

STEM CELLS

THE NEXT STEPS

Researchers hope to figure out which growth factors and nutrients are needed to guide stem cells into becoming any one of the more than 200 tissues found in the body

NERVE CELLS
Might be used to repair injured spinal cords or treat neuro-degenerative disorders like Alzheimer's disease

MUSCLE CELLS
Might be used to replace damaged cardiac tissue

PANCREATIC CELLS
Might serve as replacements for defective insulin-producing islet cells in certain diabetics

NERVE CELLS

MUSCLE CELLS

STEM CELLS

PANCREATIC ISLET CELLS

O NE OF THE MOST SIGNIFICANT SCIENTISTS OF 2001, Rudolf Virchow, died in 1902. Virchow was a German physician and pathologist who was the first to realize that in living organisms, each different kind of cell (muscle, bone, brain … in a human being, there are more than 200) somehow springs from the small group of identical cells that are present at the beginning of life. Today we call that undifferentiated raw material stem cells.

Such cells harbor enormous promise: enthusiastic medical researchers believe they can cultivate stem cells to create new heart tissue for cardiac patients, insulin-producing cells for diabetics, healthy neural cells for victims of Parkinson's or Alzheimer's. But because such stem cells are taken from human embryos, opponents of the research fear a day when unborn human embryos might be misused, cultivated and harvested like a cash crop.

The dilemma began to take shape in 1998, when University of Wisconsin researcher James Thomson figured out not only how to harvest stem cells from human embryos but also how to keep them alive and reproducing indefinitely. Thomson's discovery signalled that meaningful research could at last begin on the cells that Virchow had predicted more than a century earlier. But it also meant that vexing ethical questions—does such research amount to strip-mining unborn children for spare parts?—were no longer theoretical. Parsing this paradox demanded the wisdom of Solomon—and the political skills of Lincoln. The decision fell in the lap of new President George Bush: he would have to decide whether to commit federal funds to such research and if so, under what conditions.

SMALL WONDER THAT BUSH BUTTONHOLED A WIDE spectrum of people in the spring of 2001, asking what they thought about the issue and why. The answers sometimes surprised him: G.O.P. icons and rock-ribbed abortion foes like Senator Connie Mack (a cancer survivor), Senator Strom Thurmond (whose daughter suffers from diabetes) and former First Lady Nancy Reagan (whose husband suffers from debilitating Alzheimer's disease) supported stem-cell research. Other answers were less surprising: Pope John Paul II (who suffers from Parkinson's) condemned stem-cell research as infanticide during a meeting with Bush in late July.

So nearly everyone (especially detractors who seldom uttered Bush's name in the same breath with those of Solomon or Lincoln) was surprised when the new President managed to find a middle ground. Bush seems to have been determined from the beginning to split the difference between seemingly irreconcilable positions. He was enticed by the possible scientific advances but repelled by the free market in human tissue that might emerge in the absence of a regulatory role for the Federal Government. The idea of using federal law to ban stem-cell research entirely wasn't an option: the votes for such a measure were not available in either house of Congress. So it was a choice between figuring out a role for government or simply walking away from the issue entirely.

The President did not want to force the vanguard of stem-cell researchers to flee the U.S. for a less restrictive environment in Europe. But he was also resolved to kill an alternative plan floated by Senator Bill Frist, a Tennessee Republican who is an important Bush adviser on medical and health-care issues. As the only Senator who is also a physician, Frist wields considerable authority on such subjects. His plan would have allowed research on stem cells soon to be harvested from as many as 1 million currently living embryos that are slated for destruction in the near future.

But after Bush ordered an inventory that turned up more than 60 lines of stem cells currently in stock at various facilities around the world (significantly, taken from human embryos that were already dead), he made his decision: to support a limited program of federally funded research on existing stem cells but ban federal money for research on new tissue or material from embryos created specifically as a source of stem cells.

Bush went public with his choice, and the process that led to it, on Aug. 9, in his first major televised address, speaking to the nation from his home in Crawford, Texas . "I have made this decision with great care," he said, "and I pray it is the right one." Such disparate figures as James Thomson and the Rev. Jerry Falwell claimed they were pleased by his plan. But scientists around the world soon cautioned that many of the 64 stem-cell colonies Bush had approved for use were not yet—and might never be—useful for such research. To skeptics, the evidence on which the President made the stem-cell decision was beginning to look more like the haul from a political scavenger hunt. Despite Bush's Solomonic intentions, the debate over stem cells may rage for years to come. ■

MANNY CENETA—AFP—CORBIS

STEVE LISS FOR TIME

HOT TOPIC John Borden, a foe of stem-cell research, testifies before a congressional committee as he holds his twins, who were conceived in a Petri dish; above, George Bush prepares to announce his decision from his ranch in Crawford, Texas

The ABC's of
Yoga

It limbers, relaxes and soothes—and yoga also seems to be good
for what ails you. Research is proving this ancient physical regimen
helps fight disease. So why isn't it just what the doctor ordered?

CREEN STARS DO IT. LORDS OF SPORTS DO IT. JUDGES in the highest courts do it. Let's do it: that yoga thing. A path to enlightenment that winds back 5,000 years in its native India, yoga has suddenly become hot, the exercise-cum-meditation for the new millennium, one that doesn't so much pump you up as bliss you out. Yoga now straddles the continent— from Hollywood, where $20 million-a-picture actors queue for a session with their guru du jour, to Washington, where, in the gymnasium of the Supreme Court, Justice Sandra Day O'Connor and 15 others take their weekly class.

Everywhere else, Americans rush from their high-pressure jobs and tune in to the authoritatively mellow voice of an instructor, gently urging them to solder a union (the literal translation of the Sanskrit word yoga) between mind and body. These Type A strivers want to become Type B seekers, to lose their blues in an *asana* (pose), to graduate from distress to de-stress. Fifteen million Americans include some form of yoga in their fitness regimen— twice as many as did five years ago; 75% of all U.S. health clubs offer yoga classes. As supermodel Christy Turlington, a serious student, says, "Some of my friends simply want to have a yoga butt." But others come to the discipline in hopes of restoring their troubled bodies. Yoga makes me feel better, they say. Maybe it can cure what ails me.

Sounds good. *Namaste,* as your instructor says at the end of a session: the divine in me bows to the the divine in you. But let's up the ante a bit. Is yoga more than the power of positive breathing? Can it, say, cure cancer? Fend off heart attacks? Rejuvenate postmenopausal women? Just as important for yoga's application by mainstream doctors, can its presumed benefits be measured by conventional medical standards? Is yoga, in other words, a science?

By even asking the question, we provoke a clash of two powerful cultures, two very different ways of looking at the world. The Indian tradition develops metaphors and ways of describing the body (life forces, energy centers) as it is experienced, from the inside out. The Western tradition looks at the body from the outside in, peeling back one layer at a time, believing only what can be seen, measured and proved in randomized, double-blind tests. The East treats the person; the West treats the disease.

The few controlled studies that have been done offer cause to believe in yoga's health benefits. A 1990 study of patients who had coronary heart disease indicated that a regimen of aerobic exercise and stress reduction, includ-

TWO BOATS Sharon Gannon and model Christy Turlington demonstrate contact yoga, amplifying their combined energy

ing yoga, combined with a low-fat vegetarian diet, stabilized and in some cases reversed arterial blockage. The author of that study, Dr. Dean Ornish, is in the midst of a new study involving men with prostate cancer. Can diet, yoga and meditation affect the progress of this disease? So far, Ornish will say only that the data are encouraging.

To the skeptic, all evidence is anecdotal. But some anecdotes are more than encouraging; they are inspiring. Consider Sue Cohen, 54, an accountant, breast-cancer survivor and five-year yoga student at the Unity Woods studio in Bethesda, Md. "After my cancer surgery," Cohen says, "I thought I might never lift my arm again. Then here I am one day, standing on my head, leaning most of my 125-lb. body weight on that arm. Chemotherapy, surgery and some medications can rob you of mental acuity, but yoga helps compensate for the loss. It impels you to do things you never thought you were capable of doing."

Is this series of exercises as old as the Sphinx the medical miracle of tomorrow—or just wishful thinking? Since it was first glimpsed by Americans as an enthusiasm of Allen Ginsberg, Jack Kerouac and other icons of the Beat Generation in the 1950s, yoga has endured an ever-changing array of evolutions in popular consciousness. First it signaled spiritual cleansing and rebirth, a nontoxic way to get high. Then it was seen as a kind of preventive medicine that helped manage and reduce stress. "The third wave was the fitness wave," says Richard Faulds, president of the Kripalu Center for Yoga and Health, in Lenox, Mass. "And that's about strength and flexibility and endurance."

SIDE CROW Sharon Gannon, co-founder of New York City's Jivamukti Yoga Center, defies gravity in a strength *asana*

At each stage, the most persuasive advocates were movie idols and rock stars—salesmen, by example, of countless beguiling or corrosive fashions. Today yoga is practiced by so many stars with whom audiences are on a first-name basis—Madonna, Julia, Meg, Ricky, Michelle, Gwyneth, Sting—that it would be shorter work to list the actors who don't assume the *asana.*

So much for the stars; what about the science? Yoga can massage the lymph system, says Dr. Mehmet Oz, a cardiac surgeon at New York Presbyterian Hospital in Manhattan. Lymph is the body's dirty dishwater, a network of vessels and storage sacs that crisscross the entire body, in parallel with the blood supply, and carry a fluid composed of infection-fighting white blood cells and the waste products of cellular activity. Exercise in general activates the flow of lymph through the body, speeding up the filtering process; but yoga in particular promotes the draining of the lymph. Certain yoga poses stretch muscles that from animal studies are known to stimulate the lymph system.

Researchers have documented the increased lymph flow when a dog's paws are stretched in a position similar to the yoga "downward-facing dog."

Yoga relaxes you and, by relaxing, heals. At least that's the theory. "The autonomic nervous system," explains Kripalu's Faulds, "is divided into the sympathetic system, which is often identified with the fight-or-flight response, and the parasympathetic, which is identified with what's been called the Relaxation Response. When you do yoga—the deep breathing, the stretching, the movements that release muscle tension, the relaxed focus on being present in your body—you initiate a process that turns the fight-or-flight system off and the Relaxation Response on. That has a dramatic effect on the body. The heartbeat slows, respiration decreases, blood pressure decreases. The body seizes this chance to turn on the healing mechanisms."

How does yoga finesse the stress? "We know that a high percentage of the maladies that people suffer from have at least some component of stress in them, if they're not overtly caused by stress," says Dr. Timothy McCall, an internist and the author of *Examining Your Doctor: A Patient's Guide to Avoiding Harmful Medical Care.* "Stress causes a rise of blood pressure, the release of catecholamines [neurotransmitters and hormones that regulate many of the body's metabolic processes]. We know that when catecholamine levels are high, there tends to be more platelet aggregation, which makes a heart attack more likely."

So instead of a drug, say devotees, prescribe yoga. "All the drugs we give people have side effects," McCall says. "Well, yoga has side effects too: better strength, better balance, peace of mind, stronger bones, cardiovascular conditioning, lots of stuff. Here is a natural health system that, once you learn the basics, you can do at home for free with very little equipment and that could help you avoid expensive, invasive surgical and pharmacological interventions."

McCall, it should be said, is a true believer who teaches at the B.K.S. Iyengar Yoga Center in Boston. But more mainstream physicians seem ready to agree. At New York Presbyterian, all patients undergoing cardiac procedures are offered massages and yoga during recovery. At Cedars-Sinai Medical Center in Los Angeles, cardiac doctors suggest that their patients enroll in the hospital's Preventive and Rehabilitative Cardiac Center, which offers yoga, among other therapies. According to Dr. Noel Bairey Merz, the center's director, patients opting for yoga show "tremendous benefits." These include lower cholesterol levels and blood pressure, increased cardiovascular circulation and, as Ornish's 1990 study showed, reversal of ar-

CAREFUL! Don't try this at home: Gannon and Turlington have mastered yoga's intensely demanding exercises

terial blockage in some cases. Other studies and programs have shown yoga is a promising treatment for alleviating insomnia and mood swings in postmenopausal women and for relieving pain caused by carpal tunnel syndrome.

In 1998 Ornish published a new study, in the *American Journal of Cardiology,* stating that 80% of the 194 patients he had monitored in an experimental group were able to avoid bypass or angioplasty by adhering to lifestyle changes, including yoga. He noted that such changes would save money, for the average cost per patient in the experimental group was about $18,000, whereas the cost per patient in the control group was more than $47,000. The researcher also said he was convinced that "adherence to the yoga and meditation program was as strongly correlated with the changes in the amount of blockage as was the adherence to diet."

Ornish hoped for more than the respect of his peers; he wanted action. "I used to think good science was enough to change medical practice," he says, "but I was naive. Most doctors still aren't prescribing yoga and meditation. We've shown that heart disease can be reversed. Yet doctors are still performing surgery; insurance companies are paying for medication—and they're *not* paying for diet and lifestyle-change education."

Why haven't more studies tested the efficacy of yoga? For lots of reasons. Those sympathetic to yoga think the benefits are proved by millenniums of empirical evidence in India; those who are suspicious think the benefits can't be proved. Further, yoga's effects on the body and mind are so complex and pervasive that it would be nearly impossible to certify any specific changes in the body caused by the practice. The double-blind test, beloved of traditional researchers, is impossible when one group in a study is practicing healthy yoga; what is the control group to practice—bad yoga? Finally, the traditional funders of research studies, the pharmaceutical giants, see no financial payoff in validating yoga; no patentable therapies, no pills, no profits.

At the heart of the Western medical establishment's skepticism of yoga is a profound hubris: the belief that what we have been able to prove so far is all that is true. At the beginning of the 20th century, doctors and researchers surely looked back at the beginning of the 19th and smiled at how primitive "medical science" had been. A century from now, we may look back at today's body of lore with the same condescension. In the meantime, we can assume a favorite *asana*, feel the benefits—and wait for the scientists to catch up. ∎

HOW IT WORKS

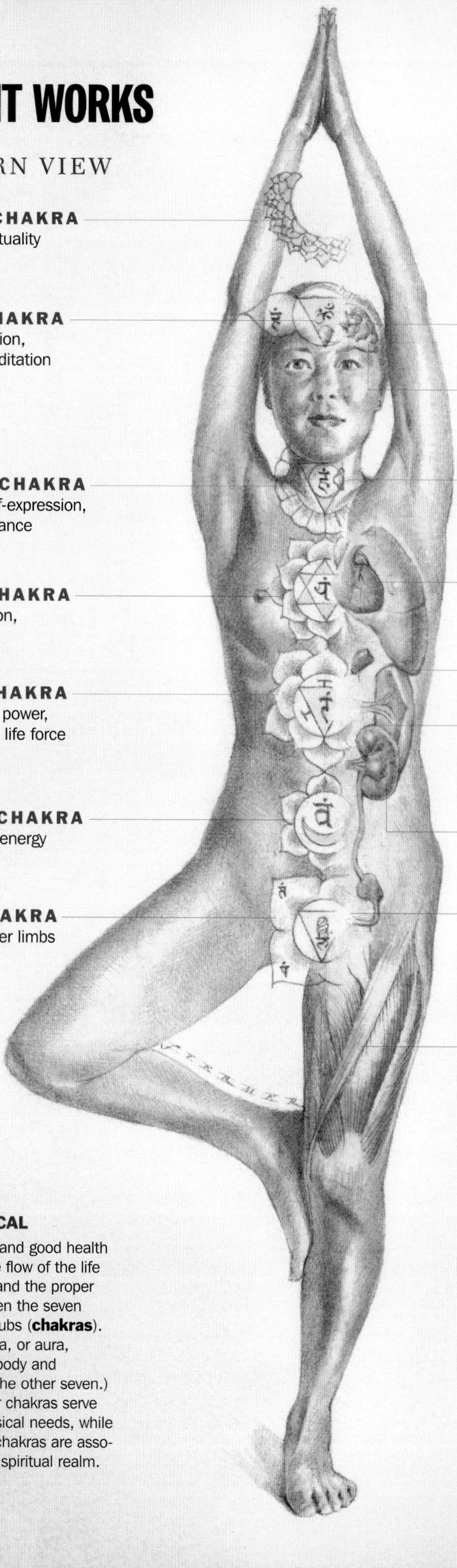

EASTERN VIEW

CROWN CHAKRA
Intuition, spirituality

BROW CHAKRA
Senses, intuition,
telepathy, meditation

THROAT CHAKRA
The ether, self-expression,
energy, endurance

HEART CHAKRA
Air, compassion,
love of others

NAVEL CHAKRA
Fire, personal power,
storage of the life force

SACRAL CHAKRA
Water, sexual energy

ROOT CHAKRA
Earth, the lower limbs

WESTERN VIEW

BRAIN
Triggers relaxation response

PITUITARY GLAND
May signal glands to secrete
fewer stress hormones

THYROID GLAND
May signal glands to secrete
fewer metabolic hormones

HEART
Strengthens circulatory
system, lowers blood pressure

LUNGS
Improves deep breathing

ADRENAL GLANDS
May deactivate stress response
by suppressing adrenalin

KIDNEYS
Enhances drainage of waste
from lymphatic system

**REPRODUCTIVE
ORGANS**
May influence secretion
of sex hormones

MUSCULATURE
May improve muscle tone
and prevent injury

THE MYSTICAL
Enlightenment and good health
require the free flow of the life
force (**prana**) and the proper
balance between the seven
major energy hubs (**chakras**).
(An eight chakra, or aura,
surrounds the body and
encompasses the other seven.)
The three lower chakras serve
the body's physical needs, while
the five upper chakras are associated with the spiritual realm.

THE SCIENTIFIC
Breathing exercises have been
shown to decrease **blood
pressure** and lower levels of
stress hormones. Stretching
the body through various poses
promotes better drainage of
the **lymphatic vessels,** the
body's waste removal system.
Holding postures may build
muscle tone, which enhances
physical well-being and protects
delicate **joints** against injury.

QUIET TIME **Sisters congregate in their Community Room**

The Nuns' Story

In the decades-old writings of elderly sisters, a young scientist found clues that may help us reduce the effects of Alzheimer's syndrome

THE FIRST CROCUS SHOOTS HAVE VENTURED ABOVE ground; it's the day after Easter at the convent on Good Counsel Hill. But this is Minnesota: the temperature is 23°F, and it feels much colder. Still, even though she's wearing only a skirt and sweater, Sister Ada, 91, wants to go outside. She needs to feed the pigs.

But the pigs she and the other nuns once cared for have been gone for 30 years. Sister Ada simply can't keep that straight. In recent years, her brain, like a time machine gone awry, has been wrenching her back and forth between the present and the past, depositing her without warning into the days when she taught primary schoolchildren in Minnesota—or to the times when she and the sisters had to feed the pigs several times a day.

Like some 4 million other Americans, Sister Ada (not her real name) is suffering from Alzheimer's disease; as the years go by, she will gradually lose her memory, her personality and finally all cognitive function. But advanced age does not always lead to senility. Ada's fellow nun, Sister Rosella, 89, continues to be mentally sharp and totally alert, with no sign of dementia, as she eagerly anticipates the celebration of her 70th anniversary as a sister.

In a very real sense, these two retired schoolteachers haven't finished their teaching careers. Along with hundreds of other nuns in their order, the School Sisters of Notre Dame, they have joined a long-term study of Alzheimer's disease that could teach the rest of us how to escape the worst ravages of this heartbreaking illness.

COLLEAGUES **David Snowdon visits the convent frequently**

The groundbreaking research they are helping conduct probably won't lead directly to any new drugs, and it's unlikely to uncover a genetic or biochemical cause of Alzheimer's. Doctors know, however, that preventing disease can be a lot easier and cheaper than trying to cure it. It was by studying the differences between people who get sick and people who don't—the branch of medical science known as epidemiology—that doctors discovered the link between smoking and lung cancer, between cholesterol and heart disease, between salt and high blood pressure.

Now it's Alzheimer's turn. Precious little is known about this terrible illness, which threatens to strike some 14 million Americans by 2050. Its precise cause is still largely mysterious, and effective treatments may well be years away. But epidemiologists are beginning to get a handle on what kinds of people are most seriously ravaged by Alzheimer's and, conversely, which people tend to escape relatively unscathed.

Much of this knowledge comes from a single, powerful piece of ongoing research: the aptly named Nun Study, of which Sisters Ada and Rosella are part. Since 1986, scientist David Snowdon, first at the University of Minnesota and now at the University of Kentucky, has been studying 678 School Sisters—painstakingly researching their personal and medical histories, testing them for cognitive function and even dissecting their brains after death. Snowdon and his colleagues have teased out a series of intriguing, revealing links between lifestyle and Alzheimer's.

Snowdon wasn't planning to study Alzheimer's disease when he first began visiting the sisters' convent in Mankato, Minn; he was simply trying to find a research project that would secure his position at Minnesota. He was a young assistant professor of epidemiology at the time—a field he had been introduced to as a young boy who raised chickens to earn money. "I learned a lot about what it takes to stay healthy from taking care of those chickens," Snowdon recalls. "That's what epidemiology is all about—the health of the whole flock."

Chicken studies wouldn't cut it with the Minnesota administration, though, so Snowdon got interested when a graduate student, an ex-nun, told him about the aging sisters at her former order, living out their retirement in a convent just two hours away. He was already familiar with the advantages of studying religious groups, whose relatively uniform backgrounds mean fewer variations in lifestyle to confound the data. An order of nuns whose economic status, health care and living conditions were especially similar would be an excellent starting place for an epidemiological study of the aging process. So he went out for a series of visits. Both Snowdon and the sisters had to overcome inhibitions—theirs at becoming research subjects, his from a Roman Catholic school background that made him uncomfortable asking personal questions of a nun. But they finally agreed that he would quiz them periodically to learn about what factors might be involved in promoting a healthy old age.

At first, the study didn't look as if it would reveal much. Snowdon had to count on the nuns to recall those aspects of their lives, including the years before entering the order, that had differed—and memory, even among the mentally competent, is notoriously unreliable. But then, after several months, he stumbled on two olive-green metal file cabinets—the personal records of all the young women who had taken their vows at the Mankato convent.

POSTMORTEM **Most of the nuns allow Snowdon to examine their brains after death to trace the effects of Alzheimer's**

What Alzheimer's Does to the Brain

Spreading from the bottom to the top

The disease is characterized by the gradual spread of sticky plaques and clumps of tangled fibers that disrupt the delicate organization of nerve cells in the brain. As brain cells stop communicating with one another, they atrophy—causing memory and reasoning to fade

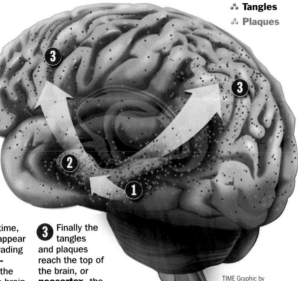

⋰ **Tangles**
⋰ **Plaques**

❶ Tangles and plaques first develop in the **entorhinal cortex,** a memory-processing center essential for making new memories and retrieving old ones

❷ Over time, they appear higher, invading the **hippo-campus,** the part of the brain that forms complex memories of events or objects

❸ Finally the tangles and plaques reach the top of the brain, or **neocortex,** the "executive" region that sorts through stimuli and orchestrates all behavior

TIME Graphic by Lon Tweeten

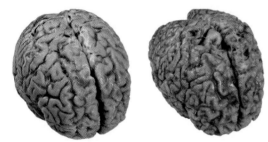

GRAY MATTERS

A brain ravaged by Alzheimer's, right, shrinks in size and weight as the disease destroys neural tissue. The once tightly packed ruts and grooves on the surface of a healthy cerebral cortex, left, become visibly pitted with gaps and crevices

The reason, according to one leading theory, was that some folks might have an extra reserve of mental capacity that kept them functioning despite the loss of brain tissue.

So he and Mortimer, along with University of Kansas psychologist Susan Kemper, began analyzing the autobiographies for evidence of such extra capacity. Kemper, an expert on the effects of aging on language usage, had earlier shown that "idea density"—the number of discrete ideas per 10 written words—was a good marker of educational level, vocabulary and general knowledge. Grammatical complexity, meanwhile, was an indicator of how well memory was functioning.

Applying these measures to the sisters' autobiographies, Snowdon and Kemper found to their astonishment that the elderly sisters who showed signs of Alzheimer's had consistently authored essays low in both idea density and grammatical complexity a half-century or more earlier. Idea density turns out to be a surprisingly powerful predictor of Alzheimer's disease. Snowdon found by reading nuns' early writings, he could predict, with 85% to 90% accuracy, which ones would show the brain damage typical of Alzheimer's disease about 60

Because the records were relatively standardized, Snowdon could extend his study of aging over many decades. The autobiographies written by each sister on her entry into the order were full of basic information about where the sisters were born, who their parents and siblings were, and why each one decided to join the order. With these documents Snowdon now had an objective measure of the sisters' cognitive abilities while they were young and in their prime. The first results confirmed earlier studies suggesting that people with the most education were most independent and competent later in life (most of the sisters were teachers; many had master's degrees).

When Snowdon joined forces with James Mortimer, an eminent researcher on aging then at the Minneapolis Veterans Administration Medical Center, to study the nuns' youthful autobiographies in more detail, their relationship led to an interesting discovery. Autopsies by other scientists had shown that the physical destruction wrought by Alzheimer's didn't inevitably lead to mental deterioration.

years later. While all the sisters show age-related decline in mental function, those who had taught for most of their lives showed more moderate declines than those who had spent most of their lives in service-based tasks. And that, says Kemper, supports the commonsense idea that stimulating the brain with continuous intellectual activity keeps neurons healthy and alive.

Snowdon's studies have provided further clues into the nature of Alzheimer's: that strokes and other brain trauma could contribute to the dementia of the disease, and that nutrition may play a role in helping stave it off. Sisters with high levels of the nutrient folate, also called folic acid, showed little evidence of Alzheimer's-type damage in their brain after death.

And more discoveries may be in store, for on Good Counsel Hill the Nun Study goes on—so that future generations will continue to benefit from lessons that women like Sister Rosella and her fellow nuns are teaching us about how to age with grace and good health. ∎

THE SCOTTSMAN—CORBIS SYGMA

Images

SPOILED SWINE
Foot-and-mouth disease, the highly infectious livestock illness, began breaking out on farms around Britain in February. In short order, hundreds of thousands of pigs, sheep and cows were slaughtered. These pig carcasses are awaiting cremation at Burnside Farm in Heddon-on-the-Wall, Northumberland. The USDA quickly banned the importation of meat and meat products from the 15-nation European Union.

Hail to the Buff Chief

Can you match workouts with a guy in his 50s? Here's George Bush's routine—and don't forget to run 5 km (3.1 miles) in under 21:30!
1. CURLS: Sets: 3. Reps: 10. Weight: 50, 60, 70 lbs.
2. INCLINE BENCH PRESS: Sets: 1 to 3. Reps: 10. Weight: 100 to 135 lbs.
3. FLYS: Sets: 1 to 3. Reps: 10. Weight: 20 to 25 lbs.
4. BENCH PRESS: Sets: 1 to 3. Reps: 10. Weight: 155 lbs.
5. LAT PULLDOWNS: Sets: 1. Reps: 30. Weight: 135 to 155 lbs.

RON EDMONDS—AP/WIDE WORLD

TED THAI—TIMEPIX

BUSHED? Not this fitness fanatic

JEWISH HOSPITAL—AP/WIDE WORLD

PIONEER Tools, center, with surgeons

Death of a Pioneer

In June Robert Tools, a retired tech librarian from Franklin, Ky., became the first person to receive a fully contained mechanical heart. Surgeons Robert Dowling and Laman Gray installed the buzzing, 4-lb. grapefruit-size plastic-and-titanium lump after doctors had given the 59-year-old grandfather only 30 days to live. The device, called the AbioCor, was implanted as part of a federal clinical trial at Jewish Hospital in Louisville. Doctors installed four other AbioCors, but high hopes for the pioneer of the process were set back after Tools suffered a stroke and died on November 30.

Move Over, Rover!

We love seeing-eye dogs, but why should one animal have a monopoly on helping the blind? Enter the seeing-eye pony: miniature horses, roughly 2 ft. tall at the shoulder, that come equipped with a good memory, excellent night vision and absurdly cute sneakers to provide traction indoors. And the ponies' 25- to 35-year life span ensures they can share many years with their grateful owners.

LISA CARPENTER

AID Horse sense

All the Hues That's Fit to Eat

For the nutrition-obsessed, this year's news is hues. Some experts are convinced that the pigments in foods, called phytonutrients, play a key role in preventing disease. The blue in blueberries, they say, may protect the brain, while the orange in carrots may promote heart health. Light-beige carbs such as breads and cookies are, well, beyond the pale.

The Arts

July 4

Age cannot wither her, nor custom stale her infinite variety. In other words, it was time for another Madonna world tour. Unbowed by age (she turned 43 in 2001), unfazed by marriage (she wed movie director Guy Ritchie in a castle in Scotland in 2000), unhindered by parenthood (son Rocco, her second child, turned one in August), the Material Mom was back in harness in her Drowned World Tour 2001. Slithering, sashaying and sweating, she was the hard-bodied barker of a carnival that called for aerial stunts, a mechanical bull, a kimono with 52-foot cuffs—and some all-too-prescient gas masks.

THAT'S SHOW BIZ!

Give 'em hell, Mel! Veteran funnyman Mel Brooks brings laughs, gaffes and dancing Nazis to Broadway in his triumphant *The Producers*

HOTCHA! Nathan Lane and Matthew Broderick are a match for the film's Zero Mostel and Gene Wilder

PAUL KOLNIK (3)

WHO KNEW? BROADWAY, NEW YORK CITY'S ETERNALLY fabulous invalid, wasn't dying—it was simply in need of a strong dose of fabulosity. For years, most of the street's big musical hits have been operatic British imports. *The Lion King* was a great homegrown boost, but producer the Walt Disney Co. and director Julie Taymor were, and still are, outsiders. Enter veteran comedian Mel Brooks with *The Producers*, his hilariously over-the-top adaptation of his 1968 movie about a schlocky Broadway producer who connives with his nervous accountant to raise money for an awful Nazi musical so they can abscond with the funds when the thing flops. Sweep-ing all before it (including conventional notions of good taste and political correctness), *The Producers* opened in April to rapturous buzz, fawning reviews and monster advance ticket sales ($13 million worth), then went on to dominate Broadway's Tony Awards, bagging a cool dozen.

Brooks' recipe for success? The best possible modern substitutes for the film's stars, Zero Mostel and Gene Wilder—Nathan Lane as producer Max Bialystock and Matthew Broderick as nebbishy Leo Bloom. Choreography by Broadway's hottest musical director, Susan Stroman *(Contact, The Music Man)*. Music and lyrics by a previously unknown musical genius, Mel Brooks. And support from a gaggle of Broadway backers so eager that one producer had to hold a lottery to decide which of his investors got the privilege of putting money into the show.

The sublime result: *The Producers* is one of the best translations of a beloved movie to the stage ever. Most of Brooks' famous lines and bits are here, including the memorable *Springtime for Hitler* production number, staged by Stroman with goose-stepping pizazz, a flock of pigeons doing the Nazi salute and more gay jokes than have crossed a stage since Liberace.

People had been bugging Brooks for years to turn *The Producers* into a musical. But he resisted them all until 1998, when DreamWorks exec David Geffen talked him into giving it a try. It helped that Brooks' movie career was in a slump and that Geffen had—"unbeknownst to David Geffen, but knownst to me," says Brooks—tapped into a longtime dream of the comedian's: to write a Broadway score. Though he has played drums since age 9, the 74-year-old Brooks has little musical training; he is what is known among music professionals as a "hummer": an unschooled composer who comes up with melodies and leaves it to others (on *The Producers,* it was arranger Glen

Kelly) to translate them into notes, chords, arrangements. His songs are a sprightly retro pastiche, ranging from mock *Fiddler on the Roof* to mock Astaire and Rogers to mock Bavarian beer hall. The music came easily, Brooks said; harder was the task of reshaping the movie into a cohesive show. For help with that, he turned to an old pal, Thomas Meehan, writer of *Annie* and a collaborator on several Brooks films, who helped structure the show, suggested spots for music numbers and pitched in with jokes.

Brooks' search for a director landed him at the doorstep of Mike Ockrent (*Crazy for You*) and his wife, choreographer Stroman. "I opened the front door," Stroman told TIME, "and he launched into *That Face,* one of his songs from the show. He danced down the hallway and wound up on top of the sofa. Then he said, 'I'm Mel Brooks.'" The performance won them over, but not long afterward Ockrent became ill with leukemia; he died in December 1999. After a few months' hiatus, Stroman resumed working on her own with Brooks. "I needed someone to make me smile," she says. "Who better than

Mel Brooks?" By all accounts, Stroman and Brooks were a smooth-running team, the old Catskills *tummler* deferring to the sure-handed Broadway director—though Brooks attended every rehearsal and made some slight suggestions (example: "You're ruining my masterpiece!").

The show is a crowning touch to Brooks' career—and his life. The onetime combat engineer in the European theater in World War II is still satirizing Hitler without apologies. "You can't compete with a despot on a soapbox," he said. "The best thing is to make him ludicrous." Today Brooks is seeing more of himself in the wacky show-biz satire he wrote more than 30 years ago. "It's the story of a caterpillar who becomes a butterfly—that's Leo Bloom. And that's me. A little kid from Brooklyn who finally made it across the vast East River to Manhattan, to Broadway. That's a journey that is as great as from the Alleghenies to the Rockies." You made it, Mel. ∎

MAIN MAN The ever-exuberant Brooks saw Leo Bloom in himself. Above left, a Broadway first—a chorus line of little old ladies with walkers—is topped by the show's second-act show-stopper, *Springtime for Hitler,* top.

JUST MILD ABOUT HARRY

The first movie based on J.K. Rowling's fantasy series about a boy wizard is magic at the box-office, but some critics aren't spellbound

WOULD THE MAGIC SURVIVE THE MUGGLES? THAT was the question as millions of fans of J.K. Rowling's novels about a boy wizard braced themselves for perhaps their hero's most perilous adventure, one that might be titled *Harry Potter and the Hazards of Hollywood.* Muggles, you see, are the vision-challenged nonwizards of Rowling's series—a category that generally embraces most of those who toil in Hollywood. Now, with *Harry Potter and the Sorcerer's Stone,* Warner Bros. and director Chris Columbus were bravely going toe to toe with the imaginations of readers who have purchased 100 million Potter books since *Harry Potter and the Philosopher's Stone,* as the first book is known in Britain, was published there in 1997. The fledgling wizard is one of the most beloved figures in literary history—and Rowling, once a struggling single mom in Edinburgh, Scotland, is an international celebrity. So fans held their breath: could the enchantment of her pages be captured on the big screen?

Columbus (*Home Alone, Mrs. Doubtfire*) and screenwriter Steven Kloves (*Wonder Boys*) worked closely with Rowling on the development of the film, ensuring it stayed remarkably close to the novel. "Fans would have been crushed if we had left too much out," said Columbus, whose adaptation runs a whopping 143 minutes. "Instead of trying to overtake the readers' imagination, we've just given them the best possible version of the book, which means steeping it in reality ... I wanted kids to feel that if

HARRIED Radcliffe played Potter, Grint and Watson his pals

they actually took that train [the Hogwarts Express Harry rides to school], Hogwarts would be waiting for them."

While Rowling didn't have final say over the movie, her contract gave her a consulting role, and she will receive a share of its profits. Although she rarely visited the set, Rowling was involved during preproduction when crucial design and plot decisions were being made. Columbus wondered early on where to put the hero's lightning-bolt scar, a souvenir from Harry's infancy, when he had his first run-in with the evil Lord Voldemort, who killed his parents. Editions of the books all over the world showed the scar in various places, so the director went to the source. "I drew a face with a wizard hat, and I had her draw in the scar," says Columbus. She described it as "razor sharp" and drew it vertically down the right side of the young wizard's forehead. Done.

Rowling also had a hand in choosing most of the adult cast members. She specifically requested Robbie Coltrane, the veteran Scottish comic who plays Hagrid, the lovable, gigantic Hogwarts dogsbody. Others, like Richard Harris as headmaster Albus Dumbledore, Maggie Smith as Professor McGonagall and Alan Rickman as Professor Snape, came straight from a wish list of actors that Rowling provided the producers. The film's critical younger stars include Rupert Grint, 13, and Emma Watson, 11, who play Harry's friends Ron and Hermione. Following what British producer David Heyman called a "brutal" search, the role of Harry was cast only weeks before the film went into production in September 2000. Daniel Radcliffe, the 12-year-old who took on the title role, had starred in the BBC's 1999 production of *David Copperfield* and in the 2001 movie adaptation of John le Carré's *The Tailor of Panama*.

SNAPE **Alan Rickman was another of Rowling's casting suggestions**

MC GONAGALL **Rowling had a hand in casting Maggie Smith**

And the verdict? Audiences embraced the film's eye-popping grandeur, dazzling special effects and sumptuous production values (the budget: more than $125 million). After it hit 3,500 screens just before Thanksgiving, *Harry* scored the highest-grossing opening weekend in Hollywood history. But its spell didn't take on some critics and audience members; many found the movie, well, *too* steeped in reality. Said TIME critic Richard Corliss: "In choosing to be true to the words, [Columbus] made a movie by the numbers. The film lacks moviemaking buoyancy—the feeling of soaring in space that Rowling's magic-carpet prose gives the reader. The picture isn't inept, just inert … An adapter of a famous work need not choose between fidelity and poetry; the King James version of the Bible had both. But Columbus is content to make a student's copy of the original master portrait. This is a magic act performed by a Muggle."

No matter: the week after *Harry Potter and the Sorcerer's Stone* opened in America, the lights went up on the filming of *Harry Potter and the Chamber of Secrets*, scheduled for release at Thanksgiving of 2002, with Columbus back at the helm. The entire *Sorcerer's Stone* cast will return, and Kenneth Branagh will join them in the role of the preening new defense against the dark-arts teacher, Gilderoy Lockhart. Meanwhile, Kloves has begun adapting the third book for the screen. In Hollywood a critic may bark, but the franchise moves on. ∎

ONSCREEN, A WAR OF THE WIZARDS

To millions of readers, British fantasy means Tolkien, not Rowling. On Dec. 19, New Line Cinema released *The Lord of the Rings: The Fellowship of the Ring,* the first of three films to be drawn from Oxford don J.R.R. Tolkien's classic trilogy. Squaring off against Richard Harris' Dumbledore in *Harry Potter* was Sir Ian McKellen's Gandalf

People

Return of the King

His fans will always love him, but Michael Jackson's long-planned comeback—intended by the self-proclaimed King of Pop to be a major cultural event of 2001—fizzled. Michael, now 43, cooked up a two-pronged assault: a gala, two-night, star-studded 30th-anniversary celebration at New York City's Madison Square Garden, followed by the release of his first album of new material in six years, the humbly titled *Invincible*. One got the sense it was not to be Michael's year when the first of his gala

MICHAEL Eager to regain his throne

nights, with seats costing up to $2,500, began with a supersized Marlon Brando, seated on a La-Z-Boy, asking for charitable donations. The date of the next gala summed up Michael's bad karma: it took place on the night of Sept. 10.

But to give the Thriller his due, the galas did offer him a chance to share a groove with his reunited brothers, to prove that he is still one of the hardest-working men in show business and—once you waded through the stifling layers of production hype—to remind us that he is still the most innovative and gifted popular dancer since Fred Astaire. But the comeback dream was centered around *Invincible,* a $30 million effort that was four years in the making—and spent only one week atop the charts.

SEAGULL Streep and Kline fire up

Havin' a Heat Wave

Was it because the tickets were free—or because New York City was enduring a record heat wave? Hundreds of folks camped out in Central Park in August for a place in, literally, the town's hottest seats: an all-star outdoor production of Chekhov's *The Seagull* featuring Meryl Streep, Kevin Kline, John Goodman, Marcia Gay Harden, Philip Seymour Hoffman, Natalie Portman and Christopher Walken. It was Streep's first stage turn in 20 years, and as for John Goodman's performance: no sweat *(not!)*.

When Booty Calls

The diva profession is tougher than it looks: imagine wearing

those 3-in. heels 24/7. Just ask the top divas of 2001, the double-Grammy-winning Destiny's Child, an R.-and-B. trio led by singer Beyoncé Knowles, a break-out superstar and the writer (and, we suspect) the subject of the group's monster hit, *Bootylicious*. To paraphrase Louis Armstrong, If you have to ask what that is, you'll never understand it.

Hands Across the Water

Music, we're told, has powers to soothe. No wonder the Taliban outlawed it. But music has other powers as well: to uplift, to voice defiance … to get phones ringing with pledges of money. Such were the goals of the Concert for New York City, the Oct. 20 benefit at Madison Square Garden whose audience included 5,000 New York City police and fire fighters. The show for Gotham turned out to be Made in Britain: David Bowie opened with Paul Simon's *America* and Paul McCartney closed with an injunction to *Let It Be.* Along

PAUL *Let It Be*

the way, the Who, Mick Jagger and Keith Richards chipped in. The bottom line: more than $30 million for Sept. 11 relief efforts.

TRIPLE PLAY Beyoncé, center, began the group as a quartet in Houston in 1990

MOBY Showing off his high-tech crib

Star Chambers

This is our unspoken deal with the wealthy: we don't begrudge them their money too much as long as they blow some of it on the sort of ludicrous, solid-gold-birdbath, mansion-envy fantasies that get us through our bitter little lives. Now, in another triumph for reality TV, cable channels have crafted hit series based on guided tours of celebrity homes—or, as MTV's home show put it—*Cribs*. And MTV wasn't alone: E! presented *Celebrity Homes*, and HGTV offered a raft of such shows, including *At Home with …* and *TV Moms at Home.*

What's the appeal? "It's informational voyeurism," said HGTV president Burton Jablin, coining a fine new synonym for old-fashioned snooping. Celebrities love doing the shows, observed Nancy Glass, host of many of HGTV's celeb tours, because "it's not a gossip show. We don't ask who they're sleeping with. We ask what they're sleeping on." Besides, where else would you get a chance to see Larry King's one-of-a-kind portrait of Larry King, a mosaic made of jellybeans?

Morris Dances

How long does it take to evolve from bad boy of modern dance to grand old man of the dance world? In the case of Mark Morris, 20 years—the anniversary he celebrated with his

company at the Brooklyn Academy of Music in March. On view: 16 of the master choreographer's 100-odd dances—from *L'Allegro, il Penseroso ed il Moderato*, a full-evening extravaganza for 24 dancers, four singers, chorus and orchestra, to *Peccadillos*, a duet for Morris and a toy piano. Meanwhile, across the street, the company moved into the brand-new $6 million Mark Morris Dance Center, its first permanent home (with a new school) in the dance capital of the world.

REVELS The Morris company shines in *Four Saints*

THE 2001 BEST

DESIGN | CINEMA | TELEVISION | MUSIC | THEATER | BOOKS

Though the turning point for America's moral agenda in 2001 was surely Sept. 11, chroniclers of the arts and other leisure activities still observe the Julian calendar. Hence TIME's annual review of cultural events, recalled with fondness or contempt. Except for the film *Kandahar* and David Letterman's TV show, the items cited here do not relate directly to the attacks on the U.S. But they do speak to our need to look back: to Greek myths (reinvented off-Broadway), to John Adams (in a new biography), to '70s punk (rekindled by the Strokes). We also look up (at the winged victory of a Milwaukee museum) and, for therapeutic escape, look away (to the generous sweetness of *Monsters, Inc.*, and the snazzy zip of the new Mini Cooper S sports car). Art can take us out of ourselves or deeper within. In soft times or tough, the Best will endure. And the Worst—well, the Worst is always with us.

Milwaukee Museum of Art Addition

Throughout Europe, the Spanish engineer-architect Santiago Calatrava is famous for elegant bridges and public buildings that are descendants, in their different ways, of London's 19th century steel-and-glass Crystal Palace, the greenhouse-exhibition space that signaled the beginning of pure engineering as the new form of beauty. For his first completed work in the U.S., Calatrava provided a showstopping new addition for the Milwaukee Museum of Art. His low-slung extension is crowned by a supreme statement, the upward arc of his *brise de soleil*, a sunscreen with "wings" made of 72 steel-pipe ribs. These great wings are pure glorious gesture, a flourish of structural brio that gives the museum a stratospheric silhouette and Milwaukee a stunning new landmark.

JIM BROZEK—MAM

2 Pocket Furniture Droog Design's multipurpose cabinets and boxes, suggested by a cigar-box manufacturer, all fit within one another and can be arranged in multiple configurations. The containers are fantastic flights of fancy that can be stamp boxes, keepsake boxes and, yes, cigar boxes.

3 The Mini Cooper S Car designers have chosen one of two roads of late: make vehicles more like trucks, or mine the archives to create the new VW Beetle or the faux-retro Chrysler PT-cruiser. But reintroducing legends can be sticky. BMW got it right with the Mini Cooper Series. The Cooper S, below, is almost as cute as its gutsy little '60s forebear. The outsize head lamps, the twin exhausts under the back fender and the squat little body mark it as a mini from the front and back. It's only from the side that one sees it has stretched, so it's cheerful and comfortable.

4 American Folk Art Museum Husband-and-wife architects Tod Williams and Billie Tsien were the perfect team for this vest-pocket New York City museum. Their famous feel for craft and

material is something that folk artists understand. But their exercises in stone, glass and ingeniously textured metals are carried out within a modernist idiom that never looks quaint or "folkloric." Who knew you could work so many delightful configurations of space and surprising vistas—plus three staircases—into a relatively small building? It's a jewel-box museum that's a jewel in itself.

5 Sagmeister: Made You Look Long revered among people who admire CD cover art, Sagmeister took a year off to prepare this book. It worked. There are cute tricks, like the red plastic cover, which, when removed, reveals hidden, much less cheerful pictures and text. But there is substance too. Sagmeister, who once carved words into his body and photographed it for a poster, bravely shows bad work as well as good and annotates it all in his spidery handwriting. This makes it, unlike most graphic-design books, a good read as well.

6 Moulin Rouge When they write the definitive history of eye candy, Baz Lurhmann's voluptuous movie should get its own chapter. Art director Catherine Martin reimagined the famous Montmartre nightclub as something like Pee-wee's Playhouse in Gotham City, stuffed to bursting with bright ideas and dark corners. The

inspirations came from everywhere—fashion photography, the technicolor "Paris" of old Hollywood, the Bhagavad Gita. Plus there's that boudoir-in-an-elephant!

7 Helmut Lang Dress What's a young fashionista who doesn't want to look too frivolous to wear these days? Helmut Lang made a fascinating suggestion in his fall 2001 collection. The dress, below right, which he did in long and short, black and white, and with and without the "holster" (the leather band around the shoulder and ribs), manages to be both austere and sexy and serious and glamorous. It's a look that will be most appreciated by the fashion cognoscenti, but it's also one that any reasonably confident woman (with great triceps) could safely wear.

8 The "Go" Chair One of this year's most heavily promoted design debuts was Go, above, the world's first chair in magnesium, a metal lighter than aluminum. For a humble stacking chair it wasn't cheap—$700 and up—but its spindly silhouette by designer Ross Lovegrove has the glamour of liquid mercury. Just sitting, the thing looks like it's launching into warp drive. An overhyped wonder? We think this chair has legs.

9 Diablo Radio With all the advances the past few years have seen in technology, consumer electronics has no

excuse for being boring. The good folks at Lexon, as well nearly the entire population of Japan, have long understood this. The hourglass-shaped Diablo radio, designed by Elise Berthier, has no switches. You swivel the top half to turn on the power and increase the volume. You swivel the bottom half to find your favored station. It's simple and satisfying. And if the news is bad, you can always look to the radio to give yourself a smile.

10 Prada Epicenter Store, New York City Rem Koolhaas had never done a store before Miuccia Prada approached him, but he had researched shopping while teaching at Harvard. His first foray into retail is a brainy roller coaster of a store with a precipitous dip, moving carriages of clothes and magic mirrors that let you see front and back at the same time. The dressing rooms alone, with glass doors that frost over at the touch of a button and a closet that transmits information about your chosen garment onto a screen, will make this a must-stop shop.

Kandahar Before Sept. 11, few knew of Kandahar; few cared about the ravages of civil war and Taliban rule in Afghanistan. Now the world can see the news value in Mohsen Makhmalbaf's tale of a woman crossing the desert incognito to find her sister. Even without the headlines, this Iranian film boasts a visual and emotional magnificence. It has a painter's acute eye for beauty within horror: the gorgeous colors of the burkas that imprison Afghan women; the handsome face of a child in a Taliban school as he expertly assembles a Kalashnikov rifle; the vision of one-legged men scrambling to retrieve prostheses dropped in parachutes from a plane. This is scoop journalism and heartbreaking poetry.

2 Moulin Rouge A never-prettier Nicole Kidman entrances hunkily soulful Ewan McGregor in an orgasmic swirl of color, design and pop music from mad Aussie Baz Luhrmann (*Romeo + Juliet*). In the age of Media Cool, this recklessly romantic burst of kinetic excess offended nice sensibilities even as it launched other viewers into rapture. I'm with the rapt.

The movie asks, *Moulin Rouge-ez avec moi ce soir?* I say, Sure. All night long.

3 Black Hawk Down Ridley Scott's harrowing replay of a 1993 Somalian debacle for U.S. troops is pure cinema in action. In nearly two hours of relentless warfare (think of *Saving Private Ryan* without the slow bits), it shows how a director can marshal images and sounds, biography and geography, to create *emotion* pictures. With *Gladiator, Hannibal* and now this ultimate war movie, Ridley's on a roll.

4 In the Mood for Love So many affairs are like the one endured here by Maggie Cheung and Tony Leung: furtive, guilty, leaving the ache of remorse. Hong Kong director Wong Kar-wai keeps the camera close to his actors—so close you can feel their heat and pain. Everyone is gorgeous and grieving in this threnody to erotic loss.

5 Mulholland Dr. David Lynch made the first 90 min. of this sexy thriller as a TV movie. When it didn't sell, Lynch added a coda that sends his characters into the weirdest Wonderland, as if *Twin Peaks* had morphed into *Blue Velvet*. It's not all intelligible, but it's always fabulous. Like the Coen brothers' excellent *The Man Who Wasn't There*, Lynch's laugh-scream of a movie dwells lusciously in the Kingdom of Noir. It ransacks old-movie style to create an avant-movie nightmare.

6 Monsters, Inc. It was a swell year for computer-generated cartoons. *Shrek* and *Monsters, Inc.* each had heart, spot-on gags and $200 million-plus domestic grosses. But if my desert island had a giant movie theater (or a DVD player), I'd choose the latest miracle from director Pete Docter and the Pixar crowd. This is a buddy movie and a daddy movie, about two creatures who inadvertently adopt a nosy little girl. It's got pictorial dazzle and an uncommon generosity of spirit, and it ends with the sweetest, rightest shot of the movie year.

7 Fat Girl *Merci*, French directors, for reminding audiences that sex, with its negotiations and lies, its beauty and messiness, its graphic, clumsy imagery, is a crucial part of the human drama. The best of a new bunch of dark, sometimes explicit French films about sex is Catherine Breillat's fable of two sisters, 12 and 15, who are rivals and comrades. Breillat juggles coming-of-age comedy with horror-tragedy in a film that lingers in the mind like the memory of a first, ill-fated affair.

8 The Lord of the Rings: The Fellowship of the Ring It's a fantasy based on a famous series of novels … a film of eye-popping grandeur and sumptuous production values … and, unlike *Harry Potter*, it's a good movie too. In the first of a Tolkien film trilogy, director Peter Jackson lays out the Middle Earth adventure with epic dash. This solid, often stirring version stops just this side of enthrallment. But then, the grand journey has just begun.

9 Amélie from Montmartre A shy girl with a runaway imagination (Audrey Tautou) forces magic on all those in her Paris neighborhood. Jean-Pierre Jeunet's scurrying narrative and cinematic gamesmanship (a style that could be called faux Truffaut) may at times weary viewers used to Hollywood's burlier, spell-it-all-out mode. But give me, any day, a film that offers a groaning banquet table of

invention and enchantment—and a showcase for the beguiling Tautou.

10 Ghost World An Amélie with attitude, teen Enid (the frighteningly assured Thora Birch) adopts orphan things and people in order to make fun of them. This daringly undarling comedy, from director Terry Zwigoff and comix writer Daniel Clowes, shows just how furtive and morose an ordeal growing up can be. It's a *Heathers* for the 9/11 Generation.

2 HBO's Sunday night Some of its efforts were mixed (*Band of Brothers*) or complete misses (*The Mind of the Married Man*). But with strong additions *Six Feet Under* and *Project Greenlight*, returning stalwarts *Oz, Curb Your Enthusiasm* and Emmy-winning *Sex and the City* and an utterly transcendent third season of *The Sopranos*, the cable network laid claim to the true must-see—albeit must-pay-to-see—night of TV.

3 Undeclared (Fox) The characters are freshmen, but the comedy is far from sophomoric. Producer Judd

Apatow (of the much mourned high school drama *Freaks and Geeks*) got a well-deserved, and more commercial, second chance with this college sitcom. *Undeclared*, starring Jay Baruchel, above, takes the eccentric sensibility of *Freaks* and applies it to smart, sharply observed coming-of-age stories of self-discovery, romance and beer.

4 Conspiracy (HBO) In a year of high-profile Holocaust dramas (ABC's *Anne Frank*, NBC's *Uprising*), an understated movie about a meeting in which Hitler's lieutenants planned the Final Solution outdid them all. Not a shot was fired, but the cool bureaucratese with which these officials rationalized mass murder showed how language can be humankind's most insidious weapon.

① David Letterman's post–Sept. 11 return Irony was dead, the pundits proclaimed. Humor was unseemly. And late-night comics, those unacknowledged legislators of America, no longer had anything to say to us. Yet it took a late-night comic to voice, movingly and indelibly, how we felt. "We're told [the terrorists] were zealots fueled by religious fervor," said the subdued but resilient host. "If you live to be a thousand years old, will that make any sense to you? Will that make any goddam sense?" And just as important, in the weeks after, he—and his counterparts at *The Daily Show*, *South Park* and *Late Night with Conan O'Brien*— gradually came back from comedy's self-imposed mourning period to show that topical, cutting satire wasn't just appropriate; it was downright American.

5 Alias (ABC) Sydney Bristow (Jennifer Garner, below left) is a waifish grad student who looks as if you could knock her over with a heavy textbook. In her spare time, she's also a karate-kicking, gadget-wielding double agent. Ridiculous? Yes, and wonderful. Reveling in '60s spy chic, this stylish, turbocharged and emotionally charged CIA serial grew more addictively complicated, involving and suspenseful with each episode.

6 Junkyard Wars (TLC) Comedy Central's robot-war show *BattleBots* has the testosterone and buxom babes. But this U.K.-imported engineering challenge has the real geek appeal. Turning teams of amiable tinkerers loose to build hydroplanes, rockets and the like out of scrap parts, it combines good-natured competition with just enough pseudo education that you don't have to feel guilty for not watching *Nova* instead.

7 Pasadena (Fox) Under-promoted and endlessly pre-empted, Fox's twisted rich-family saga was harder to find than Dick Cheney's secret secure location. But intrepid viewers were rewarded with a great cast (including Dana Delany, Martin Donovan and Philip Baker Hall) in a darkly funny story of a powerful media clan with a skeleton—perhaps literally—in its walk-in closet. Not everything in *Pasadena*, we learned, smells like roses.

8 The Bernie Mac Show (Fox) On network TV, it turns out, you still cannot say motherf____. In every other respect, however, this fresh sitcom stays true to the foul-mouthed Original King of Comedy's riotous stand-up voice. Playing a comic (surprise, surprise) who takes in his sister's troubled kids, the gruff, unsentimental but likable Mac takes the cuddly out of family comedy.

9 "Once More, with Feeling," Buffy the Vampire Slayer (UPN) You could apply the title of this audacious musical episode to the whole season of *Buffy*, which survived an acrimonious move from the WB to return smarter, funnier and dramatically richer than ever. Who would have thought creator Joss Whedon (who taught himself piano to write the episode's surprisingly tuneful score, as well as the nimble lyrics) studied his Sondheim along with his sarcophagi?

10 24 (Fox) Even before the war made heroes out of CIA agents, this thriller was the talk of TV. Deservedly so: its pulse-pounding premise (a counterterrorist agent—Kiefer Sutherland, below—has 24 hours to stop an assassination), gimmick (each episode is one hour in real time) and look (a split screen is used to relate concurrent story lines) made its pilot the most exciting of the year. Some later episodes had a draggy, shaggy-dog quality, but at its best, *24* had viewers counting the seconds.

The Strokes *Is This It* (RCA) It's nearly impossible to listen to this album without noting all the '70s punk/pop acts being ripped off left and right. It's also impossible to resist nodding your head and singing along. The Strokes may be derivative—of the Velvet Underground, Television, David Bowie and many others—but to borrow a phrase from Courtney Love, they fake it so real, they are beyond fake.

Is This It is full of great guitar hooks, dry pop lyrics ("Alone we stand, together we fall apart/ I think I'll be all right") and old-fashioned rock-'n'-roll attitude. Lead singer Julian Casablancas, 23, is right in the middle of it all, radiating a stylish, premature weariness that no doubt makes his dad, Elite modeling kingpin John Casablancas, a proud papa. Who cares if the Strokes didn't invent their sound, so long as they perfected it?

2 Marc Anthony *Libre* (Sony Discos/Columbia) Even when Marc Anthony sings English-language pop, his heart seems to pound to a Latin rhythm. Here he returns to Spanish-language salsa, the genre that made him a superstar. But the singer's sonic palette has broadened: these songs are adorned with musical touches from around the world, including tango-style accordions and Andean flutes.

3 System of a Down *Toxicity* (Columbia) In a year filled with screaming nu-metal acts, this band screams loudest and most eloquently. Front man Serj Tankian has a soaring voice, but as he demonstrates on standouts *Chop Suey!* and *Forest*, he knows how to modulate, sounding like an angry cantor one moment and a choir boy the next. Guitarist Daron Malakian backs it all up with a fierce wall of fuzz.

4 Ryan Adams *Gold* (Lost Highway) There's a feel of the young, freewheeling Bob Dylan in the organ and acoustic-guitar textures beloved by this urban folk rocker. On his lyric sheet, word games take a backseat to riffs on love, youth and empty pockets. Boomers nostalgic for their hitchhiking days, as well as their children thumbing a ride to the city for the first time, will find something to get weepy over.

5 Olu Dara *Neighborhoods* (Atlantic) The cornetist-guitarist-vocalist makes music that doesn't just grow on you; it grows around you, locking you in an inescapable embrace, like an oak tree that's knotted around a fence. Once his magical blend of jazz and blues gets hold of the listener, there's no escape—and no wanting to leave. Dara, who has played sideman to jazz greats, has become a master.

6 Lucinda Williams *Essence* (Lost Highway) Country's most lauded poet, above, turns down the volume and comes up with a slow, soft album about the soul's dark places. In songs that range from meditations on obsessive relationships to odes to backwoods religion, she exposes emotions many listeners keep inside and spins them into music other songwriters wish they had in them. Absolutely essential.

7 Valery Gergiev/Kirov Orchestra *The Rite of Spring* (Philips) Igor Stravinsky's clamorous ballet score has now received a quintessentially Russian recording: violent, brazen, full of all the blunt power of passionate peasant ritual. Gergiev has been making a big impression as principal guest conductor of New York City's Metropolitan Opera, and this CD shows why.

8 Aterciopelados *Gozo Poderoso* (BMG/U.S. Latin) Musical mavericks often reject the past; this Colombian electro-rock duo is dragging its traditions into the present. It marinates its songs in South American rhythms, including cumbia (a hot, syncopated dance music) and vallenato (a sweet accordion-led genre). This album edifies even as it enchants.

9 Dolly Parton *Little Sparrow* (Sugar Hill) Although lumped with the bluegrass revival, this album sports little of the preciousness associated with most nouveau blue. On traditional tunes and unconventional ones (Collective Soul's *Shine*, Cole Porter's *I Get a Kick Out of You*), Parton tests bluegrass's elasticity—but gently. The whole album sounds fresh and playful.

10 Aaliyah *Aaliyah* (Blackground) A siren of subtlety, never wailing when a whisper would do, the late singer, left, blended genres with alluring ease. Her voice makes hip-hop/soul and muted alternative rock seem one.

Metamorphoses

A wading pool takes up nearly the entire stage. Ten actors—some dressed in togas, others in modern-day suits—jump in and out of it to re-enact the myths of Ovid. There's Phaeton and his chariot; Midas (that's him in the chair) and his daughter; Orpheus and his underworld voyage. Writer-director Mary Zimmerman's lovely, deeply affecting work (an off-Broadway hit that will move to Broadway in March 2002) recaptures the primal allure of the theater—it's fake; isn't it wonderful? Using stage devices that delight with their low-tech ingenuity and a text that modernizes without patronizing, *Metamorphoses* shows that theater can provide escape—and sometimes a glimpse of the divine.

decade), the residents of a ghetto neighborhood in Pittsburgh struggle against the social and economic realities of the Reagan '80s. A great cast, including *Kiss Me, Kate*'s Brian Stokes Mitchell, above, and Tony Award winner Viola Davis, luxuriates in Wilson's richly impassioned and poetic language.

2 Topdog/Underdog

A reformed street hustler, who now makes a living playing Abraham Lincoln in an arcade, shares a seedy room with his brother, who calls himself Booth. No point in trying to figure out the symbolism; just revel in Suzan-Lori Parks' haunting, fractured world of losers and even bigger losers. Jeffrey Wright and Don Cheadle (in an all too short off-Broadway run that could reach Broadway in 2002) gave riveting performances in one of Parks' strongest plays.

3 The Producers

Perhaps you've heard of it? Mel Brooks' first crack at a Broadway musical looks as if it will run forever. And maybe it deserves to. Of course, the 75-year-old amateur had help from some talented pros, especially director Susan Stroman, who serves up show stopper after show stopper, and Nathan Lane (with Matthew Broderick, below left), a Max Bialystock even Zero Mostel would have loved.

4 The Glory of Living

"He's mean," says the young girl of the man who has kidnapped her. "He is?" replies the man's abused teenage wife and partner in crime. No social critic could express with more eloquence or economy the plight of the white-trash couple Rebecca Gilman chronicles in her deadpan, slice-of-lowlife drama. This 1997 play, having its New York premiere in a fine production directed by Philip Seymour Hoffman and starring Anna Paquin, is a stunner.

5 The Last Five Years

Composer-lyricist Jason Robert Brown (*Parade*) did his best work to date in this melodic and elegantly crafted chamber musical, in which a couple simultaneously tell the story of their relationship—one from start to finish, the other from finish to start. Daisy

Prince's inventive production opened at Chicago's Northlight Theater and will face the New York critics early in 2002.

6 Elaine Stritch at Liberty

Do we really need another one-woman show in which a crusty Broadway trouper recounts her show-biz war stories while belting out Sondheim and Berlin standards? Yes indeed, if she has enlisted as artful a collaborator as *New Yorker* theater critic John Lahr. And if she can still perform, at age 76, with as much energy, wit and seen-it-all gumption as Elaine Stritch, below.

7 King Hedley II

August Wilson's brand of big windy social drama is out of vogue right now, but he's still at the top of his game. In this, the eighth of his 20th century cycle (one play per

8 Urinetown

In a mythical city of the future, an evil capitalist (John Cullum) controls the water supply, people have to pee in public toilets, and the cast never lets you forget it's all a put-on. Even with the jokey excesses, this musical by Mark Hollmann and Greg Kotis—doing a pretty fair imitation of Brecht and Weill—is original, high-spirited fun.

9 42nd Street

Broadway wasn't exactly clamoring for a revival so soon of Gower Champion's 1980 musical, based on the 1933 movie. But with thousands of tapping feet, a score brimming with seemingly every great movie song from the '30s and the perfect role (finally) for the wonderful Christine Ebersole, this show is sheer joy.

10 The Drawer Boy

Will anyone pay attention to a quiet, understated play about two middle-aged brothers living on a farm—in Canada? Oh, let's give it a try. Michael Healey's comedy-drama is beautifully paced and written, and the sentiment has some sly, unexpected edges. A popular success in Canada, the play had its U.S. premiere at Chicago's Steppenwolf Theater in a little-noticed run that featured two of the year's best performances, by Frank Galati (director of *Ragtime*) and *Frasier*'s John Mahoney.

DENISE WILLIAMS

①
FICTION
Empire Falls

Forty-year-old Miles Roby seems to be one of life's born losers. Or are his problems self-made? He manages a decrepit restaurant in the dying Maine burg of Empire Falls—the place he was born and feels helpless to leave—in the wan hope of inheriting it from the widow who owns it. A limited circle condemns him to repeated and unpleasant meetings with his ex-wife's obnoxious boyfriend. He has lost parental control of his bright but troubled teenage daughter. Why doesn't he pack up and start somewhere new? In answering that question, Richard Russo's richly textured novel not only offers an enthralling and sometimes scary portrait of small-town life but also reveals a dignity, unexpected yet totally convincing, in its beleaguered hero.

①
NONFICTION John Adams

The second U.S. President lacked the charisma of such fellow Founding Fathers as George Washington, Thomas Jefferson and Benjamin Franklin (and who didn't?), but David McCullough's sprightly biography makes a strong case for John Adams' importance, both to his contemporaries and to posterity. Sensible, independent, rather prim, Adams was among the first to advocate American independence, and he displayed a crucial steadying hand during his four years as Chief Executive of

a young Republic, just stretching beyond baby steps. Filled with fascinating people, momentous events, shrewd insights and excerpts from letters between Adams and his wife Abigail, *John Adams* is a marvelous singing of a hero historically unsung.

---

2 True History of the Kelly Gang Ned Kelly, an Australian outlaw who was eventually captured, tried and hanged for murder in 1880, still remains a Down Under hero and legend. He left behind some papers,  which Australian-born author Peter Carey (*Bliss*) deftly incorporates into an exculpatory fictional autobiography of enormous imaginative power, the story of a normally flawed man who is driven to desperate acts for the sake, ultimately thwarted, of self-defense.

3 Hateship, Friendship, Courtship, Loveship, Marriage The nine tales assembled under this long title again demonstrate Canadian author Alice Munro's thorough mastery of the short story. All these tales are touched, in one way or another, by the specter of death, a topic that Munro's skill manages to make surprisingly lively.

4 Peace Like a River This engaging first novel, set in the early 1960s, follows the Land family — the father Jeremiah; son Reuben, 11; and daughter Swede, 9—as they try to track down eldest son Davy, 17, who has been convicted of murder but escaped from jail. Their trek occasions some literally miraculous events, and author Leif Enger makes the preposterous plausible and good fun in the bargain.

5 The Corrections It's a pity that Jonathan Franzen's dustup with Oprah (she chose his novel for her book club; he expressed some ill-advised concerns) has overshadowed what he wrote, for his saga about a dysfunctional family has accomplished something rare: a mix of high literary ambitions with reader friendliness.

2 How I Came Into My Inheritance No memoir about caring for elderly parents is quite like this one, a piercingly funny book without a joke in it. Dorothy Gallagher opens with the sickroom of Bella and Izzy, her Russian-Jewish mother and father, then takes their stories backward in time through the chapters of the American immigrant experience. No filial whining here, just keen observations and a steady affection.

3 Carry Me Home A white native of Birmingham, Ala., Diane McWhorter was 10 in 1963, roughly the same age as the four black girls killed in her hometown's notorious church bombing. Her adult questions about her father's hostility toward the civil rights movement has led to a comprehensive, fast-paced history of that era and its tangled racial animosities.

4 Seabiscuit Why are there so few good biographies of race horses? Well, never mind, here's one. The main character was an improbable champion: undersized, injury prone and ridden by a one-eyed jockey. Yet Seabiscuit captured America's heart, which pounded harder when he faced War Admiral in a showdown in 1938. Seabiscuit won, and Laura Hillenbrand does too with her deft blend of racing lore and social history.

5 President Nixon: Alone in the White House Those who feel they can't bear to read another word about perhaps the most peculiar man ever to occupy the White House should think again. Richard Reeves sifted mountains of evidence to get inside the President's skin. This approach works wonders. Nixon haters will still hate him, but they and less partisan readers will emerge feeling they have lived a portion of Nixon's life.

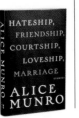

NOBEL PRIZES

Peace
United Nations and Kofi Annan, Secretary-General

Literature
V.S. Naipaul, for "having united perceptive narrative and incorruptible scrutiny in works that compel us to see suppressed histories"

Chemistry
William S. Knowles and Ryoji Noyori, for their work on chirally catalyzed hydrogenation reactions; and to K. Barry Sharpless, for his work on chirally catalyzed oxidation reactions

Physics
Eric A. Cornell, Wolfgang Ketterle and Carl E. Wieman, for the achievement of Bose-Einstein condensation in dilute gases of alkali atoms and for studies of the properties of the condensates

Economics
George A. Akerlof, A. Michael Spence and Joseph E. Stiglitz, for analyzing markets with asymmetric information

Physiology and Medicine
Leland H. Hartwell, R. Timothy Hunt and Paul M. Nurse, for discoveries of key regulators of the cell cycle

SPORTS CHAMPIONS

Baseball
- *World Series*
  Arizona Diamondbacks
- *College World Series*
  Miami Hurricanes

Basketball
- *WNBA*
  Los Angeles Sparks
- *NBA*
  Los Angeles Lakers
- *NCAA Women*
  Notre Dame Irish
- *NCAA Men*
  Duke Blue Devils

Football
- *Super Bowl XXXV*
  Baltimore Ravens

Hockey
- *Stanley Cup*
  Colorado Avalanche

Horse Racing
- *Kentucky Derby*
  Monarchos
- *Preakness Stakes*
  Point Given
- *Belmont Stakes*
  Point Given
- *Breeders' Cup Classic*
  Tiznow

Golf
- *Nabisco Championship*
  Annika Sorenstam
- *U.S. Women's Open*
  Karrie Webb
- *LPGA*
  Karrie Webb
- *Women's British Open*
  Si Re Pak
- *Masters*
  Tiger Woods
- *U.S. Open*
  Retief Goosen
- *British Open*
  David Duval
- *PGA*
  David Toms

Tennis
- *Australian Open*
  Jennifer Capriati
  Andre Agassi
- *French Open*
  Jennifer Capriati
  Gustavo Kuerten
- *Wimbledon*
  Venus Williams
  Goran Ivanisevic
- *U.S. Open*
  Venus Williams
  Lleyton Hewitt

TELEVISION SERIES

1. *Friends*, NBC
2. *ER*, NBC
3. *Everybody Loves Raymond*, CBS
4. *CSI*, CBS
5. *Law & Order*, NBC
5. *The West Wing*, NBC
7. *Becker*, CBS
8. *Inside Schwartz*, NBC
8. *Monday Night Football*, ABC
8. *Survivor: Africa*, CBS

TONY AWARDS

Best Play
Proof, by David Auburn

Best Musical
The Producers

Best Actress, Play
Mary-Louise Parker, *Proof*

Best Actor, Play
Richard Easton
The Invention of Love

THE OSCARS

Best Picture
Gladiator

Best Actress
Julia Roberts
Erin Brockovich

Best Actor
Russell Crowe
Gladiator

Supporting Actress
Marcia Gay Harden
Pollock

Supporting Actor
Benicio Del Toro
Traffic

Best Director
Steven Soderbergh
Traffic

Cinematography
Peter Pau
Crouching Tiger, Hidden Dragon

Foreign Film
Crouching Tiger, Hidden Dragon

Visual Effects
Gladiator

REED SAXON—AP/WIDE WORLD

Best Actress, Musical
Christine Ebersole
42nd Street

Best Actor, Musical
Nathan Lane, *The Producers*

BESTSELLERS

1. *Harry Potter Schoolbooks*
   J.K. Rowling
2. *John Adams*
   David McCullough
3. *Who Moved My Cheese?*
   Spencer Johnson
4. *The Prayer of Jabez*
   Bruce H. Wilkinson
5. *A Painted House*
   John Grisham
6. *Body for Life*, Bill Phillips
7. *We Were the Mulvaneys*,
   Joyce Carol Oates
8. *The Red Tent*
   Anita Diamant
9. *Harry Potter and the Goblet of Fire*
   J.K. Rowling
10. *Rich Dad, Poor Dad*
    Robert T. Kiyosaki
11. *Harry Potter and the Prisoner of Azkaban*
    J.K. Rowling
12. *Life Strategies*
    Phillip C. McGraw
13. *The Bonesetter's Daughter*
    Amy Tan
14. *Ghost Soldiers*
    Hampton Sides
15. *The Four Agreements*
    Don Miguel Ruiz
16. *Seabiscuit*
    Laura Hillenbrand
17. *Desecration*
    Tim Lahaye, Jerry B. Jenkins
18. *Dreamcatcher*
    Stephen King
19. *Jack: Straight from the Gut*
    Jack Welch
20. *Girl with a Pearl Earring*
    Tracy Chevalier

HOLLYWOOD FILMS

1. *Shrek*
2. *Harry Potter and The Sorcerer's Stone*
3. *Rush Hour 2*
4. *Monsters, Inc.*
5. *The Mummy Returns*
6. *Pearl Harbor*
7. *Jurassic Park III*
8. *Planet of the Apes*
9. *Hannibal*
10. *American Pie 2*

SOURCES. NOBELS: THE NOBEL PRIZE INTERNET ARCHIVE. SPORTS: THE NEW YORK TIMES. TELEVISION: ZAP2IT.COM. TONYS: THE AMERICAN THEATRE WING. BOOKS: AMAZON.COM. DOMESTIC FILMS (THROUGH DEC. 18): BOXOFFICEMOJO.COM. OSCARS: ACADEMY OF MOTION PICTURE ARTS AND SCIENCES.

SWEET LEMMON At right, the actor in *Three for the Show* (1955). Above, from top: *Mister Roberts* (1955); *Some Like It Hot* (1959); *Grumpy Old Men* (1993)

Photograph: Columbia Pictures—Kobal Collection

Milestones

June 27

Onscreen, he led four lives. In his first eminence, actor Jack Lemmon was usually the nice Joe getting wooed by prime kooky blonds Judy Holliday and Kim Novak. In *The Apartment* and many films that followed, he played a businessman in danger of being betrayed by his own best instincts, Job with a white-collar job. He was also at home in the blustering camaraderie of the male world, from early service comedies like *Mister Roberts* through all the odd-couple films in which he played Nellie to Walter Matthau's Butch. (And as delighted millions can attest, he fit right in with the ladies, too, when he donned drag for his hilarious turn in *Some Like It Hot*.) In Act Four, an aging Lemmon found inspiration in the works of "serious" authors—John Osborne (a TV version of *The Entertainer*), David Mamet (*Glengarry Glen Ross*), Raymond Carver (*Short Cuts*). Yet the farceur's instincts never deserted Lemmon; almost alone, he kept upper-middle-class comedy alive long past its prime. In the precision of his diction, the seeming intimacy of his asides and that dry cackle of a laugh, he was the movies' Johnny Carson. The two-time Oscar winner (and six-time also-ran) died in June of cancer. He was 76.

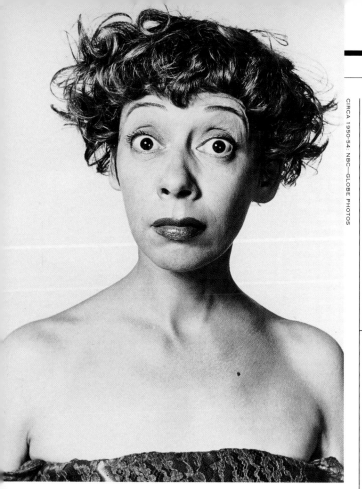

Imogene Coca
1908—2001

The wide-eyed, winsome Coca became television's first great female sketch comedian when she swept to fame as Sid Caesar's co-star in the 1950s television classic *Your Show of Shows*. Petite in stature but possessed of outsize energy, Coca won an Emmy in 1951 for her work on the program—ranging from subtle satire to zany slapstick—which aired live for 90 minutes on Saturday nights. Coca and Caesar, improvising without cue cards, acted out skits lampooning marriage, everyday life and popular culture.

Pauline Kael
1919—2001

The passionate, pugnacious, widely influential Kael was the *New Yorker's* film critic for more than two decades. In her slangy, punched-up prose, she championed such filmmakers as Brian De-Palma and Robert Altman and celebrated the appeal of pop American movies, often finding more to cheer in "trash" than "art."

James St. Clair
1920—2001

President Richard Nixon's Watergate lawyer enjoyed a storied career: chief assistant to Joseph Welch, counsel for the U.S. Army in the Army-McCarthy hearings; defense attorney for Yale chaplain William Sloane Coffin, tried for encouraging draft evasion; and counsel to the Boston school committee in its losing war against mandatory busing.

Isaac Stern
1920—2001

A brilliant classical violinist, Isaac Stern was also a generous teacher who mentored and encouraged generations of young musicians, including cellist Yo-Yo Ma, violinist Itzhak Perlman and pianist Emanuel Ax. Writing in TIME, Ax noted, "He gave unstintingly of himself for two causes that were dear to him—Carnegie Hall and music education—but he was just as enthusiastic about sharing a great meal or the wonderful performance of a colleague. In any but medical terms, the cause of his death, 'heart failure,' was the farthest thing from the truth. The one constant in his life was that his heart never failed."

Joey Ramone
1951—2001

The gangly, geeky front man of the seminal punk band the Ramones was born Jeffrey Hyman in New York City. His band's energetic, primitive sound ("simple but effective," he called it) undermined the preening pretensions of the art-rock groups of the 1970s and ushered in a new era in pop. Recalling the impact of the Ramones, U2's Bono wrote in TIME, "When I was 16, the idea of being in a band and making records seemed out of reach to me and Adam and Edge and Larry until we heard the Ramones. Something about their humility and humor just struck us when we saw them in Dublin in 1977. They seemed like the antithesis of every other band we went to see, where, intentionally or not, you felt like you were the peasants. In that sense, it was a revolution. More than a musical revolution, it felt like 'our people' were onstage. Imagination was the only obstacle to overcome. Anyone could play those four chords. You had to be able to hear it more than you had to be able to play it."

1931: NEW YORK TIMES—HULTON-ARCHIVE—GETTY IMAGES

1994: STEPHEN DANELIAN—CORBIS OUTLINE

Anne Morrow Lindbergh
1906—2001

The daughter of America's ambassador to Mexico met the renowned pilot Charles Lindbergh when he visited Mexico City after his heroic 1927 solo flight to Paris. She soon joined her husband as a pioneering aviator, becoming the first American woman to receive a glider pilot's license. She was seven months' pregnant when she and Charles set a transcontinental speed record in 1930. Two years later, their son Charles Jr. was kidnapped and killed in one of the era's most chronicled news events. The mother of six wrote 13 books; several have become classics.

Writing in TIME, Charles Lindbergh's biographer, A. Scott Berg, recalled, "She was shorter than I expected but larger than life, lit from within. Politely but directly she queried, 'Why do you want to write about my husband? He's very much out of fashion, you know'—even before we sat down. 'I'm an ordinary person who was thrust into extraordinary circumstances,' she told me, describing her role in the epochal events in her life—her marriage to the most famous man on earth, the 'Crime of the Century,' blazing air routes, the debate over America's isolationism. Because she considered no experience complete until she had written about it, she left us with volumes of poignant diaries and the landmark *Gift from the Sea* (1955), which speaks to one generation of women after another."

Eudora Welty
1909—2001

Writing for TIME about Eudora Welty, novelist Richard Ford said, "To take a walk or a Saturday drive with Eudora was to have the world narrated to you, recalibrated and transformed into language that was surprising, sometimes shocking, always sympathetic, frequently hilarious and full of perception, wonder and delight. This commerce produced 20 or so extraordinary books, a world of adoring readers, a house full of prizes and a life lived solely, though not alone, and utterly to her own measure. To know Eudora Welty was to be reminded again where the seeds of greatness are sown."

Carroll O'Connor
1924—2001

As a journeyman actor he was schooled in Shakespeare, and Carroll O'Connor left his enduring mark on U.S. culture playing a groundling: the coarse but lovable working-class bigot Archie Bunker on producer Norman Lear's *All in the Family* (1971-79). O'Connor won four Emmy Awards for his portrayal of the many-faceted Bunker; he won another for his role as a liberal-minded Southern cop on the NBC drama *In the Heat of the Night* (1988-94). In his later years, after his drug- and alcohol-addicted son Hugh committed suicide in 1995, he became an outspoken antidrug crusader. Said TIME in 1971: "Archie Bunker burst onscreen snorting and bellowing about 'spades' and 'spics' and 'that tribe.' He decried miniskirts, food he couldn't put ketchup on and sex during daytime hours. He bullied his 'dingbat' wife Edith and bemoaned his 'weepin' Nellie atheist' daughter Gloria. Archie lost most of his arguments ... But as played by O'Connor, he was daringly, abrasively, yet somehow endearingly funny."

Katharine Graham
1917—2001

Born Katharine Meyer to the wealthy family that owned the Washington *Post* and later *Newsweek*, she married the dynamic but unstable lawyer Philip Graham, who took over the Meyer concerns. Following his death in 1963, she ran the *Post* and turned it into one of the most powerful papers in the country, joining the New York *Times* in its 1971 quest to publish the Pentagon papers and overseeing the *Post*'s history-making pursuit of the Watergate story. One of America's most influential women, she was a noted Beltway socialite and the author of a Pulitzer-prizewinning memoir.

Willie Stargell
1940—2001

The proud "Pops" was captain of the great "We Are Family" Pittsburgh Pirates team that won a surprise World Series win over Baltimore in 1979. One of the few major leaguers to stick with a single ball club for at least 20 years, Stargell walloped 475 homers, a Pittsburgh record; he had more homers than any other hitter in the '70s.

John Phillips
1935—2001

Founder of the 1960s hippie folk-rock band the Mamas and the Papas, Phillips created a fresh sound: hits like *California Dreamin'* and *Monday, Monday* floated on a wave of intricate vocal harmonies. Following a brief reign atop the charts, the group split up in 1968 after Phillips' then wife and bandmate Michelle had an affair with fellow band member Denny Doherty.

Chet Atkins
1924—2001

A hero to generations of country-music fans, Chet Atkins was a pickin' prodigy, a virtuoso guitarist whose unique fleet-fingered style influenced younger musicians from George Harrison to George Benson. Atkins played on hit records with Elvis Presley (*Heartbreak Hotel*) and Hank Williams (*Jambalaya*), became a producing mogul who helped create the Nashville sound and along the way sold 75 million copies of his own albums. With Vince Gill, he led all country artists in Grammy Awards, with 14.

Ken Kesey
1935-2001

The author and '60s counterculture superhero, who died after cancer surgery, was a rebel pundit and a comic scribe, a longtime advocate of hallucinogen use and a lifelong exemplar of individualism. His acclaimed first novel, *One Flew Over the Cuckoo's Nest (1961)*, became an Oscar-winning film. In 1964 he traveled cross-country in a painted-up bus with a group of hippie pals called the Merry Pranksters. The trip, immortalized by Tom Wolfe in *The Electric Kool-Aid Acid Test*, opened the Pandora's box of the '60s psychedelic subculture. "I like to stir things up," Kesey once said. "I'm the Minister of Misinformation."

Gunther Gebel-Williams
1934—2001

The best-known animal trainer in the world, though diminutive at 5 ft. 4 in., Gebel-Williams taught his beloved tigers and leopards to jump through flaming hoops and wrap their bodies around his neck. He was born into a German circus family; in 1968 Ringling Bros. and Barnum & Bailey Circus bought out his circus just to obtain his services. A dynamic showman, he often entered the ring riding "Roman post" style, standing astride four galloping steeds. Though a gifted trainer, the "Lord of the Rings" lost teeth and bore deep scars from the huge animals with which he performed in some 12,000 shows in America alone.

Mary Kay Ash
1918-2001

The flashy yet homespun cosmetics executive nurtured her Mary Kay Inc. to sales of more than $1.2 billion in 2000. She started her company in 1963 with $5,000, after her male assistant at a direct-sales company was promoted over her at twice her salary. "I couldn't believe God meant a woman's brain to bring 50¢ on the dollar," she said. A master marketer, Ash rewarded (and motivated) her sales force of 40,000 with minks, diamonds and her trademark pink Cadillacs.

Dale Evans
1912—2001

The dulcet-voiced cowgirl was also a devoted humanitarian, the author of more than 20 books and the widow of Roy (King of the Cowboys) Rogers. Evans' boss caught her singing while she worked—as a stenographer at a Dallas insurance company—and prodded her to appear on a company-sponsored radio program. Not long after, she was cast in her first of 28 films with Rogers, beginning a long reign as the radiant "Queen of the West." Despite her immense popularity, she was often outbilled by her husband's horse, Trigger, which co-starred in 90-plus Rogers films. When Trigger died, Roy and Dale had him stuffed—a fate, Dale liked to tell talk-show hosts like Johnny Carson, that also awaited Roy upon his demise. She was just joshing.

George Harrison
1943-2001

He was the quiet Beatle only in that he was standing alongside two louder-than-life characters and in front of a guy playing drums. He held many strong opinions—on Beatlemania, on global need, on his right to privacy, on his God—and gave firm voice to most of them. But George Harrison was certainly the most reluctant Beatle, wanting out almost as soon as he was in, the leader in urging the band to quit performing live. He never succeeded in looking comfortable in his Fab Four gear, and he often said his luckiest break was joining the band—and his second luckiest was leaving it. The standard line is that Harrison was an enigma, but perhaps he was transparent: a terrific guitarist, a fine songwriter, a spiritual seeker, a celebrity who hated and feared celebrity.

After Harrison died at a friend's home in Los Angeles following a four-year battle with cancer, he was mourned and eulogized by crowds gathered outside the Abbey Road studios in London and in Strawberry Fields, the area of Manhattan's Central Park not far from where John Lennon was shot, and by his former bandmates. "He was a beautiful man. He was like my baby brother," said Paul McCartney.

The son of a Liverpool bus driver, George met Paul in 1955, and they soon began playing together, driven by a shared love of American rock 'n' roll. Harrison made enduring contributions to the Beatles, charging them up with the rockabilly jangle of Carl Perkins and later steering them into the swirling, layered sounds of Indian music. He blossomed late as a songwriter: the Beatles' last album, *Abbey Road*, included two of his best tunes, *Something* and *Here Comes the Sun*. After the group's break-up, he pioneered the rock benefit concert, summoning Eric Clapton, Ringo Starr and a then reclusive Bob Dylan to Madison Square Garden for the Concert for Bangladesh in 1971. His first solo album, that year's *All Things Must Pass*, was a masterwork that cemented his reputation. His late-career mock supergroup, the Traveling Wilburys, proved that Harrison's gift—the sharing of camaraderie that bred joyous music—was intact.

Aaliyah

Aaliyah, 22, sultry, Brooklyn-born and Detroit-raised R.-and-B. singer whose first two albums went platinum. Aaliyah and seven members of her crew were en route from the Bahamas to Florida after shooting a music video when their twin-engine Cessna crashed and burst into flames shortly after takeoff.

Mortimer Adler, 98, philosopher, educational reformer and author who helped create the Great Books program of learning and championed the universal values he believed they embodied.

Jorge Amado, 89, Brazilian novelist whose life-embracing novels (*Gabriela, Clove and Cinnamon; Dona Flor and Her Two Husbands*) enlivened the dreams of readers worldwide with the sights and sounds of the Afro-Brazilian culture of his beloved native region, Bahia.

Harvey Ball, 79, commercial artist and adman who invented the now ubiquitous Smiley Face in 1963 to put happy faces on frowny workers at two newly merged companies. Ball was paid $45 for his design and never trademarked it.

Christiaan Barnard, 78, brash, charismatic South African surgeon who performed the first human-to-human heart transplant in 1967. More dramatic than the surgery itself was that he proceeded when other heart-transplant surgeons, who had operated only on animals, were reluctant.

Byron De La Beckwith, 80, unrepentant white supremacist serving a life sentence for the 1963 murder of civil rights leader Medgar Evers. After two different all-white juries deadlocked in the '60s, the case was reopened when the long-missing murder weapon was discovered by the father-in-law of a Jackson, Miss., assistant district attorney. Beckwith was convicted in 1994.

Herbert Block, 91, fiercely nonconformist Washington *Post* cartoonist known as Herblock who illuminated issues from McCarthyism to campaign fund raising and skewered 13 Presidents. Block won three Pulitzer Prizes, shared a fourth.

Sir Donald Bradman, 92, self-taught cricket player and courtly Australian icon considered by many to be the pre-eminent sportsman of all time. When Nelson Mandela was released after 27 years in prison, his first question to an Australian visitor was, "Is Sir Donald Bradman still alive?"

Ely Callaway, 82, founder of Callaway Golf Co. He designed "forgiving" clubs, like the popular, oversize Big Bertha driver, which he introduced in 1991.

Perry Como, 87, honey-smoked baritone and seventh son of a seventh son whose casual, almost sleepy stylings rivaled Bing Crosby's and Frank Sinatra's at the top of pop charts in the 1940s and '50s.

Troy Donahue, 65, hunky, fleetingly adored studio star of the late '50s and early '60s. The blond, blue-eyed onetime Columbia University journalism student catapulted to matinee-idol status with a lead role in the 1959 teen love story *A Summer Place,* opposite Sandra Dee.

Harvey Ball

Carrie Donovan, 73, astute, flamboyant fashionista who won new fans by appearing—with her trademark oversize glasses—in recent TV ads for Old Navy.

Morton Downey Jr., 67, raucous, bellowing, chain-smoking host of the eponymous 1987-89 TV talk show.

Rowland Evans, 79, nationally syndicated columnist and television pundit. In 1963 he teamed with fellow journalist Robert Novak to write columns and books and act as hosts of a CNN show.

Meyer Friedman, 90, cardiologist who helped coin the term Type A behavior in the 1950s and posited that uptight, high-stress people were more prone than mellow types to heart attacks.

Anthony (Tony Jack) Giacalone, 82, alleged Detroit Mafia capo who was set to meet with ex–Teamsters boss Jimmy Hoffa on July 30, 1975, the day Hoffa vanished. He never spilled the beans about what he may have known about Hoffa's disappearance, except to gently suggest, "Maybe he took a little trip."

William Hewlett, 87, philanthropist and engineering whiz who, with fellow Stanford University student David Packard, started a technology company in 1938 in a rented garage with $538. Its growth launched Silicon Valley, but Hewlett was prouder of its style, which stressed creativity and teamwork.

Cliff Hillegass, 83, creator of Cliffs Notes, the series of brief study guides to literature cherished by students. His first was a summary of *Hamlet* in 1958.

John Lee Hooker, 83, Mississippi Delta bluesman and sharecropper's son whose impassioned, resonant voice and urgent electric-guitar riffs helped father rock and inspired such musicians as Van Morrison and Eric Clapton.

Sir Fred Hoyle, 86, irascible astronomer and sci-fi novelist who coined the term Big Bang theory to distinguish it, derisively, from his own belief that the universe was infinite in time and space.

Hank Ketcham, 81, creator of the impish cartoon tyke Dennis the Menace. He conceived the famed strip after his own mischievous four-year-old, Dennis, provoked his exasperated mother to exclaim to Ketcham, "Your son is a menace!" Father and son were later estranged.

Stanley Kramer, 87, producer-director and grudging bearer of the label "message filmmaker" who received nine Oscar nominations for such movies as *On the Beach* and *Judgment at Nuremberg.*

Tanaquil Le Clercq, 71, lithe-limbed ballerina who, while on tour in Copenhagen with husband George Balanchine in 1956, contracted polio, which left her paralyzed at 27 at her peak. Balanchine in 1944 had choreographed a ballet in which he portrayed a character named Polio and his elegant muse, Le Clercq, was a victim who becomes paralyzed.

Carrie Donovan

Robert Ludlum, 73, master plotter whose 21 novels, including *The Bourne Identity*, sold more than 290 million copies.

Peter Maas, 72, crime writer (*Serpico*) who chronicled the lives of Mafia insiders.

Mike Mansfield, 98, low-key but resolute Montana Democrat and longtime Senate majority leader who later served as U.S. ambassador to Japan for 11 years.

William H. Masters, 85, sex-therapy pioneer who, with research partner and second wife Virginia Johnson, studied the mating habits of hundreds of couples.

Al McGuire, 72, Hall of Fame basketball coach and broadcaster known for his effusive, unforgettable "McGuireisms."

Gardner McKay, 69, TV heartthrob of the passion-in-Polynesia series *Adventures in Paradise* who left show business to become a successful playwright.

Alfred Moën, 84, plumbing-fixture pioneer who hatched the idea for the single-knob faucet as a college student in 1937 after he was scalded by the then ubiquitous two-handled variety.

Anthony Quinn, 86, vibrant, passionate force of stage and screen, remembered most for his Oscar-nominated turn as the fiery, dancing peasant in *Zorba the Greek.* Quinn won two Oscars for Best Supporting Actor and played the sideshow strongman in Federico Fellini's first international hit, *La Strada.*

Maureen Reagan, 60, strong-willed, outspoken daughter of Ronald Reagan and actress Jane Wyman. Maureen avowed that she "was a Republican before the President was," although her opinions often—and publicly—clashed with his.

Mordecai Richler, 70, undiplomatic Canadian author whose irreverent writings, in such works as *The Apprenticeship of Duddy Kravitz* (1959), gave equal time to mocking the bourgeoisie, Judaism, life in Montreal and élitist Québécois.

Richard Schultes, 86, pith helmet–sporting father of the discipline of ethnobotany, which examines the medicinal and hallucinogenic uses of plants among indigenous peoples.

Kim Stanley, 76, protean Broadway actress most admired for portraying a dizzying range of characters—a tomboy kid sister in William Inge's *Picnic* (1953), a nightclub chanteuse in *Bus Stop* (1955)—with notable humor and pathos.

Harold E. Stassen, 93, youngest Governor of Minnesota and eternally optimistic politician who made nine fruitless attempts to win the G.O.P. presidential nomination.

Korey Stringer, 27, Minnesota Vikings Pro Bowl offensive tackle who was popular with teammates for his jovial demeanor and respected by fans for his charity work; after collapsing from heatstroke during practice in 90°F-plus heat.

John Lee Hooker

Nguyen Van Thieu, 76, controversial President of South Vietnam during the war. He survived various attacks but resigned—and fled—as North Vietnamese troops approached Saigon in April 1975.

Gilbert Trigano, 80, anti-Nazi propagandist who helped develop Club Med into a hedonistic waterside-resort chain.

Ray Walston, 86, master of quirkily cranky roles. He was the rowdy sailor Luther Billis in the movie of *South Pacific*, then won a Tony playing a stylish Satan in *Damn Yankees* on Broadway. He made his own devil's pact by joining the sitcom *My Favorite Martian* for the cash and was forever branded as an alien.

Paul Warnke, 81, outspoken Washington defense adviser who advocated disarmament during the cold war and was the highest-ranking Pentagon official in the Johnson Administration to question publicly the aims of the Vietnam War.

Anthony Quinn